TEACHING AS A MORAL PRACTICE

Defining, Developing, and Assessing
Professional Dispositions in Teacher Education

TEACHING AS A MORAL PRACTICE

Defining, Developing, and Assessing
Professional Dispositions in Teacher Education

PETER C. MURRELL JR.

MARY E. DIEZ

SHARON FEIMAN-NEMSER

DEBORAH L. SCHUSSLER

Editors

HARVARD EDUCATION PRESS

CAMBRIDGE, MASSACHUSETTS

Library of Congress Control Number 2010931409

Paperback ISBN 978-1-934742-78-5
Library Edition ISBN 978-1-934742-79-2

Published by Harvard Education Press,
an imprint of the Harvard Education Publishing Group

Harvard Education Press
8 Story Street
Cambridge, MA 02138

Cover Design: Sarah Henderson

The typefaces used in this book are ITC Stone Serif for text and
ITC Stone Sans for display.

Contents

Acknowledgments

We want to acknowledge the special contribution and effort of our colleagues in this enterprise—the case writers. These include our colleagues from the University of Denver and the Boettcher Teachers Program, María del Carmen Salazar, Andra Brill, and Karen L. Lowenstein; our colleagues from Winthrop University, Lisa E. Johnson, Rebecca Evers, and Jonatha W. Vare; our colleagues from the University of Cincinnati, Chester Laine, Anne M. Bauer, Holly Johnson, Stephen D. Kroeger, and Karen S. Troup; our colleagues from the University of Southern Maine, Catherine Fallona and Julie Canniff; our colleagues from the University of Wisconsin-Eau Claire, Robert E. Hollon, Michael W. Kolis, Susan R. McIntyre, J. Todd Stephens, and Rosemary L. Battalio; our colleagues from the University of North Carolina Wilmington, John Fischetti, Scott Imig, Abdou Ndoye, and Robert Smith; and our colleague from the University of Illinois at Chicago (UIC), Eleni Katsarou. These individuals have indeed become our colleagues in this enterprise and continue to extend and enrich the dialogue of inquiry into, and reflection on, practices of preparing ethically agentive, excellent teachers.

We would also like to express gratitude and respect to the UIC partners in teacher preparation, the two groups of mentoring teachers for Katsarou's students, all from Chicago Public Schools, who, in addition to having mentored teacher candidates, took the time to recount, reflect, and help design the DECA-UT. The first group consisted of Tim Hart, Mary Giannetos, Shannon Paolucci, Bill Giannetos, Marc Garcia, Eve Ludwig, and Alex Castaneda. The second group consisted of Tim Hart, Shannon Paolucci, Kathy Dynak, Rana Khan, Hannah Natividad, Karla Stampley, Holly Heneghan, and Carmen Jenkins.

Finally, we would like to express our deep appreciation for our TEAMC colleagues Erskine Dottin, Richard Osguthorpe, and Hugh Sockett, who served as mentors to some of our case writers and shaped the intellectual work of this project. In addition, we want to acknowledge Sharon Robinson, president of the American Association for Colleges of Teacher Education, for her charge to TEAMC to work with dispositions. Finally, we want to thank Carol Smith, Lisa Stooksberry, Alicia Ardila-Rey, and Mary Harrill McClellan for their support over the years.

Preface

The topic of dispositions is, and has been in recent years, a lightning rod of controversy in teacher preparation. The dispositional aims found in many, if not most, teacher education programs are subject to a variety of criticisms—some deserved, others not. Both the deserved and undeserved criticisms are part of a complex field of discourse concerning good assessment, what constitutes "the good teacher," and the contested meanings of social justice in the preparation of teachers and the educational system. Sorting through this field requires unpacking both the pedagogical and the political issues so as to address what amount to attacks on the use of dispositions.

For example, organizations like the Foundation for Individual Rights in Education (FIRE) criticized teacher education programs for proffering a liberal bias and imposing a politicized litmus test for preservice teachers. Similar criticisms openly rang an alarm that a liberal bent in teacher education was afoot, and warned that dispositions would become a vehicle to advance political and ideological agendas. Clearly infuriated by the concept of *social justice*, George Will articulated this sentiment in a 2006 opinion piece published in *Newsweek*. He argued that teacher education should *not* be promoting social justice or preparing preservice teachers to be change agents who "recognize individual and institutionalized racism, sexism, homophobia, and classism," "break silences," and "develop anti-racist, anti-homophobic, anti-sexist community [sic] and alliances."[1] Yet, this sentiment runs counter to what many feel is the most central purpose of education in a democracy. For example, the ongoing attention within the *Journal of Teacher Education* to the topic of teacher dispositions in recent years has highlighted the moral nature of teaching practice and its significance within teacher education.[2]

Identifying the right call to action for teacher educators regarding dispositions is no easy task because of the complexities of the issues, both within the profession and without. The battle lines of political orientation and ideology are but one set of challenges in the debate. Add to the mix the fact that there is little consensus within the professions of teaching and teacher education regarding the meaning, purpose, and use of dispositions. Stir in governmental pressure and the public's increased gaze toward teacher preparation with a clamor for increased teacher quality. Finally, fold in the genuine concern with the moral and ethical dimensions of teaching and how to prepare the best teachers.

Put all of this together, and you have a potent mix of controversy that makes it difficult for the profession to chart a proper course. The profession needs clarity on a number of questions. Where did dispositions come from? How and why did they become important in teacher preparation? What is the basis of the controversy around dispositions? How should we think about dispositions in teaching? How do we understand dispositions as something more than the third element of the "holy trinity" along with knowledge and skills? What is, or ought to be, their function in preparing the best teachers? What role do dispositions play in the profession now? Toward what practices and policies should we be moving? How do we locate the moral work of teaching in all of this?

The purpose of this book is to provide some clarity in beginning to answer these questions. In conceptualizing this book, we knew that doing this work would not simply be a matter of pouring through the professional literature, doing exhaustive analysis on that content, and then discussing our findings. We knew we had to turn to what people were *actually doing* and grappling with in the actual practice of preparing teachers and using dispositions. We knew that we had to ground our discernment in the contexts of present practice, and discover how thoughtful teacher educators in different institutional and policy contexts were *thinking* about the meaning of dispositions in teaching and learning, as well as what they were *doing* in their teacher education programs to promote the moral nature of teaching. We knew that charting a proper forward course for dispositions in teacher preparation was not going to be a matter of rendering abstract ideas and theory; this was to be a road made by walking.

The editors of this book are all members of a task force of the American Association of Colleges for Teacher Education (AACTE), called Teacher Education as a Moral Community (TEAMC). First convened by Barbara Burch in 1997 at the close of her presidential year for AACTE, the group explored issues related to the morals in teacher education for a number of years, producing sessions for the AACTE annual meeting and sparking thoughtful written pieces by its members. The genesis of this book came in 2006, when president Sharon Robinson asked TEAMC to make teacher dispositions our major focus. In the years since that request, the group has produced a monograph and several webinars, preconferences, and sessions at AACTE annual meetings, as well as individually authored articles, book chapters, and books on the topic. This book continues the conversation, both for the field and for TEAMC. It pulls together work that we've been doing and suggests a way to move forward.

This book is the product of the continuing effort by TEAMC to advance the inquiry into the moral, ethical, and professional development of candidates using dispositions. We engaged colleagues in describing their institutional practices as well as their inquiry into those practices. The result is a book that provides a window into a set of teacher education programs in which faculty have begun to look honestly at the congruence between their rhetoric and practice, and to chart a course for conceptualizing, developing, and assessing dispositions. In so doing, this volume does two things. First, it provides concrete pictures of the ways teacher educators work to ensure ethical and moral development of educational professionals. Then, from an interpretation of these pictures, the volume offers a framework of *ends* and *means* for the use of dispositions in preparation of caring, competent, capable, and ethically centered teachers. With respect to *ends*, this volume asks, What are the moral and ethical aspects of teaching, schooling, and education? And with respect to the *means*, How do we prepare teachers to act morally and ethically as professionals?

Thus, this book takes stock of where we are, both as a profession and as a community of teacher educators, with regard to ensuring the ethical and moral development of educational professionals. It also projects a future course based upon an ends-means analytical framework. With regard to these *ends*, we focused on the products that teacher educators used to conceptualize, teach, and assess dispositions, making the possibilities more discernable by contextualizing these varied frameworks in authentic contexts of work in teacher education—hence our decision to do this examination and analysis through a set of institutional case studies. With regard to the *means*, we sought evidence about the kinds of learning opportunities that programs provide to their candidates, and the kinds of formative assessments that promote the capacity for ethical and moral professional practice.

Each of the seven cases in this volume represents a rich journey of inquiry into practice. Though they explore different terrains and vistas, their paths ultimately intertwine into a new direction that advances our understanding of dispositions in teaching and teacher preparation. We invite you to partake in these journeys.

Peter C. Murrell Jr.
Professor of educational psychology and
    founding dean, School of Education,
    Loyola University Maryland
Spring 2010

Introduction

Mary E. Diez and Peter C. Murrell Jr.

The context for this book is the recent attention to teacher dispositions—within schools of education, in state policy and national accreditation, and more broadly in K–12 districts. At issue is not only the definition of *dispositions*, but also the application of the notion in screening or evaluating teachers. We begin this introduction with a brief history of the emergence of dispositions both in the teacher education literature and in policy and practice, and then provide an overview of our work in identifying and working with seven institutions to tell their stories of grappling with making the conceptualization, development, and assessment of dispositions meaningful for their teacher candidates.

A BRIEF HISTORY

How did teacher dispositions come to the fore in teacher education? In one of the earliest references to dispositions, Lilian Katz and James Raths describe a teacher who refuses to reexplain a concept for a student as punishment for the student's not paying attention. They clarify the difference between having mastery of the skill of explaining and using that mastery when requested to: "If . . . on *most* occasions of such a request, the teacher is helpful and encouraging, providing clarification and assistance, then the teacher can be said to possess not only the requisite skills for teaching, but also the disposition to use these skills" (emphasis in the original).[1] For Katz and Raths, dispositions are about specific kinds of actions and their frequency, not a set of beliefs or attitudes.

While Katz and Raths did not deal with what *motivated* the frequency of a person's actions, they did see a clear connection between patterns of action and the *ethos* of a teacher education program, which they describe as "an intellectually oriented ethos . . . in which staff and candidates exhibit, for example, dispositions to wonder, puzzle, reflect, explore, examine, study and analyze pertinent phenomena, in which the exhibition of such professional dispositions is encouraged and appreciated."[2] Again, however, they did not address the underlying values or other motivations for these professional dispositions.

While Katz and Raths were working on these ideas at the University of Delaware, we were working with colleagues at Alverno College to explicitly link dispositions as an integral part of the teacher preparation program. In contrast to Katz and Raths, we were very interested in what fuels the connection between *intention* and *action*, grounding our understanding of that connection in Alverno's ability-based approach. The Alverno faculty defines an *ability* as including a complex integration of "skills, behaviors, knowledge, values, attitudes, motives or dispositions, and self perceptions."[3] Using the ability-based approach, we were working to develop a picture of how teachers develop, not only in their subject area knowledge and in the psychological, social, and philosophical foundations of education, "but also in their sensitivity to learners as individuals, their use of moral reasoning, and their sense of responsibility for meeting learner needs."[4]

Seeing the formation of professional identity as critical to teacher education, we began to work with candidates both to understand what they bring to the program and to recognize how they grow not only in their knowledge and skill but also in their values and their understanding of how those values apply in the profession. Because *valuing in decision making* is an ability embedded across the undergraduate curriculum at Alverno, students develop language to talk about values and moral perspectives, which facilitates the conversations we have with them about dispositions. As part of our work, we also began to see the importance of the ethos of the program—that we, as faculty, also needed to model that same integration and growing depth of knowledge, skills, and dispositions that we sought to develop in our candidates. In our work we understood dispositions to be integrated with knowledge and skill and fostered in part through modeling by faculty.

INTASC AND NCATE

While the researchers and teacher educators cited above were beginning to frame dispositions in terms of teacher education *practice*, efforts by the Interstate New Teacher Assessment and Support Consortium (INTASC) and the National Council for Accreditation of Teacher Education (NCATE) moved dispositions into the *policy* arena. In the early 1990s, INTASC convened a group of state department representatives, teacher union representatives, and teacher educators to develop a set of model standards for beginning teachers.[5] The group decided to focus on "knowledge, skills, and dispositions," replacing the then current formation in many states of "knowledge, skills, and attitudes." The change was partially in response to issues raised by members of the group, including Lovely Billups, who represented the American Federation of Teachers. She challenged the teacher educators in the group, asking, "When are you going to stop recommending candidates for licensure who have high grade point averages and are mean to kids?"[6] Her question echoes the concern first expressed by Katz and Raths: the problem of having the knowledge and skills required to be an effective teacher, and yet not using them for good in the classroom.

The INTASC standards were released in 1992, and within ten years many states had used the document as input for their own standards setting. Eventually, more than thirty adopted or adapted the standards into state code. The INTASC standards language was also adopted by NCATE, further influencing teacher education programs around the country. By the late 1990s the phrase *knowledge, skills, and dispositions* was part of the discourse of teacher education, including both bureaucrats at the state level and NCATE board of examiners members who sought explicit evidence of each element in their review of programs.

NCATE's adoption of dispositions as part of its standards expectations greatly influenced what the term came to mean. This in turn led to changes in the practice of teacher education. Some teacher educators sought grounding for their work in psychology, philosophy, or moral education. But because of the high stakes of state approval and national accreditation, the focus for many institutions gravitated toward doing what was necessary to "meet NCATE" rather than focusing on the kind of thoughtful work required to rethink programs in terms of moral and ethical demands of the profession.

In addition, varied conceptions of the notion of dispositions led to political controversy, as attested to in both popular media and in the professional literature.[7] When use of the term *social justice* as an example in NCATE's glossary definition of *professional dispositions* became the object of controversy, the accreditation body eliminated it as an example. That action became controversial as well, as groups committed to addressing issues of diversity saw it as a backing-down from an important stance with regard to social justice. This in turn led to demonstrations at the American Educational Research Association (AERA) in support of "restoring" social justice as one of the exemplars in the NCATE definition of professional dispositions. In any event, the point is that the development of dispositions in teacher education programs is taking place in a politically contested terrain. Some assert that objections to the reference to social justice as a professional disposition by those on the political right signal an all-out campaign to define the goals of public education, the role of teachers, the nature of knowledge, and conceptions of learning, teaching, and learning to teach.[8] Ultimately, resolution of the larger ideological issues will rest with determining the nature of, and purposes for, assessment of dispositions—a point to which we will return presently in chapter 1.

OVERVIEW OF THE BOOK

In chapter 1 we lay out five key points that guide our thinking about teacher dispositions, address the kinds of tensions that have emerged in the last twenty years of responding to policy requirements, and outline issues with assessment that affect work with teacher dispositions. In the next seven chapters, we provide seven cases of institutions grappling with some of the issues we have highlighted here, and then conclude in chapter 9 with an analysis of those chapters.

When we began work on this book in the summer of 2007, we published a call for cases about how teacher education programs are working with teacher dispositions. Twenty-nine institutions responded to the call, representing small, medium, and large programs and public and private colleges and universities, spread geographically across the country. While we had asked for institutions to describe their practice and how they were addressing problems in conceptualizing, developing, and assessing dispositions, many of those responding provided instead documents that read like accreditation reports or academic papers; there was little sense of "story" or of serious grappling with thorny issues.

In late fall 2007, we selected seven cases that represented diversity in size and mission, from across the country, at different stages of development. We believed that each had the potential to tell a story that could be helpful to others. We worked for over a year with writing teams from each of the seven institutions selected, in an intense process of refining, reflecting and rewriting. The result of this work is not a set of *case studies* in the formal sense, but rather a set of *cases* that are, we believe, an authentic picture of the kind of work being undertaken in teacher education around issues of conceptualizing, developing, and assessing teacher dispositions.

These cases represent several kinds of diversity, including size and mission. For example, in terms of Carnegie classifications, our cases include three large research universities with high or very high research activity: the University of Cincinnati, the University of Denver, the University of Illinois at Chicago; three master's large universities: the University of North Carolina Wilmington, the University of Southern Maine, Winthrop University; and one master's medium university: the University of Wisconsin-Eau Claire. One is also an example of an emerging model, a small teacher-residency program in which a university collaborates with a local school district: the Boettcher Teachers Program at the University of Denver.

Taken together, these cases offer a picture of work with teacher dispositions across stages of development—both *individual* and *institutional*. Some have implemented programs and are examining their impacts through a systematic process of reflection using data that spans at least two years. The University of Denver, the University of Illinois at Chicago, and Winthrop University look *retrospectively* at their work, while also seeing implications for ongoing improvement. Others have recently made or are in the process of making changes in their programs, exploring *prospectively* where those changes will take them; these include the University of Cincinnati, the University of North Carolina Wilmington, the University of Southern Maine, and the University of Wisconsin-Eau Claire.

For each case's writing team, we, as editors, pushed for clarity about how their story could make meaning for the profession, asking, "What is this a case of?" These are complex and complicated stories, about a number of issues, but as a way of introducing them, we have characterized them in particular ways, recognizing that some are more single-minded than others. Two of the cases focused on issues related to assessment:

- The University of Denver's focus on the work of one student across a series of assessments illustrates how this residency program uses assessment in the service of teacher candidate development.

- Winthrop University's focus on assessment for program evaluation illustrates how an ongoing refinement process can improve assessment for both development and documentation.

Two of the cases used their experiences with candidates to examine how the program was working and what changes might be appropriate:

- The University of Cincinnati undertook a diagnostic process to reenvision the program in the light of three candidate stories.
- The University of Southern Maine examined two stories about candidates who did not succeed, to identify key pieces of the preparation program in need of review.

Three of the cases focused on the search for a unifying vision:

- The University of Wisconsin-Eau Claire used the theme of collaborative leadership as a way to integrate across three separate programs, probing a common framework to find connections and a shared vision.
- The University of North Carolina Wilmington embraced a state mandate as a way to reenvision teacher education and begin to get a large number of programs to work toward a common vision.
- The University of Illinois at Chicago story involves a faculty member in a collaborative effort with cooperating teachers to codify what was an unarticulated shared vision of good urban teaching through the development of a formalized assessment instrument.

Finally, in chapter 9, we look across the cases, identifying patterns and issues in the ways that the seven institutions conceptualize, develop, and assess dispositions, and suggesting how this work can inform the thinking and practice of teacher educators. We believe that these honest and nuanced stories offer a dynamic picture of what it means and what it takes to make professional dispositions a central outcome in teacher education.

CHAPTER ONE

Dispositions in Teacher Education—Starting Points for Consideration

Mary E. Diez and Peter C. Murrell Jr.

Rebecca T. is a second-year teacher in a large urban public school. Having graduated from a highly regarded teacher education program, she felt ready to carry out the program's social justice mission by meeting the instructional needs of the racially, linguistically, and culturally diverse students in her classroom. Yet, like many teachers, she felt stymied by the constraints that the system, and the conditions at her school, placed upon her capacity to meet her students' needs. When the citywide test scores showed a decline for African American students in her school and a widening gap between those students and their white counterparts, she participated in a data analysis retreat with other members of her school team. Rebecca felt a vague unease as the team agreed to the district supervisor's suggestion that they abandon the literacy program they had developed in her grade-level team that featured a wide range of reading and writing activities specifically designed to address the systematic grammar issues posed for African American students taking the literacy test, and replace it with a direct instruction literacy program with daily scripted skills drills. Weeks into using the new curricular program, Rebecca's unease grew into dissatisfaction, and she began to consider secretly abandoning the direct instruction program and resuming her previous efforts, thus contemplating an "unprofessional" course of action in favor of one that seemed to her more "right" for her students.

Jessica R. is a third-year teacher in a similar district and in a school with similar test results. Jessica also graduated from a strong teacher education program, one similarly dedicated to preparing teachers to meet the instructional needs of racially, linguistically, and culturally diverse students. She took on the challenges in the literacy instruction of her African American students making the transition from home speech patterns to the formal patterns of standard English, and actively sought out colleagues at her school and outside experts who shared her commitment to educating all students. After attending a forum called "Teaching Standard English in Urban Classrooms," she worked on adopting the approach she learned there that developed students' awareness of language patterns involving contrastive analysis. Then Jessica demonstrated the system to her grade-level team colleagues, just as she had seen in the video clip of Rachel Swords shown at the forum, including the part where the teacher leads students in a systematic inquiry on the differences between formal and informal speech patterns aimed at promoting the syntactic awareness they needed to code-switch appropriately.[1] The word pattern games based on contrastive analysis that she created and sent home with her students became very popular among parents, who were pleased to see the enthusiasm their children had for being "language detectives." When her district mandated a scripted phonics curriculum for the primary grades to address low test scores, Jessica and her grade-level team were able to show that they already had a direct instruction system in place—one that identified the persistent grammar issues her students encountered on the literacy achievement tests. Her grade-level team established good relationships with parents, who saw the success they were having in elevating test performance and eliminating the school's achievement gap, and convinced the district central office that what they were doing met the district goals. Hence, Jessica was able to integrate her motive for "doing what's right for her students" in way that Rebecca could not. Jessica found a course of action that was "professional" not only in conventional terms, but also in the innovation of practice that supported her moral conduct. Jessica demonstrated ethical agency in professional actions that allowed her to meet both district demands and the demands of conscience. Promoting this kind of teacher development—from Rebecca's case to Jessica's case—is what dispositions are designed for.

HOW TO THINK ABOUT DISPOSITIONS IN TEACHING

The vignettes above illustrate the importance teacher *dispositions*—which we define as habits of professional action or moral commitments that spur such actions. In effect, dispositions refer to a teaching stance, a way of orienting oneself to the work and responsibilities of teachers. Those responsibilities are ultimately about moral practice, in which the teacher mobilizes her knowledge and skills in behalf of the learners entrusted to her care. While dispositions impact the performance of all teachers, we have situated these vignettes in urban schools because these contexts make vivid and urgent the importance of attending to dispositions in teacher preparation.

As we thought about the pressing needs in urban teaching, where teachers often face not only a lack of resources but also constraints on their choices of instructional methods, we identified five key points from our reading of the literature on teacher dispositions, our work with teacher candidates, and our discussions with colleagues over the last several years. These points are critical to an emerging understanding of dispositions in teaching and teacher education. We discuss them below, returning to the vignettes to illustrate their meaning in context.

1. Dispositions Depend upon Knowledge and Skills

Though we frequently refer to dispositions as though they are distinct from knowledge and skill, they develop in tandem with them. As the vignettes above illustrate, a teacher may have a strong desire to make a difference with learners, but lack the knowledge and skills to carry it off. That is, she may be *disposed to* a particular level or quality of practice without necessarily having the *capacity to enact* it. Likewise, a teacher may have knowledge and skill needed to work effectively with young learners, but lack the commitment, persistence, and creativity to overcome external challenges. This is one key distinction between the two teachers in our opening vignettes. Both confronted basically the same dilemma and the same obstacles, but Jessica's capacity to *enact* her moral stance in her interactions with parents, teachers, and colleagues led her to a more positive outcome. Her ability to collaborate with others and improvise alternative ways to meet learner needs depended upon her knowledge and skill as well as her commitment to her learners. Steven Covey makes this point when he writes that a habit, another term for disposition, is "the intersection of knowledge, skill, and desire."[2] We agree: the strong desire to be an accomplished teacher and the requisite knowledge and skills for doing so fortify each other. An accomplished teacher's dispositions, knowledge, and skill combine synergistically in the enactment of good teaching.

Teacher educators who attend to the development of knowledge, skills, and dispositions can attest to the mutual effect each has on the development of the others. Consider, for example, a teacher candidate who comes into a program not really believing that "all children can learn" and thus not committed to finding ways to reach each learner. Perhaps he had experiences in classrooms as an elementary or secondary student where some children did not learn, and he attributed that outcome to their lack of ability. As he learns more about how children's development is shaped by the quality of their experiences and interactions and as he practices teaching approaches that more successfully address individual learners' needs, he may begin to develop some of the knowledge and skill needed to reach all learners. The experience of successfully implementing new knowledge and skills could in turn modify his disposition toward the learning capacities of all children, especially if he is surrounded by teachers and mentors who model and articulate this belief. As he engages in additional practicum experiences in classrooms where he both observes and participates in effective instruction, his beliefs about children's ability to learn change as his capacity to achieve this outcome grows. Thus, in this instance, the acquisition of specific knowledge and skill supports the development of the disposition to take responsibility for and work hard at promoting the learning of all children.

While expanding knowledge and skill can influence dispositions, it can also work the other way around. Lilian Katz suggests that dispositions can drive the development of knowledge and skill. For example, a teacher may start out with the disposition of *respecting learners*, which Katz describes as "a respectful relationship between the teacher and the learner . . . marked by treating learners with dignity, listening closely and attentively to what the learners say, and also looking for what they seem reluctant to say."[3] This disposition may lead the teacher to seek out deeper understandings of child development in a social and cultural context, and thereby refine her skills to listen and interpret how individual children learn. For example, in the opening vignettes, Rebecca and Jessica were both driven by dispositions of "respecting learners" in a context of social justice and diversity. But in Jessica's case, this disposition drove her to a deeper and broader inquiry into the literacy development of African American children and resulted in the improvisation of a system of instruction that satisfied policy constraints while at the same time truly enriching the quality of her students' literacy learning overall.

Teacher educators need to develop their curriculum in ways that make these kinds of connections explicit, reveal the complexities of practice to candidates, and place them in situations where they can use their knowledge, skills, and dispositions to help children learn. Teacher educators also need to prompt candidates to connect their knowledge and skill with the moral, ethical, and professional dimensions of good teaching by providing feedback, guiding reflection, and promoting self-awareness and critique. For example, faculty in Rebecca's teacher preparation program might have provided Rebecca and other candidates with dilemmas like the one she currently faced, and asked, "If you really believed that the new program was problematic for your third graders, what else might you do if your intention is to meet your students' learning needs?" In this way candidates would not only exhibit dispositions as "predictive patterns of action," but also be able to describe their *intentions* in their actions, analyze their impact, and reflect on how they see the need for change and growth.[4]

2. Dispositions Are About Ethical, Moral Actions

Many teacher education programs identify as key *professional dispositions* such behaviors as being on time, submitting work on time, dressing appropriately, and other aspects of professional conduct. Other programs reserve dispositions for the intellectual and relational habits exhibited by effective and successful teachers, such as seeking evidence for learning or learning about a child's outside interests in order to connect her interests to in-school learning. While both categories reflect desirable professional conduct on the part of candidates preparing to teach, only the second category goes to the heart of the teacher's role in society, the responsibility for ensuring equitable learning opportunities for all students. These deeper elements of professional dispositions relate to the ethical and moral foundations of teaching, learning, schooling, and education.[5]

All professions have ethical codes that serve as guides to practice. In many programs, teacher educators introduce candidates to ethical practice by, among other things, exploring codes of professional practice that specify norms for what is right and what is wrong. Codes of ethics for teachers explicitly address commitments to students, the profession, and society, and spell out expectations for appropriate and positive actions as well as proscriptions against improper actions. For example, with regard to students, the National Education Association (NEA) code of ethics directs the teacher to strive "to help each student realize his or her potential as a worthy and effective member of society" and to avoid "unreasonably deny[ing] the student's access to varying points of view."[6] Obviously, learning the words of such a code is not enough. Such an external guide needs to be incorporated into the teacher candidate's moral stance, so that it becomes an *internal compass*, guiding her practice and building her identity.

While professional ethics are formulated by the profession, the teacher's moral stance "stems from one's profoundly personal beliefs about the world, including the pursuit of desirable ends, the sanctity of all persons, and what is right and what is wrong."[7] Because moral perspectives are strengthened in reflection, teacher educators also need to help teacher candidates become aware of their values and belief systems, and how they influence their choices of action. This is tricky, if for no other reason than that it is hard to operationally represent an individual's moral stance.

Helping teacher candidates see how their decisions derive from their values and beliefs is necessary in helping them develop a moral stance. This is where the idea of dispositions as expressing a moral stance in action becomes important. Consider the distinction between Rebecca's and Jessica's moral stances regarding social justice in terms of meeting the educational needs of all children. Both may be commended for having a strong moral stance, but Jessica has developed an "ethics in action" stance, which she demonstrated in the face of a moral dilemma.

3. Dispositions Relate to Teachers' Professional Identity

Professional dispositions are part of a teacher's identity, influencing how she sees herself and her professional responsibilities. But they do not, by themselves, tell the whole story. We believe that the construction of professional identity for teachers must also be rooted in a broader and deeper view of what is required of teachers in a democratic society. The professional identity of a given individual can be viewed as a melding of her role (e.g., what the "good teacher" is *expected* to be like and be able to do) and how she *projects* herself in that role. The notion of dispositions offers a way of articulating what constitutes the identity of the good teacher in the two dimensions that matter: (1) what the individual as a professional *ought to do* (moral action) and (2) what the individual *chooses to do* (ethical agency).

The professional identity of the individual is perhaps the most important construct for capturing the integration of these two dimensions. In practice, candidates need to be in touch with both external expectations and their own internal agency so that they can translate external expectations into their own intentions.[8] Developing the *intentionality* and *agency* that constitute professional identity comes from being in touch with both external expectations and one's own internal decision-making processes. Our responsibility as teacher educators is to help candidates develop the habit of discerning the moral aspects of different choices in a particular professional setting. Teacher educators can also support the development of ethical agency by promoting the practice of *discernment*—critically engaging moral dilemmas in the embedded contexts of teaching, learning, schooling, and education. Such discernment becomes an ongoing guide to ethical professional conduct in practice.[9] We can also support the development/formation of a strong sense of professional identity by encouraging candidates to undertake reflection on what it means to be a professional: How am I constructing who I am as a professional who builds respectful relationships with learners through respect? How do I see myself as a professional who can be counted on to assume responsibility? The disposition to critique one's actions with questions like these is likely to lead, in an ongoing way, to the construction of one's professional identity.

4. Context Influences the Enactment of Professional Dispositions in Practice

We believe that the nested contexts of teaching—school, profession, community, and society—help create and affirm professional identity and practice.[10] At the micro level, a teacher candidate or beginning teacher, working in an environment where colleagues work to support each individual learner, might find that local context enables and reinforces her own commitment to take responsibility for every student in her class. Such support also builds her ability to fulfill her moral purpose as an educator. A candidate or beginning teacher working in an environment where colleagues show respect for each other and are open to learning from each other will build a commitment to collegial interaction, strengthened by her experiences in a community of learners.

Conversely, a teacher candidate or beginning teacher may find some work environments very challenging, calling her commitments into question or revealing the need for additional knowledge and skill to address the needs of learners effectively. For example, in the opening vignettes, where district policy and practice appear to be at odds with the commitment of the young teacher, the dilemma might be so daunting that the teacher begins to see her commitment as unreasonable. Specifically, Rebecca's commitment to her students may have been dampened in her acquiescence to the curriculum change. If she stays in teaching but just goes through the motions or gives up on the profession entirely, she may lose her sense of moral purpose. Alternatively, a beginning teacher may see the need to find support for her commitment by finding like-minded colleagues inside or outside her school community so that she can change the context she is in or by moving to another school/district that is a context where she can exercise her moral stance. Thus, teacher educators need to help candidates understand how teaching is embedded in, and influenced by, multiple contexts.

Context—social, situational, and cultural—influences professional identity. The difference in Rebecca's and Jessica's responses to their dilemma positioned them differently among their colleagues, in the school's social network, and in their profession. Some cultural psychologists refer to the *positionality* of an individual as a situation-specific social identity. A person's positionality is constituted both by the person they project and by the person others ascribe to them.[11] Jessica's agency may be rewarded by the regard she receives as someone who is resourceful, smart, and a real go-getter among colleagues, and as a teacher who "really cares" among parents. Both Rebecca and Jessica "really care" as an intrapersonal dispositional trait, but only Jessica has that trait ascribed to her in a public way by virtue of her successes as recognized by colleagues and by parents. In this way, Jessica may have advantages over Rebecca in the development of an affirming professional identity because, in her particular context, she is able to both *feel* and *live* the part of "the caring teacher." The difference in the *positionality* of these two young teachers illustrates our next point: that dispositions can be developed. In environments in which candidates experience success in exhibiting the virtues and qualities they value (e.g., being a go-getter or being the really caring teacher), they are more apt to further develop those virtues and qualities.

5. Dispositions Can Be Cultivated/Developed

Dispositions are neither invisible aspects of a teacher's psyche nor fixed personality traits. They are commitments and habits of thought and action that grow as the teacher learns, acts, and reflects under the guidance of teachers and mentors in a preparation program and in the first years of practice. They are visible in a teacher's decisions and actions over time and especially in the teacher's reflections about the consequences of those decisions and actions. Because dispositions are interdependent with knowledge and skills, their cultivation is tied to conceptual understanding, refinement of skills in guided application, and thoughtful reflection on practice.

Cultivating or developing dispositions requires making the process of growth explicit, both in terms of the kinds of ethical and moral action expected of a professional and in terms of how the teacher candidate begins to make connections between principles of action and her own choices of action in an ongoing way. While teacher educators may begin with readings and discussion based upon scenarios of practice, they also need to ground discussion in actual situations experienced by candidates in school settings. Each experience in school settings needs to be accompanied by guided reflection, with both individual and class debriefing of the issues encountered, in terms of the moral, ethical, and practical demands.

Thoughtful assessment is also a key process necessary to support dispositions development and to document student performance. Currently, teacher educators take widely different approaches to the assessment of dispositions. Some are clearly guided by a psychometric approach appropriate for what Richard Stiggins calls "assessment *of* learning"—that is, a "point in time" judgment of the candidate.[12] Others are guided by what Stiggins calls "assessment *for* learning"—looking at candidates as they participate in the preparation program and providing feedback, interventions, and support for the candidates to grow into the expected proficiencies that guide the program.

TENSIONS IN TEACHER EDUCATION POLICY AND PRACTICE

In the introduction, we looked at the history of teacher education's current focus on dispositions and some of the dilemmas and challenges that the profession faces. These dilemmas and challenges offer the potential for both richness of perspective and contradiction or confusion. These contrary possibilities are visible in a set of tensions that appear in the discourse on dispositions in teacher education and further highlight problems in how teacher educators have responded to the mandates from states and NCATE.[13]

Entity Versus Incremental Perspective

Drawing on Carol Dweck's work with notions of intelligence, we see a parallel in the discourse on teacher dispositions.[14] Dweck characterized two views that children hold regarding intelligence: an "entity" view that sees intelligence as fixed and an "incremental" view that sees intellectual capacity as able to change and grow. She points to the danger of holding a fixed view, where a child may say, "I can't do this because I'm not smart," and the promise of an incremental view for learning, where a child may say, "I can't do this yet, but I will be able to do it with help from my teacher and practice doing it."

Analogously, an entity view sees teacher candidate dispositions as fixed (e.g., as wired-in personality traits or talents). This view is reflected in the use of screening instruments at the beginning of a teacher education program.[15] It also shows up in recent research studies that explore noncognitive constructs that link to personality theory.[16] The incremental view sees dispositions as able to change and develop. Sharon Oja and Alan Reiman, for example, link the notion of dispositions to the development of professional judgment, seeing the necessary growth in teacher decision making as a complex process of integrating dispositions with theoretical knowledge and skills to meet the learner's needs.[17]

While the framing of entity versus incremental approaches to dispositions seems dichotomous, some teacher education programs begin with screening for specific dispositions as a *basis* for growth into the profession. Thus, even if teacher educators seem to hold an entity view, they can use information about dispositions as stable traits in order to make teacher education candidates more *conscious* of key dispositions they come with (e.g., core beliefs, empathy, respect for others, responsibility) in the context of the teacher's role.

Separate Versus Holistic Views

An uncritical acceptance of the assumptions of positivist empirical research methods may have influenced some teacher educators to see value in casting dispositions as separate from knowledge and skills. *Analytically*, it is possible to treat disposition, knowledge, and skills as separate categories, but in *practice,* teaching requires the orchestration of all three.

Seeing dispositions as separate from knowledge and skills is problematic because it cuts things up in a way that distorts reality. For example, separating dispositions from knowledge and skills in assessment contributes to the decontextualization of dispositions seen in the examples above. Those who argue for dispositions as separate often do so primarily on the basis of instrumentation.[18] Yet, as noted above, NCATE encourages assessment processes that connect dispositions to larger performances involving candidates' work.

Compliance Versus Construction of Professional Identity

This tension links two of our beginning points: that the ethical and moral go beyond being on time and dressing appropriately and that dispositions are related to professional identity. When teacher education programs focus on a narrow set of dispositional actions—being on time, submitting work on time, dressing appropriately, and so forth—they often don't get beyond those factors. In TEAMC sessions at AACTE annual meetings, we have observed that when these expectations dominate the discussion, the tone often turns strident, with participants asking, in effect, what they can do to *force* candidates to comply with their expectations. Because it is hard to see how compliance leads to ethical and moral agency or to a sense of professional identity, focusing on these factors preempts a richer and deeper role for dispositions in teacher education.

There may be a way out of this tension, rooted in a conversation with candidates. Returning to the common list of initial dispositions, a teacher educator could engage candidates in looking at what's beneath the disposition to be on time. "Being on time" can have at least two motivations: a person can come on time for a meeting because he'll be marked down or docked in pay for being late, or a person can come on time because he respects those he is meeting with and values their interaction. The first motivation reinforces a compliance mentality: this is what I have to do, or I'll be punished. (Note that if the impetus comes from outside, it can hardly "count" as a disposition.) The second motivation is nurtured by reflection on what it means to be a professional: How am I constructing who I am as a professional who builds relationships with learners through respect? How do I see myself as a professional who can be counted on to assume responsibility? The disposition to critique one's actions is likely to lead, in an ongoing way, to the construction of one's professional identity.

The same process of conversation and reflection can be employed with regard to dispositions that start out more clearly in the moral realm. Candidates come to us with values and beliefs that constitute a "moral filter"; whether or not the teacher is aware of them, those values and beliefs function in teacher decision making.[19] When teacher educators assist candidates to make their initial moral filters explicit, those filters can be examined against the code of ethics and moral demands of the profession. Then, through a process of reflection and self-critique, candidates can begin to construct their professional identity. It is not a matter of compliance, but of owning the profession and integrating professional values with one's individual identity as a professional.

Narrow Ideology Versus Moral Purpose

This tension bridges some of our earlier discussion about dispositions as moral and ethical actions with the recent history of controversy in teacher education. Some have critiqued the notion of dispositions, especially in teacher education, as narrowly ideological. For example, in the recent high-profile cases referenced earlier, some teacher education candidates challenged faculty for allegedly imposing political positions in the name of dispositions.[20] These highly charged cases were the backdrop for NCATE's elimination of the term *social justice* from its glossary entry on professional dispositions.

We believe that the application of narrow ideology—on either side of the political spectrum—distorts the role of dispositions in teacher practice. But some of what is going on when candidates disagree with faculty members may derive from a conflict between candidates' preconceptions and faculty members' knowledge and ethical/moral commitments. For example, candidates who come to teacher education from middle-class, white backgrounds may have a preconception that children of color, from poor backgrounds, are less able to learn. The sources of this preconception may be experiences they have had as students in classrooms where student needs were not addressed equitably or the media's constant comparison of test scores by racial groups. Labeling such a preconception as a lapse in social justice is likely to be met with defensiveness or anger. In any case, such a label is not helpful in changing the preconception.

In the process of teacher formation, faculty members contribute to a change in preconceptions in at least three ways: by presenting research-based information on teaching and learning, by exploring the ethical and moral issues related to teaching, and by engaging candidates in experiences with learners from backgrounds different from their own who are being successful as learners. Putting the research, commitment, and experience together, faculty may help candidates explore and revise their beginning preconceptions through reflection questions and dialogue. They can help them learn to use tools that allow them to act on their new beliefs. In this way, candidates can grow into an awareness of possible meanings of social justice through such reflection and interaction; the label is then less important than the understanding of how to reach all learners and to support their equitable opportunities to grow and develop.

The tension here is between perceived *indoctrination* of candidates—imposing one set of values or beliefs with political undertones; and the *formation or transformation* of candidates—bringing candidates into a profession, grounded in empirical support for the kinds of practices being taught.

Screening Versus Building a Professional Community

The tension between screening and building a professional community is another lens for looking at assessment in terms of the dual purposes of development and documentation. Teacher educators clearly have an obligation to assess candidates upon entry, especially with regard to background checks to protect children from persons who may do them harm. And teacher educators do have to be concerned about candidates (or teachers, for that matter) who are mean to kids; we need processes in place to work with candidates whose behavior sends up a red flag. Laying out key professional expectations/dispositions is one way to approach those issues. When, however, teacher educators use assessment solely for screening out candidates who don't meet disposition requirements, they stop well short of the expectations for moral and ethical practice.

Teacher educators have a larger purpose: that of preparing teachers who can effectively meet the needs of all learners, thus promoting both individual students and the ongoing creation of a democratic society. How do we build the knowledge, skills, and dispositions required for candidates to be able to work as part of a professional community to support learning for all students? How do we assess the candidate's growth in being able to work within a professional community, to encourage others to do so, and to take responsibility for leadership within such a community?

Erskine Dottin calls for a statement of candidate proficiencies as a "means by which the unit will help candidates to acquire the moral sensibilities it deems relevant to how life ought to be lived in the unit and in the world of practice."[21] Dottin's statement suggests once again the need for radical change in our perceptions of our professional role as teacher educators. How do we, for example, model in our interactions within a college/university what we want our candidates to learn and demonstrate? How do our candidates learn to model in their interactions what they want their students to learn?

Issues of Assessing Dispositions

Controversies about dispositions have also been tied to assessment, with at least one cause célèbre focusing on the right of an institution to dismiss a candidate who did not exhibit appropriate dispositions.[22] Legal scholars are clear that if an institution has clear outcomes related to professional behaviors and can document candidate performance related to those outcomes, the courts will uphold their decisions regarding candidate retention.[23] But those two criteria are critical: First, having clear outcomes related to professional behavior requires that teacher education programs both conceptualize and operationalize their understanding of dispositions. Second, documenting performance related to the outcomes requires credible assessment data as evidence. As we next look at the assessment of teacher dispositions, critical issues related to these two criteria need to be part of our conversation.

A Preoccupation with Screening

In reviewing assessment plans submitted to NCATE, we have seen more than a few that place a heavy emphasis on determining who should be admitted to teacher education programs. The assumption is that through these measures, teacher education programs can avoid admitting candidates who lack the proper dispositions. Typically, these programs use instruments that ask candidates to respond to a list of dispositions, values, beliefs, or other such elements. While it may be difficult for candidates to know what they are expected to say, it is likely that they will respond according to what they think faculty want to hear—and particularly in a high-stakes screening process, this would be a sensible approach for candidates to take. The problem is that there is no way to know whether these responses represent any beliefs, values, and dispositions that the candidate actually possesses. In such a list, for example, a candidate may not even recognize or encounter his own strong beliefs, values, and dispositions; so he just chooses from among those that come closest or those that he suspects are the "right" answer. Thus, both the criterion of clear outcome and that of documented performance are in question. (For more on issues with this kind of assessment, see Mary Diez's article, "Assessing Dispositions.")[24]

Another typical instrument is a prompt that calls for a reflective essay about the candidate's beliefs, values, and dispositions. This approach may come closer to providing the program with accurate information about what dispositions a candidate brings to the program, but because such a prompt may not situate the request in a meaningful context, many such essays are vapid, written without any sense of purpose. Again, a candidate may write what he thinks the faculty is looking for, rather than writing what represents a reflection of his own values and beliefs. As a result, the essay may not be a useful tool for making a high-stakes decision regarding admission. It would be possible, however, to shape the prompt to focus on a decision the candidate made and why he made it, or invite the candidate to analyze and respond to a dilemma. As we will discuss further below, even a more meaningful prompt may not provide sufficient information to justify denying a candidate the opportunity to pursue teacher education.

Lack of Evidence for Assessment Judgment

In some institutions, we have seen the pressure to aggregate data for NCATE—nearly always interpreted as number ratings only—result in worrisome assessment practice. For example, many programs use instruments that ask faculty to make judgments about the candidates in action, either focusing on a specific action or looking across a semester of experience with the candidate. Global ratings that cut across a whole semester (or other large period of time) are quite problematic, because they are rarely linked back to explicit evidence in the candidate's performance and thus are likely to be based upon unverified inferences. Many rating scales of student teacher observations use this approach for a whole host of judgments; but the fact that they are widely used does not negate the problematic nature of judgment sans evidence and/or valid interpretation. In addition, as Richard Osguthorpe points out, "educators exacerbate this pitfall by suggesting that this discrete set of dispositions can somehow be assessed in the absence of teaching practice (i.e. exclusively in the teacher preparation classroom)."[25] These kinds of global ratings may or may not meet the first criterion in their connection to a clearly conceptualized outcome; they do not meet the second, which requires meaningful documentation of performance.

In order to address the problematic nature of observations, teacher educators can make them less global and more connected to performance. For example, they can pair observations of candidates in action with the candidates' reflections on what happened and why they did what they did (alternatively, one could also interact with them about how they made sense of their values and beliefs in the light of their behavior). When candidates reflect on (a) what they intended to do, (b) what they did, and (c) what they see in retrospect in relationship to their actions as guided by beliefs, values, dispositions, they also become more conscious of their decision making as practitioners.

Teacher educators can also avoid global judgments by using a collection of artifacts, gathered by candidates as evidence for meeting standards or demonstrating proficiencies. These artifacts, accompanied by candidate reflections, provide a window into the thinking and decision making of the candidate and relate the choices made to their purposes, the needs of the situation, the response to professional expectations, and so forth. The quality of reflection is a key aspect here, as some programs promote a formulaic approach that may not assist candidates in probing their practice for next steps. Dottin notes that "the process of 'reflection on action' enables learners to stop and examine why they acted as they did, and, as a result, gain insight from the learning experience," adding that this process must be taught.[26] In both of the alternatives to global ratings, the possibility of collecting records of practice comes closer to meeting the criterion of documented performance.

The Largely Untapped Potential of Formative Assessment

Much of the work seen in institutions' assessment of dispositions focuses on summative judgments, again perhaps because of the NCATE expectation that data be aggregated and compiled for analysis. As a result, the potential for using assessment to support candidate growth has been minimized. Interestingly, while NCATE's supporting explanation for standard 2 indicates that "the unit embeds assessment in the preparation programs, conducts them on a continuing basis for both formative and summative purposes, and provides candidates with ongoing feedback," the rubric used to make accreditation decisions does not mention formative assessment.[27]

In the development of dispositions, formative assessment has the potential to play a key role. Consider, for example, the entry essay that many teacher education candidates are asked to write, and assume that the faculty have shaped the prompt appropriately to focus on a decision the candidate made and why she made it or on the analysis of a dilemma. A summative judgment of the essay would simply categorize the candidate's response. A formative response would begin a dialogue with the candidate about her thinking and its sources or perhaps about alternative approaches and their grounding in the literature. Such a response would combine feedback on what the candidate did, as well as questions to prod further thinking. Above all, a formative approach to assessment would feed forward to future work and assessment prompts, allowing both the candidate and the teacher education faculty to see how the candidate's performance over time shows growth in clarity, depth, and complexity of thought.

The formative uses of assessment go beyond the two criteria mentioned above. A program could assess candidates using a clear conceptualization and appropriate documentation without taking advantage of formative assessment. Without good formative assessment, candidates lose opportunities to internalize or deepen their understanding of dispositions and to learn from their documented performances.

The Complexity Required to Assess Ethical and Moral Aspects of Teaching

As we come to understand dispositions as related to ethical and moral responsibilities of teaching, we also need to think of new ways to engage in assessment. Consider the ethical and moral stance that a teacher is responsible for ensuring equitable opportunities to learn for all students. Using the first criterion, that statement is a clear outcome, although it requires some unpacking or operationalization. Using the second criterion, one would need to have a robust, complex, multifaceted assessment of the candidate in action in order to provide documentation as evidence.

For example, the Performance Assessment for California Teachers (PACT) elicits a teacher's planning, implementation in the classroom, and reflection on his impact on learners. The reflection guides that accompany all aspects of the assessment assist candidates to probe their decision making and to stand back and analyze the impact of their work on learners individually, in subgroups, and as a whole group. Very carefully designed rubrics guide faculty assessors in documenting the evidence in valid and reliable ways.[28] Table 1.1 is an example of a rubric (from the PACT Web site, www.pacttpa.org) that brings together how the clear conceptualization of teacher practice integrates knowledge, skills, and dispositions; in addition, it illustrates the kind of evidence required to document candidate performance. The rubric addresses an aspect of providing equitable opportunities for learning—in this case, focused on supporting learners' academic language development. In the progression of the rubric, it is evident *how* candidates who are rated at level 3 or 4 demonstrate a stronger knowledge/skill base, which allows them to more effectively support their learners' development of language proficiency. For example, at both levels 3 and 4, the candidate's use of support strategies is clearly designed to help the learner succeed in a meaningful task. The focus on the learner reflects a clear moral purpose, supported by knowledge and skill. At level 3, the candidate can explain why these strategies are likely to support language development. In addition, at level 4, the candidate can project ways in which instruction can be adjusted as the learner becomes more proficient. Across these descriptors, candidates' reflections also demonstrate their commitment to providing such support to their learners.

Both Stiggins and W. James Popham have recently decried a serious lack of assessment literacy in the teacher education community.[29] They note the wide variations in assessment practice, representing problematic to excellent approaches to developing appropriate instruments and using them in both formative and summative ways. While teacher educators need to be concerned with how we guide candidates in their growth in knowledge, skill, and dispositions, the efficacy of our work with candidates depends critically on how we use meaningful assessment processes to both support candidate development and document candidate performance in action/reflection.

The issues presented in this chapter are our starting points for probing practice in teacher education. The opening vignettes, showing the contrasts between Rebecca and Jessica, highlight the urgency to develop dispositions in tandem with knowledge and skills; to focus on ethical, moral action; to develop teachers' professional identity; to recognize the impact of context on the enactment of professional dispositions in practice; and to cultivate dispositions by making the process of growth explicit. The sets of tensions illustrate multiple perspectives that chal-

TABLE 1.1   Performance Assessment Rubric

Academic language/supporting academic language development

EL12: How do the candidate's planning, instruction, and assessment support academic language development? (TPEs 1, 4, 7, 8)

Level 1	Level 2	Level 3	Level 4
• The candidate gives **little or sporadic support to students** to meet the language demands of the learning tasks. *Or* • **Language and/ or content is oversimplified** to the point of limiting student access to the core content of the curriculum.[a]	• The candidate uses scaffolding or other support to **address identified gaps** between students' current language abilities and the language demands of the learning tasks and assessments.[b] • These supports **provide immediate access to core content** without providing opportunities for students to develop further language proficiency.	• The candidate's use of scaffolding or other support provides access to core content while also providing **explicit models, opportunities for practice, and feedback for students to develop further language proficiency** related to the demands of the learning tasks and assessgments. • The candidate **articulates why** the instructional strategies chosen **are likely to support** specific aspects of students' language development.	• The candidate's use of scaffolding or other support provides access to core content while also providing explicit models, opportunities for practice, and feedback for students to develop further language proficiency related to the demands of the learning tasks and assessments. • Candidate **articulates why** the instructional strategies chosen **are likely to support** specific aspects of students' language development and **projects ways** in which **the scaffolds can be removed** as proficiency increases.

[a] Core content is the set of facts, concepts, skills, and abilities that are absolutely necessary to participate at least minimally in the learning/assessment tasks in the learning segment.

[b] Such support might include one or more of the following: modeling of strategies for comprehending or composing texts; explicit communication of the expected features of oral or written texts (e.g., using rubrics, models, and frames); use of strategies that provide visual representations of content while promoting literacy development (e.g., graphic organizers); vocabulary development techniques (context cues, categorization, analysis of word parts, etc.); opportunities to work together with students with different kinds of language and literacy skills, etc.

Source: Performance Assessment for California Teachers, http://www.pacttpa.org.

lenge teacher educators to find a clear vision of teacher candidate development and a meaningful path to that development. Finally, issues with assessing dispositions invite teacher educators to develop knowledge and skill in the design of assessment that both supports development and provides meaningful documentation.

CHAPTER TWO

A Journey Toward Humanization in Education

María del Carmen Salazar, Karen L. Lowenstein, and Andra Brill

> My teachers taught me the essentials: reading, writing, and math. However, I never saw myself reflected in the content or context of my schooling. As a consequence, my teachers inadvertently taught me that people who looked like me had little value. I remember wishing my skin away in the third grade, wishing I could be white. I had come to associate whiteness with success and brownness with failure. I was overwhelmed with feelings of shame over the most essential elements of my humanity: my culture, my heritage language, and my parents.
>
> I learned to read, write, and do math . . . it came at a heavy cost.
>
> —*María del Carmen Salazar*

Editors' Case Introduction:
Boettcher Teachers Program at the University of Denver

The University of Denver is the oldest independent university in the Rocky Mountain region, enrolling approximately 11,500 students in its undergraduate and graduate programs. The Morgridge College of Education supports multiple pathways to teacher preparation including a range of university-based educator preparation programs and two urban teacher residencies, the Boettcher Teachers Program and the Denver Urban Teacher Residency.

Established in 2003, the Boettcher Teachers Program is a dual licensure and master's degree fellowship. Boettcher Teaching Fellows are specially trained and endorsed to work with culturally and linguistically diverse students. Fellows are awarded full tuition in exchange for a commitment to teach in low-income schools in the metro Denver area for four years beyond licensure. In the teacher residency year, fellows receive a living stipend and complete licensure requirements; as practicing teachers, they complete the master's degree at the end of their second year in the program.

The Boettcher Teachers Program involves collaboration among these partners: the University of Denver Morgridge College of Education, the Boettcher Foundation, the Public Education & Business Coalition, University, Adams 12 Five Star Schools, and Mapleton Public Schools.

A Journey Toward Humanization in Education illustrates how the three authors, who are also the key practitioners involved in working with Boettcher Teaching Fellows, captured their practice through an in-depth examination of one candidate's performance in a series of assessments designed to guide candidate growth as well as to document candidate progress. They identify ways in which their coaching assisted the candidate to confront issues in his understanding of learners and build skills in advocacy for them, but also recognize where they missed chances to use assessment as a support to his growth. Table 1 provides a detailed picture of five "humanizing dispositions," with both conceptual and behavioral indicators and table 2 documents how these dispositional indicators are assessed in the program's series of performance assessments.

• • • • •

Teacher educators across the nation recognize that children in U.S. schools receive the message that they must sever their cultural and linguistic roots in order to succeed in mainstream U.S. society. This message is often fueled by teacher candidates who come with prior experiences that do not foster a belief in the potential of culturally and linguistically diverse students. Furthermore, teacher candidates may view students' cultural and linguistic resources as barriers to overcome rather than resources to develop and build on. As core faculty in an urban teacher residency known as the *Boettcher Teachers Program*, we, the authors of this chapter, respond to the current state of schooling through advocacy for humanization in teacher preparation. Our vision is that academic success should not result at the expense of the cultural, linguistic, and familial resources that children need to thrive and that "humanize" their experience in schools. Thus, we hold a strong conviction that teacher educators have a moral and ethical responsibility to foster humanizing dispositions in teacher preparation. *Humanizing dispositions* are attitudes, values, and beliefs that advance the dignity, humanity, and achievement of culturally and linguistically diverse learners.

This is a case of our efforts as teacher educators to identify and develop humanizing dispositions in teacher preparation. We describe performance assessments developed for teacher candidates to internalize humanizing dispositions. We also describe the experience of one teacher candidate who navigated our efforts to develop humanizing dispositions. We further detail how we unpack what it means for teacher candidates to develop humanizing dispositions through targeted beliefs and actions, and how we link this work back to our performance assessments. Finally, we address challenges in infusing humanizing dispositions into teacher preparation and discuss our overall learning as teacher educators.

IDENTIFYING HUMANIZING DISPOSITIONS IN TEACHER PREPARATION

In 2009, the Boettcher Teachers Program successfully reached its fifth year of operation, an important milestone for any program. María, Karen, and Andra engaged in collective reflection as to the strengths and areas of growth for the program. Our reflections were based on our previous professional experiences, personal experiences, theoretical knowledge, and practical expertise in teacher education. A consistent theme emerged as a result of our dialogic interaction about the importance of classroom teachers' providing students with a humanizing experience. We began to conceptualize humanization as promoting the notion that students' cultural, linguistic and familial roots are essential to their academic achievement. As a result, we pushed each other to articulate the humanizing dispositions we seek to foster in teacher preparation. Through reflexive deliberation involving critical analysis of teacher candidates' program feedback, we identified the following five core humanizing dispositions that we seek to foster:

- Commitment to being a learner of diversity and its impact on teaching and learning
- Relentless belief in the potential of culturally and linguistically diverse youth
- Conviction to coconstruct knowledge with students and their families
- Willingness to accept, embrace, and navigate the complexity of teaching and learning in collaboration with others

• Persistence in advocating for students and their families

The sections that follow provide a detailed description of each of the five core humanizing dispositions.

Commitment to Being a Learner of Diversity and Its Impact on Teaching and Learning

Humanizing dispositions originate through a quest to discover one's own diversity. Sonia Nieto and Patty Bode assert that "an educator must accept their own diversity and delve into their own identity before they can learn about and from students."[1] We provide opportunities for our teacher candidates to examine their own diversity, including privileges and biases and how these impact their educational philosophy.

As part of the ongoing process of exploring their own diversity, our teacher candidates are asked to continuously learn about the *other* and appreciate how diverse experiences inform worldviews, perspectives, aspirations, self-concepts, and opportunities.[2] In learning about the diverse experiences of the *other*, teacher candidates come to understand that educators, students, and parents experience multiple identities and navigate multiple worlds. It is vital that teacher candidates understand the ways diverse populations of students and parents experience the world, and that their ways of knowing and being in the world are equally valid.

We also believe that teacher candidates need to understand how their own conceptions and understandings of cultural differences and cultural diversity affect teaching and learning. We emphasize that teacher candidates envision students' language and cultural needs as the nucleus of effective educational practice.[3] Furthermore, we prepare our teacher candidates to hold a deep understanding that there are different pathways to student learning and these pathways develop within a culture and community.[4] We encourage teacher candidates to be lifelong learners of their own diversity and the diversity of the students and families they serve.

Relentless Belief in the Potential of Culturally and Linguistically Diverse Youth

We are aware that a vast body of research shows that students who have caring relationships are more motivated and perform better academically.[5] We envision caring as an essential ingredient in the goal to advance high achievement for all students. Teacher candidates who develop caring relationships with students get to know the multiple identities of their students, and they share their own identities as well. They build trusting learning environments where risk taking by students and teachers alike is valued and protected. We hold our teacher candidates accountable for demonstrating caring and asset perspectives of children, families, and communities. Teacher candidates are expected to view parents and community members as partners in education.[6] We prepare our teacher candidates to guard against the *pobrecito syndrome*.[7] The word *pobrecito* means "poor little one" in Spanish. Educators who adhere to a pobrecito mentality may not believe in the potential of every child to excel academically; rather, they lower standards for the children who they perceive are born to unfortunate circumstances. We expect our teacher candidates to act on the belief that all children have the potential to reach high academic standards, especially in the face of challenges.

Above all, we envision our teacher candidates as warm demanders.[8] The term *warm demander* is frequently used to describe culturally responsive teachers who are successful with culturally and linguistically diverse learners because they hold high expectations, they teach with authority, and they are caring. We expect our teacher candidates to believe that all students *will* learn given the enactment of effective practices. This implies that teacher candidates must hold a relentless belief in the capabilities and vast potential of students and their families, and they actively communicate their high expectations. Furthermore, we expect our teacher candidates to examine their own practices when students are not experiencing academic growth.

Conviction to Coconstruct Knowledge with Students and Their Families

We foster the disposition that learning requires that students feel visible and accountable to teachers and to one another.[9] Teacher candidates support students in feeling visible and accountable to one another by coconstructing knowledge with students and their families. We encourage teacher candidates to engage their students in examining social constructions of privilege and structural inequalities and how these impact opportunities for students and their parents. We encourage teacher candidates to express humility in the impact of their own privilege, particularly in the lives of the *other*. We provide opportunities for teacher candidates to develop critical consciousness in examining inequities and building opportunities for student empowerment. Most importantly, we foster the belief that teacher candidates cannot empower students and their families; instead, they can create spaces to help students and their families discover and act on their own power.[10]

Willingness to Accept, Embrace, and Navigate the Complexity of Teaching and Learning in Collaboration with Others

Teacher candidates who work with culturally and linguistically diverse learners often describe a greater sense of uncertainty due to the complexity of meeting the needs of students and families who are culturally, socially, economically, and linguistically diverse. We ask our teacher candidates to embrace complexity and acknowledge that there are no simple solutions. We provide opportunities for teacher candidates to develop beliefs and attributes to navigate the complexity of teaching and learning in diverse communities, including (1) being open to navigating multiple definitions of success; (2) being curious, adaptable, and willing to take risks; (3) being creative and resourceful; and (4) being courageous, patient, passionate, and compassionate. In addition, teacher candidates are prepared in a cohort model, and they navigate the complexity of teaching in collaboration with experienced mentors for an entire school year. Teacher candidates learn to teach in the same context where they become teachers, immersed in the complexities of working with diverse learners throughout their apprenticeship. Thus, teacher candidates count on a strong network of collaboration as they engage in the complex work of teaching and learning.

Persistence in Advocating for Students and Their Families

We challenge our teacher candidates to understand that schools are not structured to value diverse human experiences and enable learning for all.[11] We provide opportunities for them to understand the systemic inequities in the educational system and develop a vision of their role in improving the system. Most of all, we encourage teacher candidates to advocate for marginalized students and families by challenging themselves, students, and the role of educational institutions and educators in maintaining inequitable systems. We are informed by the National Board for Professional Teaching Standards, which advocates that the role of teachers is not just to reinforce the status quo; rather, "accomplished teachers encourage students to question prevailing canons and assumptions to help them think for themselves."[12] It is our goal that our teacher candidates "prepare students to affect change in society, not merely fit into it."[13] Finally, we prepare teacher candidates to appreciate that they need allies to bring about systems change, and they need to enlist the expertise of various human resources, including colleagues, administrators, students, parents, and community members.[14]

NURTURING HUMANIZING DISPOSITIONS

We engage in a systematic effort to nurture humanizing dispositions in our teacher candidates in order to promote the principle that teachers honor and expand on students' resources. We immerse teacher candidates in critical readings, group discussions, reflective writing, multimedia presentations, interactions with native informants, daily opportunities to enact their learning, and routine classroom observation and feedback cycles. In addition, we have devised a performance assessment system that scaffolds students' learning in the development of humanizing dispositions. In the first year of the program, we begin with a *personal education history project* that requires teacher candidates to examine their own experiences and diversity and how these impact their assumptions about teaching and learning. Second, in a *child study project* we ask teacher candidates to contrast their educational experiences and diversity through a case study of a diverse learner. Third, we engage teachers in an *analysis of teaching and learning project*, which asks them to critically reflect on their knowledge of self and *other* and connect this knowledge to instructional strategies that support student learning. Fourth, teacher candidates complete a *praxis project* designed to weave theories of equity into everyday practices in classrooms. Fifth, we ask teachers to develop a *critical case study* to deepen their understanding of multiple perspectives of problems or dilemmas and competing solutions. Finally, in a culminating assessment we ask teachers to engage in critical action research in collaboration with colleagues and students in an effort to address crucial student needs in their own classroom. The ultimate objective is that our performance assessment system scaffold novice teachers in developing humanizing dispositions that result in student achievement and sociocultural competence.

TRACING THE DEVELOPMENT OF HUMANIZING DISPOSITIONS

This section highlights the experience of one teacher candidate as he navigated our efforts to nurture humanizing dispositions through our performance assessment system. Like the vast majority of teachers, John

Henry (pseudonym, hereafter "JH") is white and middle class. He speaks French fluently and is mathematically and musically talented. He is currently in his second year as a full-time teacher. His enthusiasm for his students and his content area is evident in his middle school mathematics classroom, serving predominantly Latino students.

In looking back at our initial impressions of JH, we recalled his comments around "appreciation" and "celebration" of diversity. In our work with JH and others like him, we have come to understand that preservice teachers typically need opportunities to move beyond the surface, to develop a deep knowledge and a repertoire of skills to meet the complex needs of diverse youth. The sections that follow describe evidence of his development of humanizing dispositions through our performance assessments, as well as our interventions as teacher educators to scaffold JH to a deeper awareness and enactment.

Personal Education History

In the first performance assessment of the program, the personal education history, teacher candidates are asked to explore how their own identities and key educational experiences have shaped their beliefs about teaching, learning, and the purposes of education. This particular learning experience is intended to serve as a catalyst for teacher candidates to examine their own humanity and diversity. JH described his personal education as one that was marked with fulfilling experiences that often mirror the experiences of middle-class youth in U.S. schools. He recollected participating in spelling bees and math competitions, learning French, developing his musical talents, and engaging in sports. In identifying his own high academic achievement and positive memories of schooling, he shared an experience that was typical of many of our white, middle-class teacher candidates.

In addition to sharing his own educational accomplishments, JH described one teacher in particular who encouraged him to excel and believed in his potential. He felt connected to this teacher who believed in his abilities and challenged him. He articulated an important element of humanizing dispositions in examining his connection to one particular teacher and relating the importance of identifying students' strengths and providing them with unwavering support. In describing his own identity, JH identified himself as a musician and a mathematician. Like many of our white, middle-class teacher candidates, JH described himself in individualistic terms, particularly in regard to his interests. He did not articulate an awareness of essential elements of his diversity, such as his own cultural background, ethnic identity, or socioeconomic status. We have found that, like JH, many white teacher candidates initially see themselves as individuals and not as members of a group unless they describe elements such as hobbies or familial roles.

In describing his interactions with diverse learners, JH related one particular experience of teaching as a long-term substitute in a U.S. school whose population consisted of East African Muslim students. He described an incident where a Somali student did not engage in prayer with his fellow classmates. Instead, the student yelled out an expletive in French, the equivalent to the words *female dog*, or the expletive *bitch*. The students who had been praying were deeply offended. JH met with the student and the principal to address other students' concerns with the exchange. The principal revealed that in Somali history, dogs were used by Italian invaders to strike fear in the Somali people, and dogs were still feared as a sign of enslavement.

JH articulated his learning from the incident in terms of handling situations calmly and encouraging students to learn from their mistakes. While he learned an important lesson in classroom management, he did not consider that he needed to develop greater consciousness of cultural norms and how cultural identity impacts learning. Again, we found this to be common for white, middle-class teacher candidates who lack consciousness about race, culture, and ethnicity.

We understood that we had to help JH develop a deeper understanding of his worldview by examining his own diversity and privileges, as well as the experiences of the *other* in urban schooling. We wanted JH to examine schooling through the eyes of a diverse learner, contrasting his own experiences with those of the *other*.

Child Study

The second assessment in the program is a child study. The objective of the child study is to know a child in multiple systems, such as the classroom, school, social settings, and family, in order to improve their academic achievement. JH selected Jose, an English language learner in the ninth grade who was born in Mexico and had moved to the United States when he was eight years old. In the school context, JH shadowed Jose for a day throughout his classes. He most often described how Jose was disengaged from the content of his schooling. He related that in classes Jose often socialized and did not complete his work, and he also neglected to turn in assignments. He noted that Jose often mimicked students around him; if they disengaged, he followed. He placed the responsibility of success or lack of success squarely on Jose's shoulders. He noted that Jose chose not to engage. He stated, "He needs to take more responsibility for his learning." While it is definitely the case that students must take responsibility for their learning, JH did not identify greater systemic factors impacting Jose's success, such as a lack of support for English language learners, or the disconnect between the content of schooling and the content of students' lives.

JH also concluded that Jose was "living a successful bicultural lifestyle." In addition, in his conclusion to the child study assessment, he wrote, "As teachers, we see students in one-hour windows, in a setting they may or may not be comfortable with. We have to realize that not all of our students will feel successful in a classroom environment. When we see the student in his or her known surroundings, we can gather a greater picture of the student's personality to incorporate into our classrooms that will help the students to become more successful."

While he acknowledged the importance of knowing a student outside of school and bringing a student's background into the classroom, as his instructors, María, Karen, and Andra believed that JH needed to examine the complexity of Jose's experiences on a deeper level. We challenged him through questioning strategies to continue to observe Jose and probe more deeply into his strengths and struggles. We also asked him to discuss instructional implications for improving Jose's engagement and achievement in school. We typically challenge teacher candidates to delve more profoundly into their initial observations by asking probing questions, such as: How do you know the student is living a successful bicultural life? What indicators can you identify that led you to state your observation as fact? How do the student's experiences with his classmates either support or limit his engagement? How do you know the student is bilingual, fluent in English and Spanish? What does your mentor teacher state about the student's abilities? JH's child study assessment is but one example of how we scaffold teacher candidates to probe the experience of the *other* beyond the surface. We exercise patience because understanding the experiences of the *other* is a developmental process that happens across time, and so we use questioning strategies to prod and push our teacher candidates to probe more deeply.

JH revised the child study four weeks later, and it reflected a greater understanding of the complexity of Jose's experiences. For example, he identified that Jose was having difficulty reading texts and whether this was impacting his engagement and achievement. He noted that a lack of personal connections to the material or a lack of strong reading habits might be further impacting his academic performance. In making instructional connections, JH stated that, as a teacher, he would find an entry point into Jose's literacy development by introducing him to texts he could relate to. He noted the need to create an intentional cooperative grouping between Jose and high-achieving Spanish-speaking students because Jose was motivated by his peers. He also noted Jose's sense of pride toward his home life, and he wondered how he might develop Jose's sense of pride as a student. Upon examining Jose's experience in greater depth, JH was able to articulate concrete instructional decisions that could impact Jose's achievement; these decisions reflected a desire to build on Jose's interests and skills. His connections reflected an increasingly asset-based perspective. This was especially evident in his final statement: "When magnifying the lens of analysis on Jose, I found that when he wasn't always showing success, usually it was because he needed reinforcement of traits he already possessed." JH demonstrated a desire to grasp the complexity of his students' lives inside and outside of school. He also began to articulate the importance of building on students' resources.

As we analyzed JH's progress through the performance assessments, we discovered that we must explicitly identify how we, as teacher educators, model the importance of building on students' strengths. In our program we intentionally look at teacher candidates from the perspective of the assets they bring and the background knowledge they start with. We do not berate them for their inexperience with diverse learners or for their racial, linguistic, and socioeconomic privileges, to name a few. We strongly believe that viewing teacher candidates from the perspective of their deficits only serves to *disable* teachers with regard to the instruction of culturally and linguistically diverse learners. Instead, we build on what they bring, in an effort to *enable* them to be successful. As we make sense of our work with JH, we seek to become more intentional about demonstrating our own metacognitive processes in modeling humanizing dispositions and actions. As for JH, at this point we wanted him to articulate a conviction to coconstruct knowledge with students and their families. We also wanted to see him engage in student-centered learning in the classroom.

Analysis of Student Learning

An analysis of student learning is intended to increase knowledge and skill in adapting instruction and assessment to second language learners. In this assessment, JH stated that he began to see himself as an educational planner, yet he identified the need to delve more deeply to support students in constructing meaning. He noted improvements in many important aspects of his educational planning, including time management, clear objectives, consistent assessment practices, accessing students' background knowledge, and differentiated instruction. He continued to challenge himself, noting, "Initially, my planning was more of a survival strategy, where I just wanted to get through the lessons as smoothly as possible. A lot of the time I was trying to deposit the information to the students instead of having them construct meaning on their own. Discipline issues led me to feel most confident leading the class instead of having more student-centered learning."

JH envisioned himself as an educator who incorporated inquiry-based learning, and he was especially committed to students' constructing their own meaning from mathematics. He stated, "It is a teacher's job to present students with material they can construct meaning from." He also identified his struggle to enact these ideals because he was focused on building classroom management skills.

At this point in the program, students typically express a growing sophistication in their vision of themselves as teachers. They often express a strong desire to engage students in meaningful learning. Although the teacher candidates can visualize their ideal, as novices, they grapple with the immediacy of planning, assessment, and classroom management. JH expressed the sentiment that the enactment of his ideal was a challenge as he attempted to master the basics. As we analyzed his progress through his performance assessments, we became aware that we had missed an opportunity to help JH develop a deeper knowledge of the benefits and challenges associated with coconstructing knowledge with students and families. We could have been more intentional with questioning strategies to help him explore various methods to coconstruct knowledge with students. We could have used questioning strategies to get JH to identify how he could create opportunities for parents and families to engage in the coconstruction of knowledge. While we missed an opportunity to help him develop a deeper understanding of the importance of the coconstruction of knowledge, we saw encouraging growth in his ability to connect theory and practice in his classroom context.

Praxis

The praxis assessment is designed to be a synthesis of one's emerging beliefs about teaching and learning, and reflection on the interconnections between theory and practice. It is titled after Paulo Freire's concept of *praxis*, or reflection and action upon the world in order to transform it.[15] In this assessment JH described many of the conceptual understandings of humanizing dispositions, including the importance of building relationships with students, knowing who students are in order to engage them, a desire to advance the achievement of all students, and a belief in the success of all learners.

In his praxis assessment, he specifically highlighted the importance of building relationships with students. He stated, "By getting to know my students, it shows them I care about them as individuals. They don't see me as just a teacher, but as someone who knows something about them. Building relationships is the first step towards a student being successful in the classroom." He also revealed a desire to build relationships by sharing his life experiences with his students. He stated, "By building relationships with my students and being honest about who I am, I show my students I value honest and personal relationships." JH also expressed admiration for his students and a deep desire to support their success, and he added, "Many of my students don't equate school with success. My job is to give these students the confidence they need to succeed and then give them the strategies to help succeed. Without confidence and previous success in school, I admire them for showing up every day. I want them to know I value their presence."

In describing pedagogical decisions that set students up for success, JH described the importance of getting to know students in order to provide a sense of immediacy and relevance for students. He further emphasized the importance of students' mastery of learning strategies, including reading comprehension strategies. Most of all, he emphasized the importance of communicating high expectations. He concluded his paper with the following: "I believe every student wants to learn and is capable of learning. He or she must feel there is a reason why they should learn a particular topic. My job is to provide that reason. As a teacher, I need to make sure everything I do is backed with the intention of contributing to the success of my students."

At this point, we expect teacher candidates to envision equity as a compass that guides their instructional decisions. JH was developing a strong sense of equity in that he acknowledged that relationships were the foundation for learning and he articulated strong beliefs in the potential of all learners. Equally as important, he identified instructional strategies to help his students succeed. He had reached an important milestone, clearly articulating various humanizing dispositions and how these dispositions can be enacted in the classroom. In examining his progress, we have come to understand that we need to continue to push students on the enactment of humanizing dispositions and base their competency not only on their identification of such skills, but also on observable behaviors in the classroom.

Critical Case Study

In the final assessment of the first year in the program, JH completed a critical case study, which is a description and analysis of a moral dilemma encountered in teaching. He described an incident with a student who articulated his desire to engage in a violent act. He was conflicted by the actual intention of the student, and he conferred with other teachers, who encouraged him to report the incident to administrators. He described his angst over the fact that the student did not return to school after he reported the incident, and the student was subsequently listed as a runaway. JH was deeply bothered and reflected on this incident. He wrote, "Was there a way I could have affirmed to the student that I cared about him, while still taking the necessary measures to bring this incident to the deans? Was I in some way responsible for this student running away from home? What message did I give this student about how I cared about him? Would this be his last experience in school?"

JH had internalized the importance of caring and relationships, reflecting a growing awareness of the impact of his decisions and his interactions with students, as well as an increasing awareness of the complexity of students' lives outside of school. He subsequently committed himself to affirming students and the challenges they faced on a daily basis. He examined his own role in supporting students' achievement and well-being, versus focusing on what students and their families lacked. Again, JH had reached an important milestone in the program, focusing on what he could impact, thereby increasing his sense of self-efficacy as a teacher. In reflecting on JH's progress, we could be more explicit about helping him identify resources for students who are dealing with difficult issues. This knowledge would be especially relevant as he transitioned into his first year of teaching. The final performance assessment takes place in year two of the program. At this point, JH is the teacher-of-record in a high-needs school.

Critical Action Research

In year two of the program, the teacher candidates become licensed teachers with their own classrooms. They undertake a yearlong critical action research project intended to engage novice teachers in systematic inquiry. Critical action research engages teachers with issues grounded in their own classroom practice, through the creation of research questions, theoretical frameworks, data collection, and analysis and interpretation, in an effort to increase student achievement. Through this assessment, his growing consciousness of glaring inequities in the education of Latino students cemented his commitment to diverse learners.

JH's critical action research project was titled *Building Access to Higher Level Math for Latino Students*. He engaged in extensive research on mathematics as a gatekeeper for the academic success of Latino students. The knowledge he gained from this project sparked a flame of indignation that led him to champion mathematics for Latino students. He was especially struck by the fact that Latino students perform progressively worse on mathematics national assessments in fourth, eighth, and twelfth grades.[16]

As in previous assessments, JH emphasized the need for teachers to consider not only the curriculum, but actually knowing their students. He acknowledged his students' negative experiences with math and looked for solutions to help them be more successful. He focused on building relationships with students, and he worked hard to individualize his instruction and find out each student's strengths and challenges. He engaged students in his action research project by asking them to identify effective classroom practices. While he felt that he had made progress with students, he articulated that he had a long way to go in providing students with access to higher-level math.

In the conclusion of his project, JH described the challenges he faced and his commitment to his students:

> It has been a challenge this past year to always keep an asset-based mindset towards all students. There was very little expected of the students in math class the previous year and with the revolving door of math teachers, I faced constant skepticism from the students that I actu-

ally cared about them. The more I keep the students engaged, without sacrificing rigor, and the more I validate the work the students are doing, the more successful my students will be. Ultimately, the word I am striving for my practice to be described as is purposeful. The purpose, in the end, is giving access to high level math for my students. The best way for me to do this is by developing relationships with them and holding them to high expectations.

In retrospect, the focus on critical action research is ideal in providing novice teachers with opportunities to analyze real-time challenges and create real-time solutions. We extensively use questioning strategies in helping teachers craft their critical action research projects in order to keep them focused on humanizing dispositions in their own classroom; for example: How do you know your assessment is authentic? How do you know your lesson is relevant? How do you know your students are learning? How can you engage parents in student learning? How will you use your data to improve student learning? As a result, teacher candidates typically state that critical action research is essential to fostering equity in education.

Summary

In looking back at JH's development, we asked ourselves whether he had internalized humanizing dispositions that honor and expand on students' resources. Throughout our time with JH we observed conceptual and behavioral indicators of his developing humanizing dispositions. He held strong convictions about the potential of all learners, and he expressed the pressing need for all learners to have access to higher-level learning. He valued the humanity in others through his emphasis on caring and relationships. He demonstrated a commitment to coconstructing knowledge with students. He consistently acknowledged the challenges he faced and yet was unwavering in his conviction to advocate for students' access to a quality education that would prepare them for future success.

We observed behavioral indicators in JH's planning and delivery of instruction in that he strived to present material in a manner that was relevant to students' lives inside and outside of school. We participated in his efforts to build trust with his students and validate their experiences. We noted that JH continued his commitment to reading the most recent literature on the mathematics attainment of Latino students and using this information to improve his instruction. We witnessed him advocating for access to higher-level math with school leaders, and he even took on a leadership role in the mapping of math standards in the district.

Because of our relationship with JH over time, we were able to have continued conversations about his developing vision of himself as a teacher and his challenges in enacting that vision. At the present time, while he consistently reiterates a belief in the potential of all learners, he also admits that it has been difficult to honor and expand on students' cultural, linguistic, and familial resources because of the challenging school environment he teaches in. JH is currently building his knowledge in the area of culturally responsive teaching and equity through scholarly readings and participation in district leadership teams. JH also secured a grant to attend the National Council of Teachers of Mathematics annual meeting in order to advance his objective of building his knowledge of practices that promote equity in mathematics.

LINKING HUMANIZING DISPOSITIONS TO CONCEPTUAL AND BEHAVIORAL INDICATORS

Since the inception of the Boettcher Teachers Program in 2004, we have worked with many teacher candidates who have experienced a developmental flow similar to the one JH experienced. When we analyzed his progress through our performance assessments, critical questions emerged about the experience of teacher candidates in the program, including these:

- How do we know teacher candidates have internalized humanizing dispositions?
- How can we ensure that teacher candidates enact humanizing dispositions in their classrooms?
- How do we build on our teacher candidates' assets to help them grow in their understanding and skills?
- How can we help teacher candidates maintain resiliency and asset-based perspectives in challenging contexts?
- How can we continue to provide opportunities for our teacher candidates to extend their learning and enactment of humanizing dispositions once they have completed the program?
- How can we work with schools and districts to more deeply cohere humanizing dispositions and professional development of teacher candidates?

In examining these big questions, we have come to a clear understanding of our progress as teacher educators and the goals we want to pursue, including the following:

- Explicitly name humanizing beliefs and actions with teacher candidates as a foundation for educational equity.
- Identify precise humanizing beliefs and actions that teacher candidates are expected to master.
- Use assessments diagnostically to track solid evidence of growth in mastering humanizing beliefs and actions in addition to constructing rubrics that demonstrate teacher candidates' growth.
- Explicitly identify and describe the intervention strategies that scaffold teacher candidates in developing a deeper understanding and enactment of humanizing beliefs and actions.
- Support teacher candidates to seek out their own professional development opportunities.
- Increase collaboration with school districts to promote deeper coherence in mentoring and induction programs and humanizing dispositions.

While we continue to wrestle with these issues, we decided to take action and explicitly define what it means to engage in humanizing actions. We returned to the work of Paulo Freire, who states, "Thought has meaning only when generated by action upon the world."[17] It was through the description and analysis of the experiences of teacher candidate JH that we became aware of the distinction between teacher candidates' conceptualization of humanizing dispositions and the enactment of those dispositions.[18] We are committed to fostering opportunities for our teacher candidates to link beliefs and actions, and so we packed the conceptual and behavioral indicators that would provide evidence of humanizing dispositions. Table 2.1 describes them.

We also looked back at our performance assessments to align them with humanizing conceptual and behavioral indicators. This process helped us to determine whether we were providing learning experiences that foster humanizing dispositions. We became more explicit about how our candidates demonstrate humanizing beliefs and actions through the performance assessments. Furthermore, in the future, every assessment will be linked with the opportunity for teacher candidates to demonstrate application of their knowledge in observation and feedback cycles conducted by program faculty. By linking assessments to classroom observa-

TABLE 2.1   Conceptual and behavioral indicators of humanizing dispositions

Humanizing dispositions	Conceptual indicators	Behavioral indicators
Commitment to being a learner of diversity and its impact on teaching and learning	• Develop awareness of one's own diversity and multiple identities and how these impact teaching and learning. • Identify own privileges and biases and how these impact teaching and learning. • Commit to investigate the diversity and multiple identities of *others.* • Accept one's own worldview is not universal and *other* worldviews are equally valid. • Understand that learning can be culturally mediated. • Recognize students' cultural and linguistic resources are essential to their achievement. • Support different pathways to student learning. • Envision a learning community that honors, respects, and validates diversity.	• Actively inquire into students' perceptions and experiences in the world through scholarly research and student/community engagement. • Validate and build multiple perspectives into classroom activities and assignments. • Actively seek out and incorporate content and curricular resources that reflect students' experiences. • Identify bias in curricular materials, pedagogical practices, and assessments, and make appropriate adjustments. • Supplement prescribed curriculum to include content and materials that reflect students' experiences. • Differentiate instruction in lesson planning, delivery, and assessment, including strategies for ELLs, gifted and talented, special education, and multiple learning styles. • Consistently incorporate culturally responsive practices in delivery of instruction, such as cooperative learning, storytelling, and acceptance of code-switching in oral and written discourse.
Relentless belief in the potential of culturally and linguistically diverse youth	• Honor multiple identities of students. • Commit to share own identities. • Emphasize the importance of developing a trusting learning environment. • Foster asset perspectives of students and families. • Guard against deficit views. • View parents and community members as partners in education. • Believe that all students *will* learn given the enactment of effective practices.	• Actively inquire about students' lives inside and outside of school. • Share own identities with students through • classroom dialogue, pictures, and personal narratives. • Build respectful relationships with students and families. • Incorporate students' experiences into curriculum, assessments, and material culture of the classroom. • Communicate high expectations through design and delivery of challenging curriculum and assessments that foster high-level skills. • Consistently scaffold instruction to give students access to high-level skills. • Take responsibility for student learning through differentiated strategies and data-driven instruction. • Explicitly call students capable, and dialogue with students and parents about their potential and possibilities, including college readiness and postsecondary careers.

TABLE 2.1   Conceptual and behavioral indicators, *continued*

Humanizing dispositions	Conceptual indicators	Behavioral indicators
		• Engage in consistent, respectful, and caring classroom management through clear structures, expectations, and norms
Conviction to coconstruct knowledge with students and families	• Believe that learning requires that students feel visible and accountable to teachers and to one another. • Acknowledge that visibility comes through the coconstruction of knowledge and the development of critical consciousness. • Encourage students to question prevailing canons and assumptions, and become independent thinkers. • Express humility as to the impact of privilege in own life and the lives of *others*. • Understand that teachers cannot empower students; instead, they can create spaces to help students and families discover and act on their own power.	• Develop critical thinking about systems and power through classroom dialogue, readings, and assessments. • Supplement prescribed curriculum through integration of multicultural literature and content. • Create curriculum and assessments to increase understanding of inequities and foster student agency. • Challenge inequity in the curriculum by explicitly pointing it out to students and having students identify inequities themselves. • Develop critical frames and cultural competence in own professional development. • Facilitate structured opportunities for families to construct knowledge inside and outside of school.
Willingness to accept, embrace, and navigate the complexity of teaching and learning in collaboration with others	• Acknowledge that there are no simple solutions. • Be open to navigating multiple definitions of success, including one's own, students/parents/communities, colleagues/administrators, and district/state/national standards. • Foster own and student curiosity, flexibility, risk taking, creativity, patience, resourcefulness, pride, passion, and compassion. • Promote a sense of efficacy for self and students. • Value learning as an ongoing, lifelong pursuit. • Develop systematic thinking to navigate complexity.	• Develop students' understanding of what it means to hold multiple identities through dialogue and class assignments. • Seek input from multiple stakeholders to develop a plan for student success. • Dialogue with students around gains and losses of acculturation and educational success. • Participate in professional development opportunities, including professional learning communities, scholarly endeavors, and teacher research. • Continuously include and assess student/family/community resources to facilitate learning inside and outside of school. • Plan and deliver differentiated instruction based on personalized student and family needs. • Use multiple forms of data on a daily basis to gauge student growth.

TABLE 2.1   Conceptual and behavioral indicators, *continued*

Humanizing dispositions	Conceptual indicators	Behavioral indicators
Persistence in advocating for students and their families	• Understand schooling is not structured to value diverse human experiences and enable learning for all. • Challenge self, students, and role of educational institutions and educators in maintaining inequitable systems. • Believe in the need to prepare students to effect change in society. • Promote collaboration to bring about systems change.	• Pursue leadership roles in schools to advocate for students and families. • Communicate asset perspectives with students, families, colleagues, and administrators. • Create innovative solutions to classroom challenges. • Advocate for school reform that includes the voices of students and their families. • Collaborate with others to advocate for students and families, including professional learning communities, teacher research, etc.

tions, program faculty can collect and analyze observation and feedback data in order to gauge teacher candidates' progress in the conceptualization and enactment of humanizing dispositions. Table 2.2 describes the conceptual and behavioral indicators of humanizing dispositions linked to each performance assessment.

OPPORTUNITIES TO INFUSE HUMANIZING DISPOSITIONS AND ACTIONS IN TEACHER PREPARATION

We have made significant strides in infusing humanizing dispositions and actions in teacher preparation through the work of linking humanizing beliefs and actions with our program's performance assessments. We have many opportunities to infuse humanization in teacher preparation. For example, we need to identify what is developmentally appropriate in terms of a growing awareness of self and *others*, and whether there are typical or differentiated trajectories for white teachers and teachers of color in their deepening awareness of diversity.

Mentor development is also an opportunity for continued alignment of program goals. As we make adjustments to the curriculum for our teacher candidates, we need to provide mentor teachers with a parallel curriculum. Although we have significantly less time with mentors, we strive to help them develop a deeper reflection of their pedagogy and professional development. Being more explicit about the humanizing

TABLE 2.2   Performance assessments linked to conceptual and behavioral indicators of humanizing dispositions

Performance assessment	Objective	Conceptual indicators of humanizing education	Behavioral indicators of humanizing education
Personal education history Reflective synthesis of own educational experiences and how these shape one's beliefs about teaching and learning	• Explore how own identities and key educational experiences have shaped beliefs about teaching, learning, and the purpose of education. • Identify own values, knowledge, and skills that facilitate good teaching in an urban context. • Specify promising classroom practices.	• Develop awareness of one's multiple identities and relative privileges and biases. • Name how one's identities impact perceptions of education, teaching, and learning. • Commit to explore and appreciate the diversity and multiple identities of *others*.	• Share own background with students in order to build relationships. • Dialogue with students about their lives inside and outside of school. • Interact with students in a respectful manner to build open communication. • Demonstrate willingness to learn from multiple stakeholders.
Child study Analysis of a child across multiple contexts, and connection to teaching and learning	• Know a child in multiple systems (e.g., classroom, school, social settings, and family). • Apply understanding of how this knowledge can impact teaching and learning, identifying specific classroom practices.	• Honor multiple identities of students. • Commit to share own identities. • Understand one's own diversity influences teaching and learning. • Understand schooling is not structured to value diverse human experiences and enable learning for all. • Foster asset perspectives of students and families.	• Actively inquire about students' lives inside and outside of school. • Directly engage in dialogue with students in the classroom about who they are, what they know, and what they struggle with. • Share own identities with students in classroom dialogue, pictures, and personal narratives. • Deliver individualized support/instruction that is responsive to students' individual needs.
Analysis of student learning Analysis of students' learning used to refine skills in planning, instruction, and assessment	• Trace students' learning from preassessment to summative assessment. • Increase knowledge and skill in adapting instruction and assessment to second language learners.	• Believe that all students *will* learn given the enactment of effective practices. • Desire to establish a trusting learning environment. • Support different pathways to student learning.	• Communicate high expectations through design and delivery of challenging curriculum and assessments that foster high-level skills. • Consistently scaffold instruction to give students access to high-level skills.

TABLE 2.2   Performance assessments, *continued*

Performance assessment	Objective	Conceptual indicators of humanizing education	Behavioral indicators of humanizing education
			• Explicitly call students capable. • Engage in consistent, respectful, and caring classroom management through clear routines, structures and norms, and relationship building. • Supplement curriculum through integration of multicultural content that reveals inequities and fosters student agency.
Praxis Critical synthesis of educational theory and practice	• Synthesize one's emerging beliefs about teaching and learning.	• Hold belief that an effective teacher is key for student achievement. • Identify links between learning theory of diverse learners and effective classroom practices. • Emphasize the importance of ongoing scholarly pursuits in creating links between theory and practice.	• Actively seek out educational research and instructional resources to promote student learning. • Effectively incorporate learning theories for diverse learners in curricular and pedagogical practices. • Incorporate research-based instructional strategies. • Deliver innovative classroom practices that are grounded in educational theory.
Critical case study Description and analysis of moral dilemma encountered in teaching	• Deepen understanding of multiple perspectives of problems or dilemmas, and competing solutions.	• Commit to coconstruct knowledge with students and their families. • Acknowledge social constructions of privilege and inequality and how these impact opportunities for students and their parents. • Understand educators cannot empower students; instead, they can create spaces to help students discover and act on their own power.	• Include multiple content perspectives for the purpose of fostering analytic and problem-solving skills. • Demonstrate ability to actively listen to other perspectives in interactions with students, parents, and colleagues. • Gather evidence from multiple stakeholders in order to make informed instructional decisions.

TABLE 2.2   Performance assessments, *continued*

Performance assessment	Objective	Conceptual indicators of humanizing education	Behavioral indicators of humanizing education
Critical action research project Teacher research in the context of own classroom, includes scholarly community presentation	• Engage in systematic inquiry alongside other novice teachers through teacher research aimed at increasing student academic achievement.	• Identify students' cultural and linguistic resources as the core of effective practice. • Acknowledge that there are no simple solutions, and be open to navigating multiple definitions of success. • Develop systematic thinking to navigate complexity. • Challenge self, students, and role of educational institutions and educators in maintaining inequitable systems.	• Actively seek out and incorporate content and curricular resources that reflect students' experiences. • Identify bias in curricular materials, and pedagogical and assessment practices, and make appropriate adjustments. • Differentiate instruction in lesson planning, delivery, and assessment. • Consistently incorporate culturally responsive practices in delivery of instruction. • Continuously assess and incorporate student/ family/community resources to facilitate learning inside and outside of school. • Collaborate with others to advocate for students and families.

belief and actions we want to guarantee from our teacher candidates also helps us target the essential learning that must be included in mentor selection and training. Being more explicit ensures that mentors serve as guides to the development of humanizing dispositions and actions.

In addition, we want to build an ongoing focus on humanizing beliefs and actions as teacher candidates advance in their careers. We appreciate the need to continue to work with our partner school districts to provide induction, professional development, and leadership opportunities where humanizing beliefs and actions can flourish.

CONCLUSION

This case represents our efforts as teacher educators to heed the moral imperative of preparing teachers for diverse learners. We detail our efforts to infuse humanizing dispositions into teacher preparation in order to build the dispositions, knowledge, and skills that teachers need to promote the academic achievement and sociocultural competence of culturally and linguistically diverse learners. Through rich descriptions of our critical reflections and deepening understanding of teacher preparation in urban schools, we weave a tapestry of our efforts to unpack what it means to foster humanizing beliefs and actions in teacher preparation.

In looking back at our growing consciousness of humanizing dispositions in teacher preparation, we acknowledge that our own learning as teacher educators has progressed along similar developmental lines as for novice teachers. Just as novice teachers find their stride in five to seven years, through hard work, critical reflection, and trial and error, we found our stride in a deepened understanding of the following: (1) dispositions are enacted only if they are explicitly linked to behaviors, and (2) targeted interventions can scaffold teacher candidates' internalization and enactment of humanizing dispositions. This learning has empowered us to be more explicit and continue to focus our work on humanization for teacher candidates and students alike.

The work of unpacking humanizing dispositions has renewed the passion and commitment of the three authors to serving culturally and linguistically diverse students and their families. While the Boettcher Teachers Program remains committed to humanization in education, the lead author, Salazar, committed to the development of an emerging urban teacher residency known as the Denver Teacher Residency (DTR). The DTR prepares teachers to serve families and children in the Denver Public Schools, the vast majority of whom are culturally and linguistically diverse. Salazar is a graduate of the Denver Public Schools and is passionate about making a difference for students who have experienced similar challenges.

The conceptual and practical knowledge generated from the work of unpacking humanizing dispositions spurred the development of innovative practices in the DTR. In collaboration with the DTR director and staff, Salazar extended her knowledge of humanizing dispositions to create a framework of effective teaching known as the DTR Framework for Equity. The framework embeds humanizing dispositions in five dimensions of effective teaching: commit, engage, plan, teach, and lead. The dimensions are delineated and packed into standards and indicators of an effective teacher, targeting teacher and student behaviors that promote learning. Furthermore, the work of unpacking humanizing dispositions resulted in enduring understandings that influenced the design of the DTR, including these:

- Start with the end in mind: identify what an effective teacher should believe, know, and be able to do to effectively meet the needs of culturally and linguistically diverse learners.
- Extend humanizing dispositions by identifying specific humanizing behaviors novice teachers are expected to engage in.
- Align humanizing dispositions to a performance assessment system in order to create incentives and accountability for the actualization of humanizing dispositions.
- Link dispositions, knowledge, and skills to state and national standards of teacher effectiveness; this promotes alignment to best practices in teacher preparation, creates a strong body of scholarship of effective practices, and builds credibility.
- Build on existing frameworks of teacher preparation to promote quality and innovation.
- Identify clear competencies of practice, being mindful that simplicity scaffolds the complexity of teaching and learning, hence the dimensions: commit, engage, plan, teach, lead,
- Factor student engagement and achievement into the equation of teacher effectiveness; a focus on teachers alone is insufficient.

Finally, the work of unpacking humanizing dispositions resulted in a strong conviction that teacher preparation programs across the nation need to adapt to the changing demographic imperative. Teacher educators can no longer afford to follow outdated teacher preparation standards that are geared toward students in Middle America. Teacher educators should exceed existing standards to intentionally build on the strengths and challenges of the communities they serve, clearly identifying the dispositions, knowledge, and skills a teacher needs to effectively meet the academic and sociocultural needs of culturally and linguistically diverse learners. Teacher educators and teachers alike should call district, state, and national leaders to reassess teacher preparation standards and bring culturally and linguistically diverse students and their families out of the margins and into the center of teacher preparation.

CHAPTER THREE

Disconnection as a Path to Discovery

Lisa E. Johnson, Rebecca Evers, and Jonatha W. Vare

Editors' Case Introduction: Winthrop University

Located in Rock Hill, South Carolina, Winthrop University is a comprehensive teaching university providing personalized and challenging undergraduate, graduate, and continuing professional education programs to its 7,000 students. Winthrop prides itself on being an institution of choice for groups traditionally underrepresented on the college campus. A former normal, Winthrop enjoys a 123-year tradition in teacher preparation and a long history of partnerships with surrounding school districts. Accredited teacher education programs include early childhood, elementary, middle level and secondary education, special education, K–12 art and music education, as well as curriculum and instruction, and reading. Winthrop is a member of the National Network for Educational Renewal (NNER).

In this chapter, the authors describe how action research on their teacher candidates' dispositions led to the discovery of a disconnect between candidates' judgments and actions. This discovery motivated further efforts to devise assessment tools, identify core dispositions, and consider more effective ways to develop desired dispositions. Eventually, the work of this core group became the basis for university-wide actions.

NNER PRINCIPLES OF TEACHING

In 1995 the College of Education at Winthrop University incorporated four principles of the NNER into the conceptual framework of its teacher preparation programs:

- Ensuring equal access to quality learning for all students
- Promoting responsible stewardship of our schools and universities
- Improving teaching and learning through pedagogy that nurtures and challenges all learners (preK–12, university)
- Providing students with the knowledge, skills, and dispositions to become fully engaged participants in our democratic society[1]

Ten years later, a core group of faculty began investigating how teacher candidates were developing these principles and what we, as faculty, were doing to promote such development, especially in relation to educational equity and teaching in a democratic society.

Teams of faculty in the College of Education offer core courses to teacher candidates in the various teacher education programs. Faculty use common syllabi, texts, assignments, and learning activities, and require at least one common summative assessment. These team efforts promote continuity, encourage generalization, and reduce conceptual drift. Courses on topics such as introduction to the profession, educational psychology, diverse learners, classroom management, assessment, and reflective practice offered a perfect platform for engaging in a self-study of how we, as "core faculty," develop teacher candidates' dispositions.

We began our inquiry by collecting responses to two assessments in the senior year. The first assessment was a two- to three-page essay written in response to the following prompt: "Describe your moral/ethical responsibilities as an educational leader in a democratic society." The second assignment was a personal leadership project designed to meet goals in our conceptual framework that relate to becoming an educational leader. Candidates create and implement a project addressing an identified schoolwide or community need. Because the project called for communication and collaboration beyond the internship classroom, we expected it to develop candidates' propensity towards leadership.

When we examined our students' responses to these assessments, we found that some candidates could recognize, reason through, and act upon their moral obligations, but most were judging their students from a "missionary position."[2] Candidates at elementary and early childhood levels expressed a need to "save" or rescue the students they were teaching through love and care, as these examples illustrate:

- Emily connected classroom management with socioeconomic status: "Some of my students are bused in from other areas, and their lower SES status does stand out in the classroom. These are the students that I have to spend extra time with during lessons. I have to walk around and make sure they are on-task."[3]
- Jonathan left little room for prior experiences or cultural competency: "Often times our students enter our classrooms with an empty plate, just waiting for information to add to their plates to transform them into the people they will become in future classrooms and in our society."[4]
- Sylvia repeated some new language that she had learned in courses, but still adhered to old patterns of thinking about norms and differences: "Special needs and ESOL students often have a difficult time because their peers ostracize them due to their differences. If a child hears a teacher talk about the normal kids and he is not one, this could be devastating. I plan to discuss with my students why some are more different than others. Being able to have open conversations with my class will prevent the odd balls from being hurt."[5]

The preK–12 students our candidates were teaching did not need to be "saved"— they needed to be served; however, our candidates were viewing their students through a deficit lens.

Our data did include some moral exemplars that helped us clarify what exactly we were aspiring to achieve. For example, Tanisha highlighted frustrating efforts to convince her cooperating teacher that differentiation was critical to achieving equity. Monique described how she could use "knowledge of the diversity of the classroom to influence instructional and behavioral methods and strategies to meet the individual needs of the classroom."[6] For her personal leadership project, Monique worked on making afterschool tutoring available to students without transportation.

This first study revealed a disconnect between the NNER mission of providing equal access to a challenging curriculum for all students and what our candidates were planning for and implementing in their classrooms. Our candidates needed to relinquish their deficit views and go beyond providing a fun, friendly classroom environment to educating students in basic skills, assisting them in finding resources in an already impoverished community, and making connections between content and survival.[7] This motivated us to pursue further action research in order to assess candidates and discover where changes in our own curriculum and pedagogy were needed.

Over the next four years, we embarked on a study of our candidates' dispositions and their development. We learned that many candidates were graduating without the dispositions outlined in our college's mission. This helped us clarify our goals and develop a model on which to base our teaching and assessments.

DEVELOPING A NEW MATRIX

We felt the need for a tool to assess dispositions based upon the NNER principles reflected in our mission and conceptual framework. We wanted our teacher candidates to use the knowledge and skills gained through field experience and coursework to carry out the moral and ethical responsibilities of teaching diverse populations. We were obligated to fulfill the National Council for Accreditation of Teacher Education's (NCATE) mandate to develop candidates with the knowledge, skills, and dispositions to help all students learn.[8] The alignment of NNER principles and NCATE standards focused us on the need to develop candidates who could help achieve educational equity. Such teachers would be committed to democratic principles, flexible, open to multiple perspectives, reflective, and effective at communicating.[9]

In order to document our candidates' dispositions, we needed a way to document trends in judgments and actions in particular contexts.[10] In addition, we assumed that fostering effective teacher candidate dispositions requires changes in patterns of moral reasoning.[11] We used a university research council grant to create a matrix for analyzing teacher candidates' work samples.[12]

The matrix (see table 3.1) has three schemata regarding moral and ethical issues, each of which represents a different level of complexity.[13] We hypothesized that teacher candidates would move through these levels, prompted by faculty who guide candidates to consider issues of equity and fairness in the context of their courses and field experience. As candidates move from the personal interest level to maintaining norms and finally to postconventional thinking, cooperation becomes a central theme along with recognition that social norms can be altered. As candi-

TABLE 3.1   Matrix of indicators for the moral domain

Moral/ethical schema	Judgments	Actions
Personal interest schema (Exclusive focus on self, egocentric orientation; i.e., "How does the situation affect me?")	• No mention of commitment to change curriculum, instruction, or assessments. • No mention of need to change focus from teacher to learner. • Views inequity/equity from teacher's personal perspective only. • No evidence of responsibility to teach all children. • Views self as authority in classroom.	• Use of generic instructional and assessment modifications. • No individualized modifications based on learners' needs. • Actions geared to meeting personal needs or interests rather than inequities in structures and practices. • Strives for learner conformity. • Displays controlling, authoritarian actions. • Easily bothered by socially defiant behavior.
Maintaining norms schema (A sociocentric perspective, maintaining the conventional status quo, a view of fairness as equality or treating all the same)	• Views fairness as equality (same for all) rather than equity (based on individual needs). • Ideas are based on working within existing school or classroom structure to achieve equity. • Considers purpose of laws and regulations to promote equity.	• May change actions, but implements actions to treat all children the same. • Adheres to rules and regulations of the school or district. • Works within existing school or classroom structure to achieve equity. • Strives to maintain established order. • Attempts various instructional strategies, but not part of natural repertoire.
Postconventional schema (Acting on convictions as a change agent, view of equity as treating students fairly by considering differences, realizes that social norms must be justified and can change)	• Realizes there are multiple perspectives on how to achieve equity. • Views issues from perspectives of marginalized persons and groups. • Considers the moral/ethical implications of instructional choices. • Takes into account a variety of learners' needs when planning instruction and assessments. • Plans actions that support equitable access within the classroom or school. • Plans actions that support equitable access in the district, profession, or community.	• Implements actions based on perspectives of marginalized persons and groups. • Takes more of a facilitator versus presenter role. • Modifies instruction and/or assessment based on consideration of moral/ethical implications. • Modifies instruction and/or assessment based on a variety of learners' needs. • Actions challenge existing structures or practices that promote inequity. • Implements actions that support equitable access within the school, district, or larger professional community.

dates progress, they become more open to varied perspectives and more prepared to take responsibility for meeting the needs of all students.

We used the matrix to analyze the data (society essay and personal leadership plans) we had initially gathered, and found it to be a useful tool for analysis and for providing feedback to candidates.[14] Table 3.2 presents illustrative quotes from students' society essays and personal leadership plans classified according to the three schemata. Candidates had an opportunity to revise and resubmit their work. Although this process is time consuming, we feel it is the most appropriate way to help candidates consider how their own experiences and biases influence their judgments and actions.

When we compared the relationships between candidates' judgments and actions, we discovered that students expressed beliefs that were not evident in their actions. For example, 75 percent of the candidates we studied expressed a personal sense of responsibility to educate all children, but less than 30 percent took actions demonstrating this belief. For instance, Janice wrote in her society essay, "Meeting a student's needs does not just mean making a modification to a lesson. It means implementing this modification in such a way that the student is reached and finds him or herself able to learn because of it."[15] However, when considering actions to take for a leadership project, Janice focused on raising test scores by holding tutoring sessions after school. During these sessions, she simply went over course content rather than constructing new tools to help students overcome their learning challenges.

In a follow-up study, several colleagues analyzed videos of candidates' teaching, with accompanying reflections. They used the matrix to assess candidates' abilities to demonstrate critical pedagogy in their classroom and to reflect on their teaching. Few candidates could do both. While university courses focused on equity, critical pedagogy, and moral reasoning, teacher candidates' reflections more often focused on logistical or superficial aspects of teaching, such as time constraints, quality of voice, organization, and use of teaching materials. For example, Shawna's reflection says nothing about providing equal access to the curriculum: "Students were talking out of turn and getting louder during group activities. I threatened to stop the group activity." After looking at his video, Taylor stated, "I did not want to use a summary sheet for this lesson but my teacher wanted me to use it so I did."[16]

These studies helped us realize that our candidates were able to reason at more complex judgment levels than they demonstrated in their

TABLE 3.2   Equity matrix applied to written artifacts

Dimension of the moral/ ethical schema	Judgments (Society essay)	Actions (Personal leadership plan)
Personal interest (Exclusive focus on self, egocentric orientation; i.e., "How does the situation affect me?")	• After the students know the rules and norms, they need to learn how to follow them. Students will be faced with many rules and norms throughout their lives; they need to know that there are consequences for breaking the rules. • The students that need extra help in reading and math also usually the ones with the most behavioral issues in the classroom. I have found that providing engaging tasks for them is not enough. They become distracted way too easily, and I constantly find them staring into space.	• The goal for this project is to provide students with knowledge and facts of famous and important African Americans. *Reflection*: This project taught me that as a first-year teacher, extensive planning is very important. Everything about a project or event should be carefully thought out for potential difficulties or ways for improving a situation. I have also learned that collaboration and communication are key factors in the personal development of an effective leader.
Maintaining norms (Maintaining the conventional status quo, view of fairness as equality)	• My ethics as an educator include treating every child equally, expecting success from all of my students, and working hard with each of my students so that they can succeed. In my classroom, no child will be singled out or feel excluded, because I feel that a classroom of students is like a team and as a class everyone has to work hard. • The ethics and morals valued in education are directly reflected in the educational laws set forth through the government including the No Child Left Behind Act and the I.D.E.A. Act.	• To create a NAHS program at XXX HS. *Reflection*: When I was in high school, I was a member of the NAHS and I felt that it helped me grow in both my art and my community involvement. It is a nationally honored society and that is beneficial to those students who may not be eligible for a math honors society or beta club.
Postconventional (Acting on convictions as a change agent, view of equity as treating students fairly by considering differences)	• Although I believe in people of all races being treated fairly, this does not mean the same treatment. Educational equity means giving all students the means to be successful. If some students need different treatment in order to succeed, then it is important that as an educator I provide it for them. • On a very different level, it seems that ability level and socioeconomic status have become the new "separate but equal" in schools I have worked in. • Meeting student needs does not just mean making a modification to a lesson. It means implementing this modification is such a way that the student is reached and finds him or herself able to learn because of it.	• My goal is to provide an after-school soccer clinic for XXX Elementary students who would not normally receive such instruction due to financial hindrances. *Reflection*: I feel that my PLP project has complemented the instruction in my EDUC 490 class, truly opening my eyes to what it means to fulfill my professional responsibilities beyond the classroom. Consequently, students need equitable opportunities to ensure their success inside and outside of the classroom, meaning that my duties of teaching to the "whole child" do not stop at the sound of the final bell or even with the subject of physical education.

actions or reflections. Although candidates expressed the belief that providing an equitable education is morally desirable, they often were unable to act on this belief. We needed to help candidates recognize and reason through the moral and ethical dilemmas confronting them in the classroom. Consequently, we developed a viewing guide for looking at videos of classroom dilemmas. Candidates were asked to present a dilemma, to describe how they resolved the dilemma (or how they would do so in the future), and to consider other possible approaches. These prompts helped move candidates from a focus on surface issues to an examination of moral and ethical challenges such as ensuring equitable response opportunities, expressing appropriate expectations, and engaging all students.

ADDING A NEW MEASURE

In looking for a way to promote and assess more advanced judgments, we turned to the Defining Issues Test (DIT-2), a multiple-choice test based on Lawrence Kohlberg's stages of moral development. The DIT-2 offered an objective means of assessing our candidates' reasoning that was compatible with our matrix.[17] When Lisa Johnson compared results from the DIT-2 to the judgment levels assessed with our matrix, however, she found that candidates who integrated moral and ethical ideals into their interpretations and judgments seemed to regurgitate readings and instructor presentations rather than consider the students and communities where they were working. For example, on the DIT-2, Sasha was assessed at the personal interest level, but she seemed to be writing and reflecting at a postconventional level on our matrix. In her description of moral/ethical leadership, she stated, "It is my moral and ethical responsibility to treat children as individuals . . . to adjust to the needs of the students to help them learn best."[18] We found a similar pattern with Holly, who scored in the postconventional level on the DIT-2. She stated, "I need to work on planning for individual difference." She saw her moral responsibility as "creating equal opportunities for all students [through] differentiating instruction and creating individualized assignments."[19] Overall, we found that candidates' scores on our matrix were significantly higher than the levels they achieved on the DIT-2.

These results pushed us to think about our own pedagogy and curriculum, including the two assignments that we were analyzing in our research. The society essay, "Describe your moral/ethical responsibilities as an educational leader in a democratic society," was very abstract, encouraging candidates like Sasha to look to others for guidance rather rely on her own judgments. So we replaced it with a contextual factors assignment that asked candidates to describe a K–12 class of students with whom they are working and to reflect on their ethical responsibilities to help all students in the class learn. We hypothesized that this assignment would encourage the application rather than the regurgitation of principles, resulting in increased congruence between the DIT-2 measure and the assessment scores. The next study confirmed this hypothesis. Although we were not yet influencing candidates' development, we were achieving more valid assessments. Both the quantitative DIT-2 and the qualitative, matrix-based assessments depicted the typical candidate with dispositions characterized by the "maintaining norms" schema.

Jordan describes how she will use the strategy shared by her mentor teacher to meet the needs of advanced thinkers: "I have three students who leave my room on Thursdays for forty-five minutes to attend a MERIT class. MERIT is also known as Gifted and Talented and is for students who make a certain score on their PACT tests. These students may need extra work if they complete their class work faster than the rest of their peers."[20] She is maintaining an established practice, although just providing extra work may not be the most effective means of meeting the needs of the learners.

Claire questions the impact of the schoolwide consequences: "Although expectations should always remain equitable, they are not necessarily the same for all of my students. I have to carefully consider my consequence to my student who has decided to have a mini-outburst because he is bi-polar. Although he should expect a consequence just like the rest of his peers, I will make sure that his individual needs are met. Instruction and classroom management are both necessary components to adjust when accommodating these students."[21] She continues to focus on everyone receiving a consequence; however, she is moving toward a schema of differentiation.

We also realized that our pedagogy lacked continuity. We were expecting seniors to complete these assignments successfully, without paying sufficient attention to the development of their dispositions. So we decided to have candidates analyze contextual factors starting in their junior year and for each semester thereafter. Doing so would provide four opportunities to examine the needs of diverse learners and consider the implications for teaching four different groups of students. For classes without field experiences, we provide hypothetical demographic data coupled with information from various assessments. To strengthen the usefulness of these data sets, faculty are currently creating "virtual" classes where each "student" has a cumulative folder of report cards, Individualized Education Plans, results of standardized assessments, and other material that teachers encounter. We plan to assess the impact of this new two-year sequence as our first group of candidates graduates. We expect to find distinct differences in candidates' first and last efforts to analyze contextual factors.

PRESENTING OUR MODEL OF ASSESSMENT

In 2008, Lisa Johnson and Rebecca Evers received a Winthrop assessment grant to share our tools for identifying and measuring specific program goals with the university community.[22] We compiled data from previous studies, using candidate work samples, DIT-2 scores, and video analyses gathered during the senior-year experiences. The first semester's work served as baseline data. At the beginning of the fall semester, the candidates completed the DIT-2 and two essays that we assessed for judgments of equity and fairness related to effective instruction and management. During the following semester, we evaluated their judgments in three written portions of their internship work sample (IWS) and a second administration of the DIT-2. Actions for equity and fairness were evaluated in detailed lesson plans and video samples of teaching. We used the equity matrix to assess both judgments and actions, and the DIT-2 to validate matrix judgments. This research yielded two significant findings:

- We saw patterns of growth from less to more complex patterns of thinking.[23] Some candidates progressed from personal interest to maintaining norms ; others progressed from maintaining norms to postconventional by the time they reached the last two semesters of their teacher education program, although the mean results continued to be maintaining norms (no statistically significant movement to postconventional).
- The disposition to act was more difficult for our candidates than the disposition to make judgments. Lesson plan accommodations and video sample data indicated that a majority of our candidates were transitioning from personal interest to maintaining norms.

Although judgments and actions shifted from personal interest, they were still less complex than what was needed to provide an equitable education for all students. Presenting this work to our colleagues transformed our project from action research among a small faculty group to a university-wide effort to examine how dispositions were being defined, identified, developed, and evaluated in teacher education.

CREATING A TASK FORCE ON DISPOSITIONS

In spring 2009, the need to revise assessments of dispositions in our teacher education programs led to the creation of a dispositions task force as an ad hoc committee of the NCATE unit assessment committee. The faculty recognized the need to think through the dispositional issues encountered during the past ten years, achieve conceptual clarity, and propose new ways to meet NCATE's mandate to assess candidates' dispositions of fairness and the belief that all students can learn.[24] The dispositions task force was charged with three tasks: (1) examine existing dispositions in the conceptual framework at the initial licensure level and make suggestions for change; (2) create assessment instruments with scoring guides linked to the conceptual framework and NCATE requirements; and (3) develop guidelines and a scoring guide for the essay used to assess candidates for admission to teacher education.

The task force, ten faculty members from across the university, began its work by reading literature about dispositions in order to survey alternative definitions and decide which definition we preferred. The group agreed on a cognitive definition of dispositions based on the work of Erskine Dottin, Alan Reiman, and Lisa Johnson, and Lilian Katz and James Raths: "A disposition is a trend in judgments, behaviors, and reflections over time." Committee members related the presence of dispositions to the frequency with which certain knowledge and skills are displayed in teacher candidates' judgments and actions.[25] Two groups, one focused on dispositions and the other on the admissions essay, met during summer 2009 to work on the following tasks:

- What characteristics of teacher candidates should we assess?
- Which big ideas indicate fairness and the belief that all students can learn, and through which behaviors will we operationalize these dispositions?
- How should we revise the teacher education admission essay?

To assist subgroups with their summer work, each member of the dispositions task force provided a list of "big ideas" connected to the conceptual framework that operationalize fairness and the belief that all students can learn. Group members also considered the four-part mission and postulate of the NNER.[26] The subgroup met to review the ideas, grouped them into dispositional categories, and named and described each disposition based on the content of the ideas. Four overarching themes emerged:

Fairness. Assumes responsibility for the learning of all students in the classroom in a caring, nondiscriminatory, and equitable manner and persists in effecting learning for all students.

Integrity. Adheres to the moral, legal, and ethical principles of the university and the profession.

Communication. Interacts in ways that convey respect and sensitivity.

Commitment. Embraces the complexity of the work of teaching through reflective practice and professional growth.

The next step was to align each disposition with multiple behaviors that indicate appropriate judgments and actions. This was a critical step, as it defined our dispositions in concrete terms: the criteria for assessment. We also matched the dispositions and their defining indicators with national standards (e.g., NNER, National Board for Professional Teaching Standards, or NBPTS) and with Winthrop's core commitments.

Table 3.3 shows how we elaborated the disposition of fairness that is particularly important for teachers in our state. South Carolina has many school children who live in poverty. The percentage of impoverished children ranges from 36 to 48 percent.[27] Further, 15 percent of South Carolina's school-age population are identified as students with disabilities, and the number of students who are not native English speakers has risen 714 percent since 1995.[28] We believe that teachers who work in our public schools must have a positive view of others, treating each individual fairly and believing in the worth, ability, and potential of all children, while taking into account a variety of learners' needs when planning instruction and assessments.

The disposition of integrity, highlighted in table 3.4, complements the second of Winthrop's core commitments: cultivating personal and academic integrity. We want our teacher candidates to recognize and act upon a sense of honor within the university, and as they become teachers,

TABLE 3.3   Description and alignment of "fairness" disposition

FAIRNESS

Assumes responsibility for the learning of all students in the classroom in a caring, nondiscriminatory, and equitable manner and persists in effective learning for all students

	Judgments	Actions
Indicators	• Has a positive view of others: believing in the worth, ability, and potential of all children. • Takes into account a variety of learners' needs when planning instruction and assessments. • Acknowledges existing structures or practices that promote inequity. • Views issues from perspectives of marginalized persons and groups, or professional community.	• Modifies instruction and/or assessment based on a variety of learners' needs. • Monitors and adjusts when presented with ill-structured problems. • Sets high expectations for all learners, providing scaffolding for success. • Teaches by invitation—invites students to increase the challenge or decrease the challenge based upon performance. • Uses authentic, relevant assessments to measure student understanding. • Advocates for marginalized students and their families. • Challenges inequities of existing structures or practices. • Addresses the behavior, not the child. • Supports equitable access to knowledge in the school, district, profession, or community.

Alignment	Principles of the National Network for Educational Renewal	**Mission 1:** Provide access to knowledge for all children ("equity and excellence"). **Mission 3:** Base teaching on knowledge of the subjects taught, established principles of learning, and sensitivity to the unique potential of learners ("nurturing pedagogy"). **Postulate 13:** Programs for the education of educators must be infused with understanding of and commitment to the moral obligation of teachers to ensure equitable access to and engagement in the best possible K–12 education for *all* children and youths. **Postulate 14:** Programs for the education of educators must involve future teachers not only in understanding schools as they are but in alternatives, the assumptions underlying alternatives, and how to effect needed changes in school organization, pupil grouping, curriculum, and more.
	National Board for Professional Teaching Standards	**Proposition 1:** Teachers are committed to students and their learning. **Proposition 2:** Teachers know the subjects they teach and how to teach those subjects to students. **Proposition 3:** Teachers are responsible for managing and monitoring student learning.
	Winthrop University's core commitments	**Refining ethical and moral reasoning:** developing moral reasoning in ways that incorporate the other four responsibilities and using such reasoning in learning and in life.

we want them to seek congruence between their intent and their actions. We want them to recognize when schools are not meeting their obligations to children and their communities and to do something about it. As teacher educators in an NNER institution, we are dedicated to moral and ethical teaching practices and want our candidates to be, as well.

In conceptualizing the disposition of communication (see table 3.5), we want candidates who share the reasons behind their judgments and show respect for others' ideas and perspectives. As noted in Winthrop's core commitment, we want to develop candidates who are committed to the collaborative process and to the search for consensus that benefits all. Teachers should also be open to critical instructional feedback.

Commitment encompasses the professional growth of a teacher through reflection on practice and continual development within a learning community (see table 3.6). The range of indicators reflects the development of a candidate in all phases of the teacher education program. The task force wanted to maintain accountability for developing candidates who present themselves as professionals. So we included indicators regarding such basic aspects of professionalism as timeliness and appropriate dress. Further, at Winthrop we emphasize three goals—to *live*, *learn*, and *lead* within our learning community. Therefore, within the disposition of commitment, we ask our students to demonstrate an ability to move beyond themselves, the university, and their local community into regional and national professional organizations as lifelong learners, potential leaders, and stewards of the profession. Commitment also includes the ability to engage in reflection as part of a continual cycle of self-improvement.

CRAFTING A BASELINE ASSESSMENT

The admission essay subgroup also met during the summer to devise a prompt, several case scenarios, and a scoring rubric to use as part of the admission process. When complete, the admission essay and rubric (based upon the four dispositions and indicators of fairness, integrity, communication, and commitment) will provide baseline data and guidance to faculty in helping candidates further develop their dispositions through additional assessments and reflection over time.[29] The subgroup has devised several scenarios, derived from situations encountered in candidates' field experiences during the sophomore year, and a prompt

TABLE 3.4   Description and alignment of "integrity" disposition

INTEGRITY

Demonstrates a recognition of and adherence to the moral, legal, and ethical principles of the university and the profession

<table>
<tr>
<td rowspan="2">Indicators</td>
<td colspan="2">Judgments
• Considers the moral/ethical implications of instructional choices.
• Considers the relative nature of rules and norms.</td>
</tr>
<tr>
<td colspan="2">Actions
• Exhibits academic honesty.
• Helps students learn and practice rules that promote equity and democratic ideals.
• Identifies and challenges potential biases in curricular materials and assessments.
• Maintains confidentiality.
• Engages democratic principles of classroom management.
• Maintains a professional relationship with students in and out of school setting.</td>
</tr>
<tr>
<td rowspan="3">Alignment</td>
<td>Principles of the National Network for Educational Renewal</td>
<td>Mission 2: Educate the young for thoughtful participation in a social and political democracy ("enculturation").

Postulate 12: Programs for the education of educators must involve future teachers in the issues and dilemmas that emerge out of the never-ending tension between the rights and interests of individual parents and interest groups and the role of schools in transcending parochialism and advancing community in a democratic society.

Postulate 16: Programs for the education of educators must engage future teachers in the problems and dilemmas arising out of the inevitable conflicts and incongruities between what is perceived to work in practice and the research and theory supporting other options.</td>
</tr>
<tr>
<td>National Board for Professional Teaching Standards</td>
<td>Proposition 1: Teachers are committed to students and their learning.

Proposition 4: Teachers think systematically about their practice and learn from experience.</td>
</tr>
<tr>
<td>Winthrop University's core commitments</td>
<td>Cultivating personal and academic integrity: recognizing and acting on a sense of honor, both by being honest in relationships and by upholding academic honor codes.</td>
</tr>
</table>

that will scaffold each candidate's response to one of the scenarios. Work is continuing to refine the teacher education admission process and to devise a common assessment of dispositions that can be used in courses prior to admission. Plans for the assessment include having trained faculty conduct conferences with candidates about the assessment results in which they highlight goals for future development.

TABLE 3.5   Description and alignment of "communication" disposition

COMMUNICATION
Interacts in ways that convey respect and sensitivity

Indicators	*Judgments*	*Actions*
	• Values as educational partners: (1) families, (2) colleagues, and (3) students.	• Strives for high standards in written and oral communication.
	• Holds high tolerance for ambiguity and frustration while maintaining confidence and poise.	• Employs active listening techniques when faced with dissenting opinions.
	• Integrates multiple sources of information when making judgments.	• Builds effective teacher–student connections.
		• Fosters communication that is inclusive where differences are explored and celebrated.
		• Exhibits positive communication in teaching and learning environments.
		• Respects self and others.
		• Provides constructive advice by integrating feedback into practice.
		• Avoids use of sarcasm and put-downs.
		• Communicates respect and understanding for cultural and linguistic diversity.
		• Maintains confidence and poise when communicating with others.
		• Works collaboratively.
		• Participates productively in all classroom interactions.
Alignment	*Principles of the National Network for Educational Renewal*	**Mission 2:** Educate the young for thoughtful participation in a social and political democracy ("enculturation").
	National Board for Professional Teaching Standards	**Proposition 5:** Teachers are members of learning communities.
	Winthrop University's core commitments	**Taking seriously the perspectives of others:** recognizing and acting on the obligation to inform one's own judgment; relinquishing a sense of entitlement; and engaging diverse and competing perspectives as a resource for learning, citizenship, and work.

THE JOURNEY CONTINUES

We have made significant progress in clarifying dispositions and thinking about their development in the context of our teacher education programs. Five years of action research has produced a matrix of four dispositions made concrete with specific judgments and actions based on a theoretical foundation of cognitive development in the moral domain.

TABLE 3.6   Description and alignment of "commitment" disposition

COMMITMENT

Embraces the complexity of the work of teaching through reflective practice and professional growth

		Judgments	Actions
Indicators		• Strives to develop content and pedagogical knowledge. • Sets high standards for (1) personal behavior and (2) professional growth.	• Demonstrates persistence. • Reflects on teaching experiences and effectiveness to improve student performance. • Takes advantage of professional development opportunities outside of the classroom. • Participates in professional organizations and activities. • Completes required tasks in an accurate, timely, and effective manner. • Dresses appropriately.
Alignment	Principles of the National Network for Educational Renewal		**Mission 4:** Take responsibility for improving the conditions for learning in P–12 schools, institutions of higher education, and communities ("stewardship"). **Postulate 9:** Programs for the education of educators must be characterized by a socialization progress through which candidates transcend their self-oriented student preoccupations to become more other-oriented in identifying with a culture of teaching. **Postulate 12:** Programs for the education of educators must involve future teachers in the issues and dilemmas that emerge out of the never-ending tension between the rights and interests of individual parents and interest groups and the role of schools in transcending parochialism and advancing community in a democratic society.
	National Board for Professional Teaching Standards		**Proposition 4:** Teachers think systematically about their practice and learn from experience. **Proposition 5:** Teachers are members of learning communities.
	Winthrop University's core commitments		**Striving for excellence:** developing a strong work ethic and consciously doing one's very best in all aspects of college. **Contributing to a larger community:** recognizing and acting on one's responsibility to the educational community, the local community, and the wider national and global society.

While we have achieved much, the journey continues as we focus on assessment and curriculum integration.

The task force is planning to pilot the new admissions essay that will provide baseline data. Candidates will come to a computer lab and respond to the prompt described above, applying ideas to one of the cases. Students will have two hours to craft their response, after which they can participate in a debriefing session. Task force members will ask students for feedback on their experience with the assessment. This process has been approved by the university's institutional review board.

Because we view dispositions as "developmental" rather than as a gateway check-off system, we need to become more deliberate about integrating the four dispositions into our teaching and assessments. As members of the task force work with teacher education faculty across the university, we will emphasize using the indicators in syllabi, assignment descriptions, assessment tools (e.g., rubrics), and formative feedback. We will also provide opportunities for faculty development on topics such as "integrating the four dispositions into class discussions" and "grouping students for instruction based on differences in dispositions." This will take place during "take thirty" sessions, in which colleagues gather thirty minutes prior to faculty meetings to engage in their own development and growth as teacher educators. We have also created sample rubrics that include matrix language. Table 3.7 illustrates one example of such a rubric for the contextual factors assignment described previously.

At the unacceptable level, the candidate focuses mainly on the self as teacher perspective. There is little indication of making changes in curriculum, instruction, or management to meet the needs of learners. Moving to acceptable, there is a widening of perspective as the candidate takes into account school and/or society as guiding forces, but lacks responsibility for and focus on individual needs. As candidates move to the acceptable level, we start to see a shift toward more complex reasoning. Students are seen as individuals for whom classroom dynamics often have to be adjusted. The main difference between the acceptable and the exemplary levels is what Lisa Delpit summarizes as "knowing their students and their students' intellectual heritage and using that knowledge in their instruction, by always demanding students' best, by fighting against societal stereotypes, and by helping students understand the important role they can play in changing their communities and the world."[30] At the exemplary level, candidates understand their moral obligation to support student success and to recognize and rectify inequities that might exist in the school and/or the classroom. They realize that at-risk students need strategies for reading and understanding material that is on their grade level; they need more, not less. As Delpit asks, "If children come to us knowing less, and we put them on a track of slower paced, remedial learning, then where will they end up?"[31]

TABLE 3.7   Contextual factors rubric with matrix language

	Exemplary	*Acceptable*	*Unacceptable*
Contextual factors Check one: R__ M__ U__	• Description highlights issues in community, school, classroom, and family that may hinder equitable access to curriculum, and includes perspectives from marginalized persons or groups. • The moral and ethical implications of the issues highlighted focus on varied perspective. • Suggested actions are specific and support equitable access to curriculum in the community, school, classroom, and family. Candidate demonstrates flexible view of curriculum, instruction, assessment, and management in order to meet the needs of all learners. • Reliable sources referenced correctly. Demonstrates mastery of English language usage and writing skills with no mechanical errors.	• Description highlights issues in community, school, classroom, and family that may hinder equitable access to curriculum. • The moral and ethical implications of issues highlighted focus on working with existing school or classroom structure. • Suggested actions are specific and center on classroom equality (same for all). Candidate demonstrates willingness to make adjustments to curriculum, instruction, assessment, and/or management in order to meet the needs of the learners as a class (versus individuals). • Reliable sources referenced correctly. Demonstrates mastery of English language usage and writing skills with few mechanical errors.	• Description is generic with questionable understanding of the issues in community, school, classroom, and family that hinder equitable access to curriculum. • Candidate does not address the moral and ethical implications of the issues. • Suggested actions are generic and focus on meeting personal needs or interests. Candidate does not demonstrate sufficient commitment to making adjustments to curriculum, instruction, assessment, and/or management to meet the needs of learners. • Some sources referenced correctly. Errors in English language usage and writing skills interfere with readability.

Since we have not yet begun using assessments based upon the new dispositions, we do not have samples of student work. We do, however, have moral exemplars from our earlier studies of graduates that illustrate our ultimate goals. We hope that our efforts will produce graduates who possess the desired dispositions. Lois Thies-Sprinthall and Norm Sprinthall wrote, "Great teachers are neither born nor made, but can be developed."[32] We began our journey with a simple action research project that led us to question our effectiveness in assessing and developing educators with the moral and ethical disposition to help all students learn. Engaging in this type of work is hard, often controversial, but we see it as *our* moral and ethical obligation to ensure that our graduates enter the teaching field with the disposition to ensure a high-quality, equitable education for all students.

CHAPTER FOUR

Moving from Reaction to Reflection

Chester Laine, Anne M. Bauer, Holly Johnson,
Stephen D. Kroeger, Karen S. Troup, and Helen Meyer

Editors' Case Introduction: University of Cincinnati

The University of Cincinnati is a large, urban, public, comprehensive research university set in inner-city Cincinnati. Of the 37,000 students, 5,000 are enrolled in the College of Education, Criminal Justice, and Human Services, which is dedicated to making a difference in the community through outreach, academic programs, and community partnerships.

The school of education recommends approximately 400 candidates a year for teaching licenses and endorsements. Nationally recognized programs include secondary English, mathematics, science, and social studies; special education at two levels of functioning, as well as a gifted endorsement and a prekindergarten special-needs endorsement; middle childhood education; and early childhood education.

In this chapter, the authors, who teach in different licensure programs, describe how they discovered discrepancies between their programs' espoused values and the actual performance of their teacher candidates. This discovery fueled a serious process of program revision. The chapter details a variety of changes in the structure, curriculum, and pedagogy of the teacher preparation programs at the University of Cincinnati, designed to achieve the goal of preparing caring, competent, and committed teachers.

ACCOMPLISHING THE MISSION

This mission statement is ambitious and ambiguous: "Our mission is to prepare committed, caring, competent individuals who have knowledge of their content, can act as change agents, and who are concerned about the education of all students."[1] The faculty who created it sincerely believed that it expressed the essence of our work, until the performances of our teacher candidates led us to question whether our efforts matched our rhetoric. As faculty members in the University of Cincinnati's teacher preparation programs, we wanted to have a positive impact on our community, and we hoped our teacher candidates would be change agents, committed to having a positive impact on students and on issues of social justice. Through field experiences and coursework, we attempted to enact what it means to be committed, caring, and competent educators so that our candidates would embrace these qualities.

We learned that while we believe that educators must be committed to their students' learning and to issues of social justice, we were unsure of our ability to develop the necessary attitudes, values, and beliefs in our teacher candidates. We wanted them to care about their students and their profession, but our programs did not always foster these dispositions. We knew that we had to change.

This chapter describes how we wrestled with the challenge of developing desirable dispositions in our teacher candidates. As we identified the discrepancies between our espoused values and our observations of candidates in the field, we were forced to revision the courses and field experiences in our programs. Our review of the literature and our own work in urban education led us to believe that the difference between more and less effective urban teachers is largely dispositional.[2] Since we believe that dispositional behaviors can be learned and changed, we realized that we needed to provide more robust and coordinated learning opportunities so that our teacher candidates would develop the disposition to teach all children with "no excuses."[3]

NOTICING DISTANCE

In 2001, in response to a new accreditation requirement from the National Council for Accreditation of Teacher Education (NCATE), faculty across licensure programs developed unit standards and dispositions that we believed addressed our institutional mission. Using the Interstate New Teacher Assessment and Support Consortium's (INTASC) dispositional standards as a springboard, a representative team of faculty members, school-based cooperating teachers, and university-based supervisors identified themes that reflected each of our licensure programs. From these themes, the group developed dispositional statements, which we posted for faculty discussion and ultimately endorsed in autumn 2001. On the basis of these statements, we developed the Candidate Dispositions Progress Report and Brief Report to use in identifying candidates with challenges.

We designed programs to prepare competent, caring educators committed to "no excuses" regarding the failure to help all children learn. We identified our dispositions—the attitudes, beliefs, and values that we wanted our candidates to possess and express. We organized them around the qualities of commitment, caring, and competence:

Commitment
- Professionalism in attendance, punctuality, and dress
- Initiative on behalf of all learners
- Responsibility to promote effort and excellence in all learners
- Commitment to reflection, assessment, and learning as an ongoing process

Caring
- Rapport with students, peers, and others
- Participation with other professionals to improve the overall learning environment for students
- Appreciation that "knowledge" includes multiple ways of knowing
- Creation of a protected, predictable, and positive classroom climate
- Recognition of the fundamental need of students to develop and maintain a sense of self-worth
- Recognition that student misbehavior may be an attempt to protect self-esteem
- Valuing all students for their potential and helping them value each other

Competence
- Competence in a discipline or multiple disciplines and accompanying pedagogy
- Appreciation of the content of the subject area, the diverse needs, assets, and interests of the students, and the need to plan

We did not expect candidates to demonstrate these dispositions from the moment they entered the program, but we did expect them to begin displaying them by the time they entered their early field experiences.

During the first year in the program, candidates took courses designed to teach concepts and strategies related to providing every child with access to ambitious learning opportunities. They tutored students in the field. As they progressed through the program, they designed teaching plans, instructed students, and faced real-world challenges, including lack of student engagement and difficult student behavior. Their plans and instruction required strategies for differentiation.

Faculty members used modeling, coaching, and reflection to help candidates develop new skills and move beyond coping strategies. We embraced the moral imperative to teach all students. We thought we had the program to develop this core commitment and the practices to support it. Early on, however, we began to notice a gap between the dispositions we embraced and the performances we were seeing in our candidates. While our candidates appeared to be knowledgeable, they did not always display the dispositions we espoused. We also found that when candidates did not manifest these dispositions in the field, faculty members did not always know how to respond.

Below we present three cases that illustrate these problems. The candidates—Ruth, Henry, and Brady—are composites, constructed from our experiences with many students. The cases grew out of conversations in program meetings and gatherings of faculty members and university-based supervisors, including an action research group of faculty, field coordinators, and doctoral students who met monthly for over a year. This group uncovered many of the concerns reported here and contributed many of the ideas about how to transform our teacher preparation programs. The cases and the questions they raised pushed our thinking and led us to make critical changes in our teacher education program.

RECOGNIZING AND REFLECTING ON THE PROBLEM

Ruth: A Problem of Commitment?

Ruth was a bright, diligent student who loved her content and imagined teaching students like herself. One spring day, she rushed into her instructional management class, having come from her field placement in the high school adjacent to our inner-urban campus. Ruth introduced herself to her peers, explaining that last quarter she had been placed at

Monroe High School, where she felt that she was back home. At Monroe, she held debates, had students write and share original poetry, and designed activities that were "a good fit" for her students. Now she was at that school across the street, with no technology, peeling paint and falling ceiling tiles, and a security guard. But at least she didn't have to park at the school, because her car probably wouldn't be safe on the streets by the school.

An early assignment in the course asked Ruth to find out about students likes, dislikes, interests, and experiences. Ruth reported on the demographic breakdown of the student population, based on information on the school's Web site—90 percent African American, nearly as many children on free or reduced lunch, and most students arriving on a city bus. Because of their test scores, the school was rated in "continuous improvement," with 85 percent passing all sections of the graduation test by the end of their senior year. When the instructor asked Ruth about her students' likes and interests, she explained that she found it hard to talk to them. Ruth also reported that her cooperating teacher, Mr. Jamison, a Caucasian master teacher with fifteen years' experience, behaved oddly toward his students, letting them walk around and talk in small groups. She didn't really feel that Mr. Jamison understood teaching.

Toward the end of the quarter, the instructor asked students to write about their relationships with their cooperating teachers and describe the types of teaching activities they had been involved in during the placement. Ruth stated that Mr. Jamison made her walk the hallways during some class periods and between classes, talk to the custodian and the security guard, and eat lunch in the cafeteria. He encouraged her to design the first few lessons, but then said that she needed to use his plans and activities because this was what the students expected. Ruth proclaimed that the field experience had been a complete waste of time. She had not learned anything more about teaching than she came with from her earlier experience. Once she had met her minimum clock-hour requirements, she would not return to Mr. Jamison's classroom or his students.

At the time, the supervisory model called for the university supervisor to observe, evaluate, and debrief Ruth, so there was no one to conduct a structured conversation with Ruth about her specific concerns and the challenges she faced in Mr. Jamison's classroom. Mr. Jamison contacted university faculty members, but her behavior was not seen as a critical concern. Ruth was an excellent student performing at an acceptable level.

Before this class, the course instructor had had no interactions with Ruth, so she mainly listened to her complaints and addressed questions about classroom assignments. Although she expressed concern about Ruth's placement and her inability to learn from her cooperating teacher, the secondary education program had used this cooperating teacher and this inner-urban high school for over a decade, with most candidates enjoying excellent experiences with Mr. Jamison and the students. It was not until a meeting of the secondary education program faculty members that Ruth's university supervisor and the faculty members closest to her revealed the complexities of the situation. Ruth's current supervisor explained that Ruth had difficulty engaging with students at the high school. Mr. Jamison had suggested the school tours and conversations with other adults in the building to help Ruth learn about the school community and culture. He felt Ruth was resisting learning about the students as individuals, and the more she resisted, the more prescriptive and teacher-directed her lessons became. That was why he offered her his plans, so she could get a feel for how to work with these students. What Ruth portrayed as unreasonable requests and odd behavior had in fact been Mr. Jamison's attempts to intervene and create learning opportunities. But were the purposes behind these experiences made clear to Ruth? Did she know why Mr. Jamison had made these suggestions?

Faculty Interpretation

When we reflected on Ruth's case, we realized that what we initially interpreted as resistance reflected a significant gap in our program. We thought Ruth's behavior was arrogant or elitist, but we came to see that it fit what Catherine Cornbleth calls a "world apart" response.[4] What Ruth observed in Mr. Jamison's class was very different from what she had experienced in her own high school English classrooms. On the basis of the beliefs and experiences she brought to the program, she was interpreting Mr. Jamison's culturally relevant teaching and his ability to interact with his students as a lack of authority and poor classroom management. Clearly, her beliefs were limiting what she could see and learn.

We began to ask ourselves how we could help candidates reframe negative assumptions about urban schools and students. How could we contextualize urban experiences so that our candidates would understand the culturally responsive teaching they encountered, especially when it looked so different from the teaching they experienced in their own schooling?

Henry: A Matter of Caring?

Henry was an undergraduate completing the first of two required special education student teaching experiences. He did his fall semester student teaching in a primary classroom for students with moderate to intense educational needs. Henry said that he had absolutely no interest in teaching students with moderate to intense disabilities. At the time, we had no way to elicit candidates' fears or concerns about working with special education students or to assess their competencies in advance of student teaching.

Ohio has two special education teaching licenses, one for mild to moderate and one for moderate to intense. Candidates at our institution earn both licenses so that they can teach children in all three groups. This requires specialized preparation that our program provides. Henry felt strongly that working with children with intense needs was not a viable option for him.

Following the protocol used in all of our licensure programs, Eileen, Henry's university supervisor, received Henry's lesson plans in advance of each visit. She was required to observe and evaluate Henry's teaching. Using an evaluation template based on the Ohio Standards for the Teaching Profession, Eileen documented each observation and sent them to Henry, who e-mailed his written postobservation reflections to Eileen. Henry also attended weekly seminars led by Eileen, which offered an opportunity to discuss questions and classroom challenges.

As Henry's supervisor, Eileen observed Henry, consulted with his cooperating teacher, Jan, and supported and assessed him in his field experience. As his student teaching began, Henry told Eileen that he was extremely frustrated with how little the students could actually do. He doubted whether his students could learn and make progress. After a few weeks, Henry's cooperating teacher, Jan, contacted Eileen to share her concerns regarding Henry's performance in the classroom. The issues she raised suggested that Henry was not demonstrating several critical dispositions on the end-of-quarter evaluation form. She thought that Henry lacked initiative, had not yet established rapport with the students, and was not engaging with them in a manner that allowed relationships to form.

Across all licensure programs, when such concerns come to a university supervisor's attention, the supervisor explores the level of concern with the cooperating teacher and the candidate. They outline possible next steps that might enable the candidate to succeed. Cooperating teachers often hesitate to address concerns explicitly and to document them formally. In this situation, Eileen and Jan communicated over the phone and by e-mail, with Jan following through at school by talking with Henry. They were explicit about their concerns.

Jan suggested ways to differentiate instruction and explained how to build this into Henry's lesson planning. She outlined specific steps that Henry could take to increase student engagement. Henry, however, failed to follow through. He came without lesson plans and frequently called in sick. Initially, neither his cooperating teacher nor his supervisor interpreted these absences as a reluctance to engage with his students. However, upon more targeted observation, they determined that he might be avoiding his students.

When Henry gave verbal directions, he did so from across the room. He seemed hesitant to make eye contact, preferring to stay busy with nonessential details, such as watching what others were doing in the classroom. It was as though he thought he could teach without actually interacting with students. He demonstrated little enthusiasm, evidenced by his quick departure at the end of the day, and a noted tendency to check the cell phone for messages during the school day. He appeared bored, instead of looking for something to do or for someone to help. When he completed a task, he waited until given the next task. "It's not my classroom," he would explain. "I don't want to step on anyone's toes."

Henry's failure to follow through on the cooperating teacher's suggestions prompted more contact with Eileen. Eileen scheduled a visit to talk with Henry about the continued concerns. At this point Eileen and Jan determined that the lack of initiative, lack of engagement, inability to establish rapport, and frequent absences were perhaps indicative of issues with forming caring relationships with the students.

A Successful Intervention

Eileen initiated an action plan. She encouraged Jan, the cooperating teacher, to document her concerns about Henry on the Candidate Dispositions Progress Report. Henry's action plan included a written schedule outlining his teaching and planning responsibilities for the remainder of the semester and the requirement that Henry videotape a lesson for later discussion with Eileen and Jan.

When they viewed the videotaped lesson, Eileen realized that Henry was avoiding his students, and Henry agreed. Eileen shared with Henry that although he had decided that this was "not the population for him," he still needed to improve his comfort level, skills, and interactions with his students so that he would be well equipped for any teaching situation. She said, "I want you to leave this experience confident that you can work with all children." This appealed to Henry. He was receptive to the feedback and agreed that this change in direction was important for his success, as well as for the students he might work with in the future.

When Henry and Eileen met to view a second videotaped lesson, the changes in Henry's demeanor were evident. He spoke enthusiastically about the lessons he had planned. Jan noticed that Henry was standing closer to the students. He was using a more engaging verbal tone and had several positive interactions with them. It appeared that their conversations about establishing rapport, respecting the abilities of all students, and planning engaging lessons and activities had affected his performance and his progress. Jan was also a good model for these dispositions, not only demonstrating a caring attitude toward her students, but also showing confidence in Henry's ability to develop these dispositions.

In an end-of-semester meeting, Jan, the cooperating teacher, noted improvement in all areas on the assessment and evaluation form. Henry showed openness to constructive feedback from his cooperating teacher and supervisor. He remedied the documented dispositional concerns. Midway through the following semester, Henry told his supervisor that those classrooms with students with more intense needs, classrooms he had initially avoided, might be better situations for him.

After graduation, Henry sought and found employment in a classroom with children who had significant cognitive and behavioral needs. His employers now explicitly seek "clones of Henry" in requests to the university program and field coordinator.

Faculty Reflections on Henry

When we reflected on Henry's original statement in light of his progress, we wondered, "What if Henry had not been challenged to grow professionally? And we asked ourselves, "How could we do a better job of identifying students like Henry who resist learning about individuals with disabilities?" How could we make sure that all of our Henrys do not slip past us, especially if the cooperating teacher is hesitant to raise concerns about dispositions or to initiate an action plan process?

As a faculty, we realized the need for earlier interventions. Significant changes in a teacher's practice can take from six months to three years.[5]

When Henry revealed his reluctance or disinterest in working with students with disabilities, we did not have a responsible program response. Had the cooperating teacher not called the university supervisor, the problem could have gone undocumented and resulted in a failed student teaching experience or the licensing of an incompetent teacher. We needed an early, proactive way to identify the presence or absence of key dispositions.

This case also highlights a new emerging role for supervisors and cooperating teachers. In our own survey of thirty-five special education and ten secondary education student teachers, 26.7 percent of the respondents reported that the university supervisor had very little or no impact on their practice during their student teaching, and another 20 percent reported only some impact. Given our supervisory model, this is not surprising. Periodic observations and evaluations of individual lessons by an "outside" supervisor were insufficient. We needed regular, structured conversations among university supervisors, cooperating teachers, and candidates.

We also realized that cooperating teachers might be more effective than supervisors in changing student teachers' behavior and dispositions because they can model, coach, and teach in an ongoing way. We needed to empower our cooperating teachers, helping them assume this new role as cothinkers and teachers of teaching.

Brady: A Problem of Promoting Effort and Excellence in All Learners?

Brady, an English student teacher at Sanders High School, was off to a good start with three general-level ninth-grade classes and two sophomore advanced-level classes. With a wide range of general and English language arts methods courses and content courses in linguistics, literature, composition, and communication under his belt, Brady felt reasonably well prepared. He had a supportive university supervisor, Joan Akers, and a particularly strong cooperating teacher, Carmine Young. Both his supervisor and cooperating teacher were very helpful as he got his sea legs at Sanders.

One day, during the third week of school, while Joan Akers, his university supervisor, was observing, a new student entered Brady's fourth-bell class, just after lunch. The student was tall, with olive skin, hazel eyes, and dark black hair. As he walked into the classroom, Brady was about to introduce a "think aloud" as an introductory activity for the next segment of his unit on "coming of age." Brady stopped in midsentence, greeted the new student warmly, and asked his name. The young man hesitated, first looking at Brady, then looking around the room, then back at Brady. He said nothing. Brady moved toward the young man, smiling, and showed him an empty seat near the back of the room. Quietly, with every student in the room looking at them, Brady again asked the student his name. Again, the young man hesitated, but finally said, "Cecilio." Brady tried to repeat his name, but realized, despite several tries, that he couldn't seem to pronounce it correctly.

Brady returned to his lesson, making a mental note to spend more time with Cecilio. However, Brady was frequently distracted, consumed with the activities he had planned for the day. He noticed that for the entire lesson, Cecilio sat and drew in a notebook while the other students participated in the think-aloud activity.

The Intervention

After the halls cleared, Brady returned to the classroom to meet with Joan. Using the existing observation assessment device, Joan described how pleased she was with Brady's lesson. Except for Cecilio, Brady's students were engaged in the metacognitive think-aloud activity. His transitions were smooth and his questioning techniques were very good. Joan observed that many of Brady's students used "fix up strategies" like tapping prior knowledge, skipping ahead, rereading, or making predictions. He achieved his goal of having students think about their own reading. Joan noted that Cecilio was isolated in the back of the room, frequently taking deep breaths, burying himself in his notebook, and looking around as Brady's lesson proceeded.

When Joan asked about Cecilio, Brady described the hallway reaction of another teacher, Rod Standish, who had Cecilio in his first-bell history class. When Brady described the situation that had unfolded in his class, Rod, in typical bombastic fashion, said, "Cecilio can't read! Why, he can't even speak any English! How do you expect him to participate in a reading lesson? Today, we were reading about western expansion. He wouldn't know anything about that, so I just left him in the corner drawing in his notebook. That kid sure can draw! I figured that it was better to have him do something he could be successful with. He didn't seem to mind, and anyway, he wasn't drawing that long. These Mexican kids don't belong in our classes. What is that ESL guy doing anyway?" Brady knew enough to disregard Rod's comments.

Brady told Joan that although he had received some instruction in the teaching of English language learners (ELLs), he had never encountered any ELL students in any of his earlier practicum experiences. He said, "I froze. I know it wasn't right to just leave him sitting in the back of the room, but I had no idea how to get him involved. I know that there is an ESL specialist who is supposed to be working with ELL students, and she was not with him today. I felt incompetent."

Faculty Interpretation

Brady had learned about teaching content-area concepts. He knew how to plan instruction and understood how to use content-specific instructional strategies to teach the central concepts and skills of his discipline; however, he was thrown by a student who did not speak English as his first language. He had never encountered an ELL student in his earlier practicum experiences and had never tried to apply what he had learned about teaching second language learners. His instructional decisions were filtered through the beliefs, predispositions, and prior experiences he brought to the field.[6]

Although Joan evaluated Brady's lesson, she did not have an opportunity to meet with Brady's cooperating teacher, Carmine Young. Nor did Joan, Carmine, and Brady have any regular opportunity to meet and talk about how things were going and what kind of resources and support Brady needed. Although Carmine was an effective teacher and modeled many valuable dispositions and teaching skills, our program and the local school district had not provided her with significant mentoring training.

• • • • •

As these cases reveal, some of our teacher candidates were challenged by the fundamental moral claim that all children can learn and that teachers must persist in helping every student achieve success. The cases also show that acting on this claim depends on having the requisite knowledge and skills as well as the relevant beliefs and convictions. Student teaching is too late to begin working on these problems. We needed a coordinated approach that began early in the program.

While our candidates were familiar with the professional dispositions delineated in professional, state, and institutional standards, the chasm between their own school and cultural experience and that of their students was difficult to cross. Given the demographic divide between our candidates and their students, we needed to address incoming beliefs early in their preparation program so that candidates could begin to understand, relate to, and feel responsible for supporting the learning of students who differ from them in learning needs, ethnicity, or social class.[7]

Knowing that dispositions cannot be developed in a single course, we had to work across the programs so that candidates acquired the knowledge and skills necessary to teach all learners effectively. We had to communicate our vision early in the program and help candidates learn to enact it in their teaching. Earlier field experiences in more diverse settings would be an important part of the redesign. This would help disrupt candidates' notions of who would be in their classes and what it means to be a teacher, so that they could begin to construct more appropriate professional identities and expectations.

The cases helped us see the limitations of casting the university supervisor as an observer and evaluator of lessons. This conventional role fails to utilize the supervisor's skills and ignores the potential for greater collaboration between supervisors and cooperating teachers. Seeing that most of our action plans occurred during student teaching highlighted the need to attention to dispositional concerns much earlier in the program so that we could address them in a more timely way.

While we wanted a teacher preparation curriculum "infused" with issues of diversity, we realized that diversity came up in separate courses taught by individual faculty members in different programs. Courses, readings, assignments, and discussions rarely built on or connected to one another. As a result, candidates were able to invoke the right dispositions without understanding them deeply or knowing how to act on them. Our conventional program structure did not help candidates rethink personal beliefs and form new ones or connect those beliefs to particular actions in the field. Candidates could progress through the program without teaching in inner-urban settings. And when they did teach in these settings, they often took a micro rather than macro view of diversity, looking at racial diversity rather than all aspects of difference. The pattern was clear: when teacher candidates' backgrounds differed from those of their students, they often did not know how to act on the "big ideas" they encountered in their classes or use the pedagogical tools they had learned about.

ADDRESSING THE NEED

Given the strong institutional commitment to inquiry, University of Cincinnati education faculty members are often engaged in action research. On the basis of the concerns outlined above, the authors of this chapter undertook an action research project. We used "study circles" to explore systematic changes of our courses and fieldwork, with the goal of eventually reorganizing our programs and teaching.[8] The study circle methodology brought together a variety of stakeholders to examine phenomena, implement changes, and collect systematic data to inform changes in the current structure.

We met in a weeklong faculty development institute to share stories about our frustrations, including stories about candidates like Ruth, Henry, and Brady, and brainstormed a wide range of initiatives. We considered having general education students' work with special education students and English as a Second Language (ESL) specialists in the field, requiring a multicultural education course for all students in our licensure programs, and finding ways to model the dispositions and teaching partnerships we wanted our students to emulate.

With multiple years of data from surveys of mentor teachers and principals, and samples of our students' work, we identified trends in our candidates' performance. Evidence from logs of conversations among cooperating teachers, candidates, and university supervisors demonstrated interesting patterns—for example, concerns on the part of special education candidates about whether they had enough content knowledge, and concerns on the part of secondary and middle education candidates about their ability to differentiate instruction for the diverse students they were encountering in their field placements. It became clear that some of the introductory courses were addressing issues related to our core commitment in superficial ways.

Individual faculty members took responsibility to explore integrated methods courses, coteaching models, and the work of the New Teacher Center. The university-wide change from quarters to semesters provided the opportunity to use backward design, beginning with candidate outcomes and reframing our programs to fit the needs of our candidates and the K–12 students they would teach. Rather than having faculty "own" individual courses, we began to take shared responsibility for our licensure programs, initiating several key changes.

Introducing a New Diversity Assessment

Every teacher education candidate is required to take several foundations courses, including Foundations and History of Special Education. The new special education course goes beyond identifying students with disabilities and introduces issues of universal design, high expectations, and "no excuses" (i.e., teacher responsibility for student learning and no blaming of students for failure to achieve), coteaching, and teaching all children. The foundations course is the first place where our candidates contemplate whether a career in teaching is realistic for them, especially given the challenges of urban teaching and the differences in background between the majority of our candidates and their future students. Here is where faculty begin to help candidates confront explicitly the beliefs and misconceptions they may harbor about the educational needs of children of color or children from socioeconomic circumstances unlike their own.

As part of the foundations course, each candidate now completes assessments that surface assumptions related to culture, race, and gender. Stereotypical responses, such as "Boys are more troublesome than girls" or "Some parents don't care about their children's education" come to light, and students are helped to see that these responses are inconsistent with the licensure programs' expectations. Readings and class materials are presented that address these misconceptions and stereotypes, and faculty members model various teaching strategies and methods that celebrate diversity. In addition, students are now expected to participate in a field component in an inner-urban school setting that is closely tied to the course and designed to challenge their ideas about educating all students, their misconceptions related to culture, and their concepts of themselves as teachers.

Revised Method Courses

Besides developing new early field experiences, we created opportunities for candidates to learn and practice a variety of differentiation strategies so that they would be better prepared to work with students from all circumstances. This included methods courses that emphasized content requirements so that special education licensure students would know content well enough to make necessary modifications. Cotaught by a general educator and a special educator to mixed groups of general education students and special education students, the new courses focused on how to deliver content to all students.

Pairing content faculty with special education faculty in developing new methods courses and strengthening the tie between these courses and the accompanying field experiences allow us to work out what it means and what it takes to teach content to diverse learners. We require students to work in pairs to design and deliver lessons and to reflect on their decisions and how they might improve their teaching. We hope such experiences will help students begin to see themselves as professionals who need and want to work with colleagues to support the learning of all their students.

The goal of breaking down barriers between programs through shared coursework originally led two faculty members, one in special education and one in secondary education, to coteach a secondary English education methods course tied to a field experience.[9] The course emphasized differentiated instruction and universal design for learning, as the twenty candidates constructed four- to six-week conceptual units.[10] These units utilized the cyclic process of assess, teach, and reassess, with special emphasis on multiple means of presentation, expression, and assessment.

During and after the course, the coteachers compared rubric scores for the conceptual units with scores for the conceptual units constructed in a course taught by a single instructor. They also compared course evaluations, a postcourse online survey, postcourse focus groups, faculty reflections, and follow-up observations during the candidates' student teaching to see whether the cotaught methods course improved teacher candidates' ability to accommodate their students' learning needs. Initial results indicate that the twenty English candidates in the cotaught methods course were more aware of the diversity in their classes, incorporated more adaptations and accommodations when planning, and were more open to collaborating with special education teachers in inclusion settings than students in the methods course taught by a single instructor.

This pilot stimulated general education faculty in other disciplines (science, mathematics, social studies) to explore the possibility of coteaching methods classes with their special education colleagues. Working together as equals, instructors demonstrate how their differing perspectives require alternative approaches to learning and help teacher candidates build a repertoire of strategies to use in their future classrooms. In addition, on the basis of the work of Marilyn Friend, professor of specialized education services, pairs of cooperating teachers are now being trained in coteaching methods, and pairs of special education and general education student teachers are being placed with them, resulting in four trained coteachers in the classroom at the same time.

Rethinking the Roles of University Supervisor and Cooperating Teacher

To introduce a more robust conception of mentoring, we needed to train and empower strong cooperating teachers to take a more active role in the preparation of new teachers. Field and practicum experiences provided our candidates with opportunities to practice what they learned.[11] Unfortunately, our traditional model of student teaching—in which university supervisors did a limited number of formal observations and cooperating teachers did not think of themselves as teachers of teaching—provided limited occasions to talk through their experiences. Introducing a collaborative model of mentoring based on "cothinking" allowed cooperating teachers, teacher candidates, and university supervisors to help student teachers get inside the intellectual and practical challenges of teaching. As all three players engage in new ways of thinking and acting, beliefs and assumptions come to light.[12]

To help teacher candidates recall and connect coursework and field experiences, cooperating teachers need to understand what the teacher preparation programs are trying to teach. Then they can reinforce new concepts and strategies and help student teachers enact practices consistent with the program's values. Our field coordinators are becoming more selective in choosing cooperating teachers. In addition, we are reducing the number of cooperating teachers by assigning pairs of candidates to strong cooperating teachers.

In evaluations of these field experiences, candidates report that having a peer to plan with and to evaluate their teaching was a positive experience. They were able to "rehearse" and talk through their rationales and plans. They engaged in more collaborative teaching and reflection. Cooperating teachers also indicated that the presence of two candidates increased reflection, conversation, and the sharing of materials and methods.

Using the Collaborative Assessment Log

Recently, we changed the focus of supervision from direct observation to three-way meetings during the cooperating teacher's planning period. We also adopted the Collaborative Assessment Log, a tool that is part of the New Teacher Center's formative assessment system.[13] The log helps structure conversations among the cooperating teacher, the candidate, and the university-based supervisor. The trio identifies what is working, what challenges the candidate is facing, next steps for everyone, and resources. All participants are present as candidates reflect on their work, describe the challenges they face, and assess their growth.

Next Steps

Even as we work on developing our candidates' core dispositions and assessing them in authentic ways, we still have more work to do. As Ohio moves from a summative entry-year teacher program, based in Praxis III, to a formative residency, instruments like the Collaborative Assessment Log, Pre-service Goal Setting Agreement, and Analysis of Student Work can help us understand how well teacher candidates are learning to celebrate diversity, differentiate instruction, build rapport, and engage students in worthwhile learning. We recognize the need to continue refining and revising such in-house practices as coteaching our methods courses and pairing our candidates for their fieldwork. To that end, our next steps include systematic reflection on the program changes we have instituted, such as earlier field experiences and early coursework related to issues of race, class, gender, religion, sexual orientation, language, ethnicity, and culture. We also must continue to work on assessment measures to document how well we are fulfilling our goal of preparing committed, caring, and competent teachers.

Becoming Committed

For beginning teachers to embrace commitment, they need to understand the context in which they will teach, and how issues of race, class, gender, and culture enter in. With a two-tiered admission system, candidates do not enter professional education until they are juniors. In addition, 80 percent of our candidates transfer into our program during their sophomore or junior years. Coursework may provide knowledge and even begin to develop skills and attitudes, but confronting beliefs through practicum experiences in real classrooms is critical.

Early experiences can validate the dispositions expected of teachers and provide an early reading on where candidates are with respect to desired dispositions. As we redevelop coursework to align with our thinking about teacher dispositions, we must also develop related field experiences so that our predominantly white, middle-class candidates can confront and address their biases and misconceptions about students unlike themselves. Using pedagogies like reflective journals in courses tied to early practicum experiences should help us identify concerns long before student teaching.

While candidates may state that all students can and do learn, they must be able to take this responsibility to heart. Early field experiences will provide an opportunity for candidates to tutor children unlike themselves and to work in afterschool social programs, where they will be helped to discover the value of all young people regardless of circumstance. Through such personal relationships, our candidates will develop empathy and compassion for young people who may not have had the chance to develop the skills needed to perform proficiently in some classrooms. Our expectations are high, and some individuals who think they want to be teachers may not be able to attain them.

Becoming Caring

We want candidates to care about the students they teach. Foundation courses, the first places many candidates explicitly encounter issues of race, class, gender, and culture, need to become reflective workshops that address why and how caring is a crucial disposition of teaching. These courses, prior to candidates' entry into a professional cohort, should provide time to work through their misconceptions or biases about urban teaching and about young people different from themselves.

Exposure, reflection, and guidance with situations and populations unlike their own may increase candidates' knowledge and comfort in working with students who differ from them in race, class, learning challenges. A sense of comfort can contribute to a sense of caring about the individuals in their classrooms. We know that this exposure must be done in an honest and sensitive manner where candidates can face misconceptions and misinformation in an environment that preserves their dignity and safety. Thus, we, too, must be caring.

We are redeveloping our foundations courses to include deeper reflection about caring and about our commitment to social justice. This will require more discussions with one another and with some school and community partners. We have also added a course in the final term of student teaching, Teaching and Learning in Diverse Classrooms, that reexposes our candidates to the problems, issues, and experiences of students from underrepresented groups based on race, ethnicity, language, socioeconomic status, and sexual identity. This course serves as a final reminder of what our candidates will be expected to be like, to know, and to do as teachers.

To document and assess expected outcomes related to caring, we will rely on student work from the foundations courses, such as journal entries and essays on commitment, competence, and caring and on teaching and diversity. The plan is to look for "aha!" moments from their work in the field and attend to the language they use in these assignments. Hopefully, these sources and the willingness of teacher candidates to learn will provide evidence that our new practices are producing teacher candidates with cultural flexibility who care about students across race, class, gender, and culture.

Becoming Competent

Competency has generally been reserved for content knowledge (e.g., language, science, mathematics). Besides the changes in cotaught methods courses, the pairing of student teachers and mentors, and the design of new field experiences, we need to work with content specialists across the university to create coursework that blends content and pedagogy. This will help candidates learn to transform their content knowledge into teachable curriculum.

We have begun to develop "shadow" courses that connect issues of content and methodology in mathematics, and specific science coursework that uses methodologies we want our candidates to use in their own classrooms. Once our candidates feel more confident about their pedagogical content knowledge, they are more willing to think about differentiation and to modify their methods of delivering content and their expectations for students. The continuous exposure to methods in content, special education, and general education courses has the potential to help candidates develop a flexible repertoire of approaches to learning that will ultimately benefit K–12 students in their future classrooms.

Assessing Commitment, Caring, and Competence

As we rethink our assessment tools, we need to consider issues of validity and reliability and figure out how to document dispositional change over time. The Collaborative Assessment Log is part of a larger assessment strategy that will include student artifacts, classroom observations, and candidate interviews. At this point we need to learn more about what tools are available, what other programs require of their candidates, and what seems to work. We are looking for assessments that help our students recognize the impact they have on their students. Recently, we began to collaborate with other universities on teacher work samples through the Performance Assessment of California Teachers (PACT). We know that our assessments need to attend to both content and pedagogy. As we work on these tasks, we are refining our current assessment plans, rethinking our capstone requirements, and creating tools to document candidates' development, which they will see as valuable.

Assessment is not only about our candidates and their dispositions. Our programmatic changes require deeper reflection on the part of all stakeholders. If our students are not discussing engagement, rapport building, and concern for students and their learning, we will need to go back to the drawing board. If they do not become partners with us in working toward social justice, we will need to revisit our program and make further changes in our own language, teaching, and commitments. We see that we must be more explicit with our candidates about their attitudes toward their students. They must recognize that they are teachers, and teachers teach, not just some students who may think and behave like them, but *all* students.

CONCLUSION

As we continue to rethink what we, as an entire faculty, want our candidates to know, feel, or do when they leave our preparation program, we recognize that this reflection includes what we ourselves must know, feel, or do. Our transformation must address issues of fear, cultural misunderstandings, ignorance, and safety. It will require willingness on the part of faculty to support candidates even when their growth includes hesitancy, resistance, or a bit of rebellion. Communication and dialogue will be essential as we make explicit what we value and expect.

Writing this chapter has helped us realize the need to change our practice and ourselves. Our teacher candidates will continue to be white, and lower middle class, and middle class. We accept the challenge of working with future teachers who need help building rapport with all students. To avoid perpetuating ineffective programs and practices, we must critically review and change our performance. If our candidates are not demonstrating the dispositions we have identified, we must find ways to develop those dispositions. We must be concerned with the quality of teachers, and how they impact the students they will serve.

CHAPTER FIVE

Learning from Getting It Wrong

Catherine Fallona and Julie Canniff

Editors' Case Introduction: University of Southern Maine

The University of Southern Maine (USM) is a public, comprehensive, regional university with three campuses located in Portland, Gorham, and Lewiston, Maine, serving approximately 10,500 students. The university's Teacher Education Department delivers its teacher education program in partnership with K–12 school districts. Each year approximately 100 teacher candidates participate in a yearlong cohort-based internship for each certification area they pursue. Cohorts consist of two groups of teacher candidates, those who have entered through an undergraduate pathway at USM and those who have entered via postbaccalaureate admission.

Undergraduates pursue certification through USM's Teachers for Elementary and Middle Schools (TEAMS) program. TEAMS results in a bachelor's degree in the liberal arts, a master's degree in teaching and learning, and teacher certification in either K–8 general education, dual K–8 general and special education, or dual K–8 and English as a Second Language (ESL). Students seeking certification through the postbaccalaureate Extended Teacher Education Program (ETEP) also receive a master's degree in teaching and learning. Through ETEP, teacher candidates earn K–8 general elementary and/or special education, 7–12 content area and/or special education, K–12 foreign language, or K–12 ESL teacher certifications.

"Learning from Getting It Wrong" begins their journey by exploring how teacher educators at USM identified and sought to foster teacher candidates' dispositions for equity. The authors explain how they attempted to embed their four core dispositions throughout their programs, aligning their courses and

assessments appropriately. Despite an explicitly articulated program vision and carefully designed assessments, two students whose beliefs or actions were incongruent with the program's vision highlight where the program had room for growth.

FOSTERING MORAL DISPOSITIONS

Dispositions are "a tendency . . . to act or react in characteristic ways in certain situations."[1] Fostering moral dispositions is at the heart of our work as teacher educators. It is our job to prepare teachers with the knowledge and skills they need to plan, instruct, assess, and manage a classroom. Equally important, however, is our responsibility to prepare teachers who are able to build on their dispositions for equitable and engaging learning. For example, our teacher education faculty teaches preservice candidates how to identify the range of learning styles and academic readiness of the students in their classrooms. The faculty systematically models and teaches the skills of designing, implementing, and reflecting on units and lesson plans that align with standards and differentiate the instruction and the assessment to increase each student's readiness for the content. All of our faculty and methods instructors expect candidates to maintain classroom momentum and engagement by drawing on a variety of responsive techniques. However, if a candidate appears to "learn" these skills but is never "disposed" to practice them, equally, with all students, it is an indication that she or he does not possess the moral dispositions to succeed in our program.

Our efforts to identify and foster teacher candidates' dispositions place morality at the core of teachers' work. Teaching is, as Alan Tom puts it, a "moral craft" built around a moral relationship between the teacher and the student.[2] Any action a teacher undertakes in the classroom is capable of expressing moral meaning that can influence students.[3] Gary Fenstermacher explains, "What makes teaching a moral endeavor is that it is, quite centrally, human action undertaken in regard to other human beings. Thus matters of what is fair, right, just, and virtuous are always present . . . The teacher's conduct, at all times and in all ways, is a moral matter."[4]

Morality is embedded in teachers' practice that results in an implicit moral curriculum that intertwines the knowledge and skills of teaching with its moral aspects.[5] Teachers must have a style or manner expressive of moral virtue.[6] Therefore, teachers need to possess moral dispositions that are expressive of moral virtue toward students, colleagues, the curriculum, their communities, and the democratic ideals that are central to educating the next generation of citizens.

As teacher educators in the College of Education and Human Development at the University of Southern Maine (USM), we have the responsibility to ensure that the dispositions of the teachers who graduate from our programs express moral virtues, by which we mean that our graduates act on behalf of the good of society and the good of all children. We have spent a significant amount of time across the last several years identifying and building consensus regarding the dispositions we value in teachers. Our work as teacher educators is guided by USM's College of Education and Human Development's mission "to foster respectful and collaborative learning communities, well-informed decision-making, valid reasoning, and a concern for equity and social justice in the fields of education and human development."[7] As a college, we value diversity, democracy, civility, equity, social justice, caring, ethical practice, and professional and continuous learning.

The USM Teacher Education Department's vision is to *instill a commitment to equitable and engaging learning* through a set of core practices related to fostering inquiry, engaging in scholarship, providing opportunities to learn, setting high expectations, being responsive, and nurturing collegiality. Our *equity framework*, which was crafted for the first time in 2007, guides us toward achieving our mission and integrating these practices into the program's university coursework, field experiences, and yearlong internship. Since then, the faculty have begun the arduous process of revising our courses and assessments to better align with our equity stance. For instance, our joint development of EDU 527, Understanding and Teaching Diverse Learners, and the integration of special education and ESL pedagogy into our ten teaching standards represent the ways in which our common assessments, field internships, and the yearlong seminar foster the dispositions for *inquiry, cultural responsiveness, setting high expectations, and collegiality*.

The vast majority (98 percent) of our interns enter our programs with a sensibility toward these dispositions, and throughout their yearlong internships, these dispositions expand as they gain experience as teachers in school contexts and develop an understanding of the moral dimensions of teaching. Most leave the program transformed to become teachers who place equitable opportunities for student learning at the very center of their practice. Yet, despite our dogged efforts, we aren't always successful. There are always a few with whom we are not successful because their dispositions remain at variance with the dispositions for inquiry, cultural responsiveness, setting high expectations, and collegiality.

Because we often learn more from our failures than our successes, this chapter focuses on those few with whom we aren't successful. It is a case of what we learn when we get it wrong—that is, when we fail to foster moral dispositions expressive of a commitment to equity in teacher candidates. To illustrate this case, we draw upon evidence from two teacher candidates whose performance on program assessments revealed significant conflict between their stated dispositions and their actions in the classroom. In conclusion we synthesize the issues and continuing questions we have about fostering moral dispositions in an intensive teacher education program.

ASSESSING CANDIDATES' MORAL DISPOSITIONS

Our approach to fostering teacher candidates' moral dispositions is a formative one. At USM, the assessment of teacher candidates' moral dispositions is an ongoing process that begins at the time of admission and extends through program completion. However, the faculty does not use a rubric to measure dispositions. Rather, the faculty has spent an extensive amount of time together over the last several years engaging in professional conversations that have led to a consensus regarding the dispositions we want all graduates of our teacher education programs to express. Drawing heavily upon our shared vision, the teacher education faculty identifies, assesses, and fosters teacher candidates' dispositions from the time of a candidate's admission through program completion. In the following profiles of Patrick and George, we explore the challenge of engaging in such work. Assessments of George's and Patrick's dispositions at various points in their programs reveal that both teacher candidates articulated a moral stance but resisted feedback from mentors and supervisors regarding their dispositions for equity as represented by inquiry, responsiveness, high expectations, and collegiality.

Admissions

At the time of admission to the graduate-level internship, our teacher education faculty assess teacher candidates' dispositions for inquiry, responsiveness, high expectations, and collegiality. The assessment of the dispositions of undergraduate teacher candidates in the TEAMS program is based upon a body of evidence that the candidate has collected via courses and field experiences over the course of two to three years in the program. The candidate prepares and presents a portfolio organized around the first five USM Teacher Certification Standards. These same standards and dispositions are assessed at the time we admit teacher candidates to the postbaccalaureate ETEP program. However, ETEP candidates' dispositions are assessed through a review of the candidate's previous experiences, a written statement about equity, and a probing interview. As a result of the success of our teacher candidates, it is clear that this process enables faculty to identify those candidates who possess the moral depositions for teaching. However, there are times, as in the cases of Patrick and George, where we get it wrong.

Patrick entered the TEAMS program immediately upon graduating from high school. His admission was based upon the strength of his academic record and prior experiences working with children. His application essay and letters of reference demonstrated Patrick's commitment and potential as a teacher. Following his admission to TEAMS, Patrick completed a series of introductory undergraduate education classes that are closely aligned with a field placement. As a part of these courses and field experiences, Patrick completed course assessments that required him to make theory-to-practice connections. The assessments that Patrick completed for the university classes and the reflections on the field experiences formed the evidence of the first five USM Teacher Certification Standards that Patrick needed when he was reviewed in the second semester of his junior year for candidacy to the graduate-level internship.

In these assessments, a disposition emerged concerning Patrick's passionate and vocal Christian beliefs. At first blush, one might think that his Christian beliefs would support moral predispositions toward teaching. For example, Patrick stated that the Golden Rule was one of his beliefs. He believed in treating others the way he would want to be treated, and he wanted "to exercise a spirit of charity and kindness." However, his strong Christian beliefs impeded his ability to be culturally responsive to students whose religious and family values were in opposition to his own. For example, at the beginning of each classroom placement, our teacher candidates are expected to write a letter home to parents and guardians to introduce themselves and share with them the role they will play in the classroom over the course of the semester.

Despite being told by his mentor teacher that he should not proselytize his Christian values in his letter home to parents and guardians, Patrick wrote a letter that framed his introduction to parents and his role in the classroom in terms of his Christianity. The missionary tone of his letter was unacceptable to his mentor, the school principal and his university site coordinator. The principal advocated to have Patrick removed from the school because he did not feel as though he had the disposition to be accepting of the approximately 30 percent of students in the school who were of Muslim faith. The principal only agreed to let Patrick stay in the building when his mentor and the teacher who was the team leader agreed to work with Patrick to rewrite his letter, and closely monitor his interactions with students, parents, and community members. With close monitoring by school and university faculty, Patrick "successfully" completed the semester and was able to continue in the program. He demonstrated evidence of progress toward meeting the USM teacher certification standards, but he was placed on an action plan for improvement as he moved on to the graduate-level internship.

Like Patrick, George was admitted based upon a strong academic background. As a secondary mathematics teacher candidate to ETEP, George had the required credit hours in mathematics as well as master's degrees in business administration and accounting. George was also admitted because of his teaching experience. While applying to ETEP, George was employed as an adjunct instructor teaching accounting courses at a local community college with a fairly large immigrant population. He also tutored students in mathematics through programs for at-risk teenagers and volunteered as a coach for the Special Olympics and Maine Handicapped Skiing. He described his approach to tutoring as providing careful, patient explanations of the task while "demonstrating my concern for their well being and being flexible to adapt to the special needs that each individual required." During his interview, George reiterated his commitment to working with students from a wide variety of backgrounds and abilities—emphasizing his willingness to bring examples from the real world into his mathematics instruction. His recommendation letters, all from university professors, commended his intellect and exceptional academic skills as a graduate student.

Despite these accolades and his experiences, the faculty did express some reservations regarding his dispositions toward providing equitable learning experiences for all students. One faculty interviewer stated that "he has a caring disposition, yet he has a fairly narrow concept of instructional possibilities [favoring teacher lecture and questioning]." This faculty member also questioned whether "he sees the equity issue." Yet, because George's essay touched on concepts of equity—taking time to know students, supporting their struggles to understand mathematics, and real experiences of working with young people with disabilities— and because his interview reinforced his written statements, the interviewers concurred that he possessed the dispositions to do well in ETEP, and he was admitted to the program.

In the cases of George and Patrick, there were clues during the admissions process that these individuals might not possess the moral dispositions to be good teachers. However, there was also evidence that these individuals possessed the dispositions to engage with our curriculum and our practica with a genuine willingness to transform themselves into effective teachers. Thus, hoping for their success, we admitted George and Patrick to the graduate-level internship.

INTERNSHIP ASSESSMENTS

When preparing candidates to meet the ten USM Teacher Certification Standards, the teacher education faculty rely on a set of common assessments that explicitly reinforce moral dispositions that are expressive of equity toward students, colleagues, the curriculum, their communities, and the democratic ideals that are central to educating the next generation of citizens. The faculty has spent three years designing common assessments and common rubrics that reflect the dispositions we expect of general education teachers, special educators, and teachers who work with English language learners. These dispositions have been described above and include inquiry, responsiveness, opportunity to learn/high expectations, and collegiality. The common assessments include the study of learners in their worlds, the teaching philosophy, reflective journals and videotape analysis, a classroom management system, a disciplinary or interdisciplinary teaching unit, and a final internship portfolio. The assessments also contribute to the interns' evidence for meeting the USM teaching standards, which is the overall, summative assessment in program completion. The following sections describe how Patrick and George approached the assessments, and the process by which their supervisors tried to foster their dispositions for equity.

Assessing the Disposition for Inquiry

We define *inquiry* as a "stance" through which teachers reflect faithfully and critically on their practices, with the goal of strengthening the knowledge and skills essential for developing culturally responsive pedagogy.[8] Hugh Sockett offers the insight that the virtues of character and self-knowledge are the outcomes of a disposition for inquiry, since "self-knowledge and its acquisition demands moral and intellectual honesty, a preparedness to re-evaluate each aspect of one's individual practice."[9] The places where a teacher candidate exhibits a disposition for inquiry that is intellectually honest are in their reflections on their practice, and in their teaching philosophies. To foster teacher candidates' disposition of inquiry, the teacher education faculty prompts interns to analyze a given lesson based on what they know about the students' readiness to meet a particular learning target, how the intern's instruction does or does not facilitate his or her students in meeting the learning target, and what the intern plans to do next. The faculty also requires interns to engage in discussions where they must interpret and evaluate the relationship between theories of culturally responsive teaching, and their implementation of such pedagogy in their placements. Next, the faculty examines interns' reflections to understand whether they actually noticed and acted on instances where their assumptions about students and their abilities were challenged, and guides them through multiple drafts of their teaching philosophies, encouraging them to ground their beliefs both in some scholarly literature, and in actual practices they implement in the classroom.

Patrick and George struggled with a stance of inquiry. Although both stated that they valued differentiated instruction and wanted to provide equitable learning opportunities for their students, their teaching was dogmatic and teacher centered. Both found critical reflection on their practice difficult.

In his teaching philosophy, Patrick stated that he perceived his role as teacher as to "instill knowledge." When he was unsuccessful in his attempts to instill knowledge, he didn't know what to do. Because he was so strong and confident in his subject matter knowledge, he had trouble conceiving that students did not have the same level of interest to learn and do well in school as he did as a student. Patrick's difficulty in comprehending some students' struggles with the subject matter resulted in a lack of inquiry on his part into how best to engage students in learning.

Similarly, despite extensive efforts by his supervisors, George was unwilling to inquire into why some students seemed chronically confused and unresponsive during his instruction, or why other students became defiant. When his supervisors asked him to reflect upon his lessons and think about how he might do things differently another time, he became defensive. He frequently referred to his teacher role in the classroom as delivering content through "chalk and talk," and that disposition remained fixed. While George offered students unlimited tutoring opportunities after class or after school, he was unable to understand or accept that differentiating his instruction during class time might help accomplish his goals. As the pressure of the program's pace and requirements increased, George's reflections became more and more revealing of his dispositions toward some students. In one of his journal reflections, he wrote:

> [I have had to separate] a few kids in the same class period, but after eliminating their opportunities to socialize with each other, they have all managed to put themselves into ongoing self-induced trances. They are literally incapable of paying attention for more than 20 seconds. At the risk of sounding sarcastic, I am actually impressed with their ability to intently focus on nothing and managing to avoid learning anything while my mentor and I have little difficulty engaging the majority of students. While theorists might argue that this is a situation where interactive activities in which there is a clearly identified learning target with numerous connections to the real world either through manipulatives or through exercise design is the obvious solution, I would argue that such theory is often times ill-equipped to provide any practical and meaningful solutions for the "in-the-trenches" teacher and his/her quest to provide the most equitable education possible.

Although George had gathered enough data on his students to be aware that a few students in each class were not meeting grade-level expectations in math, he continued to methodically cover the material in the textbook while these students fell further behind. George continued to treat his supervisors' expectations that he practice ongoing inquiry, reflection, and modification for his students as simply a university course assignment. He was not disposed to alter his manner of classroom teaching in order to respond to these students' obvious needs.

In hindsight, neither Patrick nor George could process feedback as constructive. Continually examining their beliefs and practices and acting upon findings to improve teaching and learning was challenging for them. At the time, it seemed that each of them was overwhelmed by how to address the needs of the diversity of learners in their classrooms, but upon review of their teaching stances and lesson reflections, it seems clear that each of them lacked a disposition for inquiry.

Assessing the Disposition of Responsiveness

The teacher education faculty's approach to the disposition of responsiveness is grounded in the literature on culturally responsive teaching, and universal design for learning.[10] The principles that guide our teaching and assessment include the following:

- Students from culturally and linguistically diverse (CLD) communities must achieve academically within the same context and toward the same learning standards as so-called mainstream students.
- Students from CLD communities must be able to demonstrate competence within their own cultural communities.
- All students must be given opportunities to investigate and critique the social order that discriminates against them.[11]

Developing and assessing candidates' disposition for responsiveness during the yearlong internship begins when interns are required to assemble in-depth profiles of themselves as learners. They access core beliefs through educational autobiographies, they discover learning modalities by completing a variety of personality and learning inventories, and they gain an appreciation for the environmental and cognitive barriers that influence their capacity to learn. All of this prepares them to use similar strategies to understand how their own students learn and interact with one another. When interns engage in this process with intellectual and moral honesty, it has the potential to reveal their deeply held assumptions about intelligence, ability, effort, fairness, and so forth. Confronting negative assumptions and replacing them with beliefs in the capacities of students is intrinsic to the process of becoming culturally responsive educators.

Teacher education faculty assess interns' disposition for responsiveness throughout the yearlong internship through a variety of assessments, including a profile of the communities in which interns teach, a profile of the students in one classroom or one middle or high school class section, and a profile of the capacities and barriers that those students face in meeting the learning targets for the interns' lead teaching week. In addition, interns are required to draw extensively on the three profiles to design a classroom management system and implement whole-class, preventive management strategies, and to implement specific supportive plans for a small subset of students who are the focus of a case study they produce.

Patrick clearly articulated a belief in "equality and love for all people." On the other hand, the way in which he framed his teaching around his own Christianity was not respectful of students whose backgrounds were in opposition to his own Christian values. Despite warnings to tread lightly regarding espousing his own religious beliefs, Patrick continually inserted his religious values in his teaching. For example, in the midst of a writing lesson, he told students that they should work hard out of respect for God. In response, one of his supervisors gave him the following written feedback: "The notion of respect for God is one that a student may bring into a conversation; it cannot come from a public school teacher. As a public school teacher and Catholic woman, I need to teach by example and not preach, always respecting the boundaries present in public education."

Yet, Patrick consistently resisted such feedback. When challenged, he clung to his perspective as being "right." As one of his supervisors noted, Patrick "can't conceptualize difference. He is not self-aware." His lack of self-awareness resulted in outwardly professing his religious values in school and expecting his students to share them. As a result, he alienated students and colleagues from religious and family backgrounds that differed from his personal religious values.

Like Patrick, George did not place students' background and needs at the center of his instruction. George's lack of responsiveness was evident when he could not transfer the learning embedded in the assignments that made up the Study of Learners in Their Worlds. In virtually each of his ten analyses of the classroom profile data, George stated that most of his students required "clear structure and time to collaboratively solve problems," "prefer a variety of presentation methods [from their instructor]," and "required a variety of methods to demonstrate learning"; and finally George observed that students were eager to use their laptops to facilitate their learning. The fact that George did not act on his students' stated preferences or his supervisors' frequent requests for him to implement the strategies he outlined in his profile analysis was troubling.

A few students became increasingly defiant in the face of George's repetitive, teacher-driven instruction. Despite the fact that two of his peers were placed on the same middle school team, had the same students, and did not experience the same problems, George continued to engage in power struggles with the students. In a journal entry, George defended his decision to publically expose one of the students for not doing his homework:

> My reaction to finding out the kid did not do his homework was to offer him an individualized lesson on the subject (real basic geometry). The class knew I was not my usual self and they all quieted down to complete silence as I spent five minutes going through this individualized lesson. After completing the short presentation, I asked the kid if he could now solve one of the homework questions. Being the wise guy that he is, he responded that he could not. I posed the question to the rest of the class, "don't you guys think that after that explanation, a student should be able to solve the problem?" . . . I don't know if it was appropriate to put the kid on the spot like this but he finally did answer that question as well as a number of others that I grilled him with.

This incident revealed a fundamental conflict between George's written beliefs—where he states, "I strongly feel that the concepts of fairness, equity, compassion and continual learning are essential in the development of intellectually mature, productive and socially aware citizens"—and his actions, which were consistent with an authoritarian approach to teaching his content and where making a public example of a student was an acceptable response.

George's unwillingness to differentiate his classroom instruction was paradoxically at odds with his strong advocacy of three students in his classes with whom he became quite close. Two students had learning disabilities, and one student developed an emotional problem that prompted George to seek assistance from the school's social worker. In hindsight, the two supervisors decided that George had the disposition to be responsive to students when he was in a tutoring relationship with them, but he could not integrate those skills into his fifty-minute classroom instruction. His teaching was about covering material, and students who needed additional support had to meet with him outside of class time.

At bottom, both George and Patrick considered the classroom and learner profiles as merely university course assignments rather than an essential tool for knowing their students in order to modify instruction. When it came to truly considering and responding to the diversity of students' backgrounds, each was unwilling to differentiate his classroom instruction according to students' background. In the end, their dispositions were paradoxically at odds with their articulated commitment to provide an equitable education for all.

Fostering the Disposition of High Expectations

The disposition to hold high expectations for all students is closely aligned in our equity framework with the concept of opportunity to learn.[12] The first assumption is that the candidate confidently knows and can discriminate among the key facts and concepts in his discipline. The objective, then, is first, to match the students' factual, conceptual, and procedural knowledge with the benchmarks in the state learning results; and second, teacher candidates must ensure that all students achieve a basic competency in the assessment *of* learning. That requires an intern to automatically search for multiple ways of (1) presenting material—for example, lecture plus small group discussion plus visual modeling; and (2) offering students a variety of ways to demonstrate what they know—for example, written, verbal, modeling. Most important, the instruction must include different levels of challenge that are open to all. These fundamental principles are at the heart of universal design for learning.

The disciplinary or interdisciplinary teaching unit that is part of the lead teaching requirement aligns with the teacher education faculty's efforts to foster the disposition of high expectations. As part of lead teaching, each intern designs and teaches at least one unit during the internship year. A unit is operationally defined as a topic, theme, or project that is substantial enough to warrant both ongoing assessments and a culminating, or final, assessment of student learning. It must relate to topics in the grade-level curriculum, pay special attention to applicable Maine learning results, and use a backward-planning methodology. An analysis of resulting student work and a reflection on instructional implications are expected as part of the finished product.

Because Patrick and George struggled to enact an inquiry stance and displayed stances toward teaching that prevented them from being responsive to students from different backgrounds with varied academic abilities, it was difficult to determine whether Patrick and George truly had high expectations for all students. Neither wrote lesson plans based upon the information they gathered about their students' cultural backgrounds, interests, prior content knowledge, or learning modalities that would reflect a commitment to responsive pedagogy so they might differentiate their delivery, assessments, or levels of challenge.

According to one of Patrick's supervisors, "He doesn't realize his weaknesses or what he needs to do." For example, he framed his philosophy for working with students "from all backgrounds and ability levels" around creating a "welcoming place for students who either shy away from learning or have tremendous obstacles to overcome in the classroom because of physical or mental abilities." Although this is extremely important, Patrick does not appear to recognize that meeting the needs of an array of learners involves much more than constructing a classroom climate that is welcoming. According to one of his supervisors, Patrick lacked "basic competencies" as a teacher, and that resulted in his inability to establish and communicate clear, challenging, and attainable standards for all learners. The result is a lack of an equitable education for all the students in his classroom because he is not responsive to individual students' needs.

Like Patrick, George lacked the competencies needed to implement the principles embedded in universal design. After the midplacement conference in October, George's primary supervisor wrote up an action plan that outlined a very specific set of performances George needed to complete each week. This included submitting lesson plans for each lesson that identified the specific learning targets, the modifications for students not meeting the learning target, a variety of presentation and assessment strategies, and most important, reflections on what was successful and how he would reteach material the students had not learned. While George endeavored to comply with these requirements by utilizing the overhead projector in two lessons, he eventually abandoned any effort to deviate from the chalk-and-talk method of delivery, stating that "students didn't seem to care if he used the overhead or not."

The teaching unit description and learning targets George submitted prior to his lead teaching week in December indicated that his lessons on statistics and data displays would be an inquiry into the theme of poverty in Maine. In actuality, George's teaching followed, precisely, the day-to-day sequence prescribed in his math textbook. None of his lessons required students to use the data analysis skills to analyze poverty.

Expressing a disposition for high expectations implies that the teacher assumes each student has the capacity to meet the learning objectives within a reasonable time period and that it is the teacher's responsibility to explore every reasonable strategy to make sure students reach this goal. By the final week of George's lead teaching, it was evident that his expectations for his seventh-grade students were simply to complete nine different worksheets representing nine different data representations. It is possible that George simply did not know how to put inquiry at the center of his teaching by letting students research real data, discuss what it meant, and then choose appropriate data representation formats to interpret their findings. However, after a full semester of watching his instructors model this process and listening to his peers discuss the units they were designing, George clearly did not hold high expectations for his students, and as a consequence he was disappointed in their final, lackluster performance.

Fostering the Disposition of Collegiality

Sharon Feiman-Nemser has argued persuasively for teacher educators, district administrators, and teacher association leaders to consider the ways in which new teachers can be strengthened and sustained through their professional careers.[13] This involves a consistent and coherent approach beginning with the teacher preparation program, in which candidates have opportunities to (1) examine their beliefs and values that form the basis for their philosophy of education, (2) establish a beginning repertoire for instruction and assessment aligned with state standards, and responsive to diverse learners, and (3) cultivate a disposition for inquiry within a peer cohort, where they engage in the intellectual give-and-take that characterizes a collaborative professional culture.

From our perspective as teacher educators, the nexus for fostering all of the dispositions described above is the internship cohort. Feiman-Nemser states that the central tasks of developing responsive and intellectual educators occur through "conversations in communities of practice. [These conversations] focus on the particulars of teaching, learning, subject matter and students. By engaging in professional discourse with like-minded colleagues grounded in the content and tasks of teaching and learning, teachers can deepen knowledge of subject matter and curriculum, refine their instructional repertoire, hone their inquiry skills and become critical colleagues."[14]

Placing all our teacher candidates in an internship cohort is a bedrock commitment in our programs. Building, strengthening, and sustaining the cohort is a continuous process in and of itself, beginning with a variety of bonding experiences including overnight camping trips to an outdoor experiential education setting, and continuing via weekly seminar meetings that are a mixture of conversation, instruction, and feedback on drafts of the program's key assessments.

Because we want our teacher candidates to have "colleagues with whom they can talk, argue, invent, discover and weave their craft," we require interns to go through an intense process of discovering and/or confronting the beliefs they hold about teaching and about students, and the actions they will take on behalf of all their students.[15] We ask them to engage with one another in pairs, in small groups, online, and in whole group discussions, to make sense of their classroom experience in light of their private beliefs. Thus, the teacher education faculty depends on the cohort to become a community that is guided by a strong moral contract where, through "the development of critical teacher reflectivity, values can be openly and honestly explored."[16] The cohort also provides the teacher education faculty with an opportunity to determine whether an intern's disposition for collegiality with his or her peers can also be observed with his or her mentor teacher, an administrator, and students.

Patrick's values were often in opposition to many of his colleagues'. He often challenged others who did not share his values. For example, Patrick challenged a university professor regarding a course she was teaching. He wrote:

> I read the description of the course. Although you didn't mentioned the word "homosexual," it appears that your course is probably intended to support and reinforce a positive outlook of homosexuals (and even possibly transgenders) in the workplace/public sphere. I say this because these are among the major groups discussed in reference to diversity in the workplace.
>
> However, I hope that this is not the case. Despite the recent decision of the courts in California, upstanding Americans from around the country are fighting around the clock to outlaw homosexual marriage, special rights and behavior. A course like LOS 316 would only damage the efforts of countless Americans who are struggling to save our country from licentious and inappropriate relationships/identities. LOS 316 also sounds like it might try to malign individuals with values that frown on homosexual/transgender behaviors and pursuits of special rights. As a Christian, I love all people, but that doesn't mean that people can do whatever they want. It also doesn't mean that I, among many others, have to condone their desire to flaunt their lifestyles in the public sphere. I could be wrong in assuming that LOS 316 will be

talking about the aforementioned. If so, I am deeply sorry about this email. Otherwise, I want to inform you, in all serious and frankness, that there are students at USM and patriotic citizens around the country who neither approve of nor want to see LOS 316 (one that wants to forward inappropriate behaviors and identities) commence in the upcoming semester/s.

Interestingly, as Patrick notes, the course instructor never specifically mentions homosexuality in the course description or objectives. According to the syllabus, the course "challenges students, from a personal and professional perspective, to think knowledgeably and creatively about diversity, inequality, cultural competency and privilege in order to nurture respectful, open individuals and organizations for today's complex, internationalized society." Without specific reason, Patrick assumed an oppositional stance and an opportunity to express his own values.

This oppositional posture was common for Patrick when it came to issues relating to sexual identity and religious freedom. It mirrors Patrick's exchanges with his colleagues when they proposed that, as teachers, they needed to support students from diverse family backgrounds and religious beliefs and those students who were exploring their sexual identity. Patrick was incapable of respectfully engaging in dialogue with those with whom he disagreed, and he refused to consider the diverse perspectives of his colleagues and refine his stance based upon input of those perspectives.

Similarly, George often dismissed the perspectives of his colleagues. He appeared bemused by the energy and antics of the younger members of the cohort. The rare times that he spoke in discussions revealed that his interpretations were not connected in any way to the students he met with every day, but were simply summaries of the text assigned for a particular day. In spite of listening to his peers describe examples of how they used the information gathered from their student profiles to design a multilayered activity complete with a differentiated assessment, George never contributed examples of where he had tried out similar experiments in his math classes.

The evidence that George regarded the cohort seminar as simply one of the university courses he was required to take, came when he announced via e-mail that he intended to leave an hour early for three weeks in a row so that he could volunteer his time to teach a personal finance course at the local correctional center. When an instructor reminded him that he was expected to attend the seminar meetings for the full time, he immediately sent a sarcastic and verbally abusive response. After similar reports began to surface where his professionalism with students and school administrators was called into question, George's supervisors met with him to begin an action planning process that outlined a series of specific benchmarks they wanted George to meet before his week of lead teaching. His supervisors increased their classroom observations and provided specific verbal and written feedback on progress toward the benchmarks and areas that needed more attention.

During this time, George became more and more withdrawn in the cohort seminar sessions, and spent his free time by himself instead of with peers who were teaching in the same building. We later learned that he never visited his peers' classrooms, rarely asked to collaborate on assignments, and did not ask about how they were using what they were learning in the seminar in their teaching.

During the action plan period, George's supervisors focused on helping him implement strategies to plan, instruct, and assess with the needs of all his students in mind. We did not, however, inform him that he was officially "on probation." George completed his lead teaching, convinced that he had been successful, only to be confronted with the decision that we were withdrawing him from the program. George fully proved that he could be a good graduate student—he turned in work on time, attempted to follow the directions, and accepted feedback on written assignments. However, when it came to applying approaches to differentiate instruction or foster student independent learning, or devising a range of assessments to meet a particular learning goal, George was unable or unwilling to embrace the concepts from his university courses as integral to his day-to-day teaching. Regrettably, George's supervisors did not fully understand the source of conflict between George's beliefs, his practices, and the expectations of the program. They were ultimately unsuccessful in helping him take seriously the program's commitments to culturally responsive teaching, differentiated instruction, high expectations for all students, and ongoing inquiry into one's teaching.

WHAT WE LEARN WHEN THINGS GO WRONG

The analysis of these cases serves to highlight the challenges in detecting problematic dispositions during the admissions process. They also caution us to take care in drawing conclusions from intern self-assessments, classroom observations, or feedback from mentors and peers. The majority of interns meet our high expectations, but the Patricks and Georges motivate us to learn from those times when "we get it wrong," and challenge our complacency around the coherence of our program's vision.

As the title of our chapter suggests, the faculty learned a great deal from reflecting on the evidence we gathered from these two interns throughout their candidacy and internship. As we reviewed the patterns that emerged, we considered ways to trace more faithfully a candidate's predispositions in situations likely to pose challenges. We discussed how we could be more proactive in documenting the consistency (or lack thereof) between interns' dispositions in university courses or cohort experience with dispositions evident in day-to-day interactions with students and their curriculum. As a result of our review, we have:

- Revised our USM Teacher Certification Standards review rubric to be more explicit about the dispositions we expect to see exhibited throughout the program, and to be clearer about basic, proficient, and exemplary levels of performance.
- Adopted a uniform action plan template for supporting teacher candidates who are struggling and in jeopardy of being dismissed from the program, requiring faculty to be extremely explicit and collaborative with struggling interns so that the intern has clear goals and benchmarks for improvement and very specific timelines for meeting those goals and benchmarks.
- Revised the process for dismissing teacher candidates who do not possess the dispositions required of effective teachers.

In George's and Patrick's cases, each of these actions may have better supported their success in our program and in becoming teachers. For example, the USM teaching standards rubric would have provided them with an "official document" in which the indicators for each standard clearly and consistently described *actions* expected of each candidate related to the dispositions for inquiry, high expectations, responsiveness, and collegiality. When it became obvious to their supervisors that they were not *acting* on these indicators, they could have taken a number of explicit steps in order to meet the standards. For example, George and Patrick could have been required to visit other classrooms, where they would see veteran teachers or cohort peers enacting these standards. Their supervisors could have followed those observations with focused conversations, including their mentor teacher, to elicit a firm commitment from them to begin applying these principles to their teaching.

Failure to comply with these actions then would have allowed supervisors to follow the newly revised probation and action planning process with full disclosure that the process could end in their being withdrawn from the program.

These faculty efforts over the course of a year bring more clarity to how faculty might respond when interns don't express dispositions for inquiry, responsiveness, high expectations, and collegiality. We also realize that identifying and fostering moral dispositions is not an exact science. We'll never be able to be 100 percent certain at the time of admission that all the candidates possess the appropriate dispositions for teaching. However, with clear behavioral indicators related to our Teacher Certification Standards, we can continuously assess and provide teacher candidates with explicit feedback that will support the achievement of their goal to become teachers. We can also continue to learn from those cases in which we get it wrong.

CONCLUSION

Over the course of the last few years, our faculty has been engaged in framing our program's stance around *a commitment to equitable and engaging learning* through a set of core practices related to fostering inquiry, engaging in scholarship, providing opportunities to learn, setting high expectations, being responsive, and nurturing collegiality. The process of writing this chapter and looking at specific cases of interns has assisted us in clarifying our processes for identifying and fostering moral dispositions related to these practices.

Writing this chapter has forced us to reflect upon how we identify, foster, and assess teacher candidates' moral dispositions. Because our methods of identifying, fostering, and assessing moral dispositions are fairly implicit, we needed help in articulating our practices. Our mentors for this chapter helped us to make our beliefs and practices explicit. Beginning with how we define a disposition, they encouraged us to critically reflect upon our own moral stance related to moral dispositions in teacher education and how we enact that stance. As a result of multiple rounds of feedback and revision, we can more clearly articulate what we do and why.

As the two of us have become more clear about how our program identifies, fosters, and assesses teacher candidates' moral dispositions, we have come to realize the importance for our entire program faculty to have a shared understanding of the moral dispositions we believe all teachers should express. Developing this shared understanding takes time and is difficult to achieve when faculty are busy and are often off in different directions engaged in their own work. It has to be a priority for faculty to take the time they need to be together to talk and learn from one another and to integrate those learning experiences into our program. Recognizing this, our faculty meets one day monthly, two full days during the academic year, and two days each summer. Our time together focuses on departmental business as well as programmatic development. As a part of this work, we are attempting to integrate what we have learned from writing and rewriting this chapter.

Writing and rewriting this chapter has helped us to realize our goal of identifying and fostering moral dispositions for equitable and engaging learning. Some of our key accomplishments that have been informed by writing this chapter include:

- Analyzing and revising our syllabi for principles of culturally responsive pedagogy and universal design for learning, and working together and independently to better integrate these principles into our courses.
- Revising the writing prompts for the application to ETEP in the hopes that it will better elicit responses that reveal potential teacher candidates' dispositions toward equity.
- Aligning the rating scales between the admissions processes for students who enter the graduate-level internship through TEAMS and through ETEP.

Each of these program activities directly relates to better identifying and fostering moral dispositions for equitable and engaging learning. Through careful attention to these practices, we will continue to better understand the moral dispositions we hope to foster and how to assess those.

CHAPTER SIX

Putting Dispositions in the Driver's Seat

Robert E. Hollon, Michael W. Kolis, Susan R. McIntyre,
J. Todd Stephens, and Rosemary L. Battalio

Editors' Case Introduction: University of Wisconsin-Eau Claire

The University of Wisconsin-Eau Claire (UWEC), located 90 miles east of Minneapolis/St. Paul, is a comprehensive institution serving 10,350 undergraduate students and 550 graduate students. Ranked fourth among the top regional public universities in the Midwest in the 2009 edition of America's Best Colleges, UWEC awards approximately 350 undergraduate and graduate degrees in teacher education each year through traditional, online, and cadre-based or cohort programs.

Students can earn bachelor's degrees in Middle Childhood to Early Adolescence (grades 1–8), Early Adolescence to Adolescence (grades 6–12), Special Education (grades preK–12) , and Early Childhood to Adolescence (grades preK–12); and graduate degrees in elementary education, various secondary fields, some special education fields, reading, communication sciences and disorders, and school psychology. Strong collaborative partnerships with area schools support multiple levels of field experience. The typical teacher education undergraduate has 300 hours of classroom experience before a full semester of student teaching.

"Putting Dispositions in the Driver's Seat" describes how faculty in three different programs made dispositions the driving force for teacher preparation at UWEC. Despite a successful program review, the authors chose to make collaborative leadership dispositions more central in their programs. Creating a rubric detailing the collaborative leadership dispositions they wanted to foster

was only the beginning. Their story highlights the challenges of embedding and enacting a common, dispositionally focused mission into three programs with diverse philosophies and differing degrees of faculty buy-in.

FOCUSING ON COLLABORATIVE LEADERSHIP DISPOSITIONS

It would be tempting to tell a story about professional dispositions as one outcome of the process of developing a conceptual framework for teacher education. It would have been equally tempting to frame dispositions in terms of reflective philosophical framing, structured analysis of trends in teacher education, and careful mapping of curriculum. The real story here is not about developing our conceptual framework or our dispositions. It is a story about how our conceptual framework of *collaborative leadership* dispositions has emerged as the primary focus for three very different teacher education programs in our institution.

In 2002, the University of Wisconsin-Eau Claire (UWEC) faced an upcoming state program review, which demanded the articulation of a conceptual framework, an assessment system, and a clinical experience progression. All three of these components needed to be aligned with the new Wisconsin Teaching Standards (WTS) that were based on the Interstate New Teacher Assessment and Support Consortium (INTASC) framework. The faculty prepared for the accreditation visit by looking at existing program practices, forming work groups focused on identifying conceptual patterns, and forming still other work groups focusing on transforming program materials and course syllabi into forms that reflected the WTS. We brainstormed characteristics of our graduates that represented our "signature"—personal and professional characteristics that identified our graduates to school leaders. The central theme that emerged from the analysis of data such as employer surveys, feedback from graduates, and conversations with our students and area educators was *collaboration.* Our unit engaged students, regional educators, and university faculty in a variety of collaborative activities involving shared goal setting, project design, and presentation of results in this alignment process. We discovered that many of our candidates were already assuming leadership roles in school and community service programs. After many conversations and work group deliberations over a period of a year, the teacher education faculty committed to making collaborative leadership explicit and intentional as a unique characteristic of our education programs and the basis for our conceptual framework.

Our education faculty set out to develop a plan of action to highlight our newly stated identity and set out to articulate the knowledge, skills, and dispositions that would characterize an emerging educator and effective collaborative leader. We developed a conceptual framework that was acceptable to three very different programs within our unit. Our special education programs drew heavily on behaviorist perspectives, while the elementary education and secondary education programs were an eclectic mix of constructivist and critical pedagogy approaches. The motto "Preparing Collaborative Leaders" was interesting but benign; the behaviorists, constructivists, and critical theorists among us could find something in it without feeling threatened. Our review was successful, and so we felt as if it was a mission accomplished. Or was it?

We emerged from the process in 2003 with program approval and much positive feedback, but the review also revealed a need to be more explicit about collaborative leadership in our assessment system and program structures. Some faculty breathed a sigh of relief upon successful review and returned to teaching and scholarly activities. Others of us, namely faculty and students from the three teacher education departments and the conceptual framing group, continued planning to better articulate the collaborative leadership framework.

It made sense at the time to think about knowledge, skills, and dispositions in that order; our state standards, professional literature, and everyday ways of thinking and acting with our students focused on knowledge and skills. Students were reminded to demonstrate professionalism and heard tales of the repercussions when their predecessors failed to demonstrate them. The Wisconsin teacher education program approval framework allows dispositions to be integrated with knowledge and skills and inferred from practice—no formal articulation or assessment of dispositions was required. As a faculty, we recognized that students who failed in our programs almost always did so for reasons identified as professional dispositions—such as a mediocre commitment to pupil learning as a priority; lack of responsibility for themselves, their cooperating teacher, or their pupils; deliberate disregard for basic professionalism; or their inability to foster productive relationships. Students rarely failed because they lacked content knowledge or could not demonstrate effective planning skill or implement management and teaching strategies. Each program had support systems in place to address gaps in knowledge and skills. Our shared perceptions pointed to concerns that we viewed as issues of professional dispositions. Yet, our conceptual framework—and the processes by which we developed it—did not seem to bring those issues of professional dispositions into focus. We were all about knowledge and skills.

In 2005, the teacher education faculty formally approved an effort to further develop the collaborative leadership knowledge, skills, and dispositions guided by the College of Education and Human Sciences Center for Collaborative Leadership (CCL). The CCL secured funds from the University of Wisconsin System to support a two-year process to examine collaborative leadership principles; identify the collaborative leadership knowledge, skills, and dispositions; transform them into program goals and assessments; and produce field-tested and approved program materials.

The process began with a three-day collaborative leadership seminar in the summer of 2006. The seminar blended students, faculty, and field professionals from all six departments in our College of Education and Human Sciences. Each department was encouraged to bring a team including at least one faculty member, one student, and one field professional. Twenty-eight participants worked for four full days in the summer with an expert consultant on collaborative leadership to conceptualize the collaborative leadership knowledge, skills, and dispositions that would have common value across multiple programs. Each team also developed an action plan to field-test assessments, curriculum tools, and teaching strategies during the 2006–2007 academic year. Monthly meetings were held in the evenings during the entire academic year to provide feedback opportunities, discuss emerging concerns, and learn from each other's work.

An interesting thing happened during the summer seminar—a spontaneous cross-program consensus on dispositions. As groups shared stories and experiences about student success and failures, and discussed the potential of striving toward collaborative leadership, we reached the consensus that dispositional issues were by far the most challenging for programs across our college. Participants agreed that they recognized "bad" dispositions when they were exhibited, and acknowledged that they were addressing them more reactively than proactively. As a result of this acknowledgement, the entire seminar group agreed that working on dispositions held the most promise for immediate program improvement. The effort shifted away from struggling to articulate detailed knowledge and skills, and toward clarifying what we believed were key collaborative leadership dispositions and the behaviors associated with them.

The primary product that emerged during the summer seminar was a draft set of five collaborative leadership dispositions with a developmental-focused rubric (see table 6.1). The work group dialogued and discussed differences among teacher as manager, teacher as leader, and teacher as collaborative leader. They looked at the differences in view of student experiences over time and with the notion that making the dispositions explicit and part of our daily language would allow more students to succeed and grow into educators representative of our program. We designed the rubric with behavioral anchors that designate the observable actions that represent different levels of development for each disposition. The progression from a focus on self toward a focus on effective relationships with others demonstrates the developmental nature of the rubric. The rubric has three levels of advancement: students at application-to-program level are expected to be at level 1 (understanding); students ready to student teach, level 2 (independent); and students exiting from the program, level 3 (collaborative).

In addition to the dispositions and rubric, the summer seminar group proposed a set of collaborative leadership *knowledge* statements and *skills*. The products from these cross-program discussions were particularly important because they were the first step in establishing elements common to all three programs. They served as the common denominator of our programs and helped us to find common ground for further conversations about developing the dispositions of a collaborative educator.

In spring 2007, after two semesters of field-testing and revising program-specific assessment tools and evaluation practices, the teacher education faculty formally approved the collaborative leadership dispositions, along with the initial statements of knowledge and skills. It was clear that the dispositions work served as the rallying point for program development, though how programs interpreted and implemented dispositions occurred quite differently. For some programs, discussion of dispositions progressed from "we need to get this done" to more fundamental conversations about what UWEC teacher education programs might really accomplish with beginners. Dispositions became a catalyst—a way to move beyond conversations about the mechanics of maintaining programs that complied with state standards.

UWEC teacher education programs increasingly operate with the perspective that dispositions provide the lens through which prospective teachers come to value and therefore act in ways that develop the specific knowledge and skills of the collaborative leader. In other words, we

TABLE 6.1   Collaborative leadership dispositions

Dispositions	0	1 Understanding	2 Independent level	3 Collaborative level
Strives for shared under-standing	• Chooses to do most tasks inde-pendently	• Asks relevant questions of "safe" person • Compromises, or asks others to do so, to complete tasks	• Asks clarifying questions for self • Paraphrases for personal clarifi-cation • Cooperates when working with others	• Asks clarifying ques-tions for self and/or group needs • Solicits responses from all parties • Paraphrases for bet-ter self and group understanding • Redirects counter-productive partici-pation • Demonstrates active listening during collaborations
Seeks beneficial solutions	• Does not try to change what has already been done—"it is good enough"	• Describes situations and solutions from multiple perspec-tives • Articulates potential barriers to situations • Lists people who may be potential resources for tasks	• Describes current condition • Tells why change might be neces-sary • Independently finds resources to support change • Defers judgment in order to come up with unique and workable solutions	• Seeks input from and works with oth-ers to describe cur-rent condition • Works with others to determine need for change • Considers others' ideas and perspec-tives to generate possible solutions and meet multiple needs

believe that *dispositions drive the moral choices that an individual makes.* Those choices are enacted—and thus evidenced—through one's ethical behavior. One example is our disposition "seeks beneficial solutions." Embedded in this statement is the idea that individuals need to know their own beliefs and values, know their own motivations, realize how their experiences have influenced them, and also know how they deal with change. It also requires them to realize at what point and under what conditions they are willing to be flexible and search for alterna-tives. Knowing these parameters then leads one to apply specific skill sets, such as active listening, reframing questions, seeing issues from multiple perspectives, and clarifying and stating fundamental prob-lems. Indicators of successful integration of the disposition, knowledge, and skills associated with seeking beneficial solutions include choos-ing empathy versus sympathy, taking a problem-solving approach, and

TABLE 6.1   **Collaborative leadership dispositions,** *continued*

Dispositions	0	1 *Understanding*	2 *Independent level*	3 *Collaborative level*
Accepts **responsibility** for self and takes on responsibility for others	• Blames others and circumstances when problems occur	• Lists possible personal responsibilities • Articulates the responsibilities of others	• Accepts responsibility for tasks when asked to do so • Assists with meeting the needs of others when within own control	• Accepts and seeks out responsibility for tasks • Advocates for others' needs, regardless of personal beliefs/needs • Actively seeks out assistance from others to meet identified needs
Displays **perseverance** for projects and **interpersonal relationship management**	• Follow-up attempts not made when first attempt does not succeed or meet expectations	• Completes tasks on time • Makes repeated, but minimal, attempts to correct or continue a task • Makes weak attempts to better understand others	• Asks questions to find out more in order to make more productive future attempts at a task • Describes options for approaching others for assistance	• Actively seeks out others for contributions in order to make change and persist with tasks • Acknowledges all participants contributions, concerns, and ideas • Depersonalizes negativity from others and contributes positive responses
Demonstrates a passion for **excellence**	• Does just what is required	• Reflects on how experiences have impacted their thinking about education • Articulates the meaning of excellence in a context of learning	• States expectations that go beyond the status quo • Independently uses the meaning of excellence in a context of learning for individual growth	• Active and positive member of groups • Uses excellence in a context of learning to collaborate with and influence others • Celebrates group successes • Exhibits an appropriate sense of humor, a positive manner, and enthusiasm during interactions

seeking first to understand and then be understood. It is crucial to note that different dispositions (lenses) point to different knowledge bases and skill sets. Although the term *disposition* is typically defined as "the *tendency* to act in certain ways under certain conditions," we would substitute "choice" for "tendency" to emphasize the active process of making evident the interconnections between the dispositions, knowledge, and skills.

We now view the development of dispositions, knowledge, and skills as a complex recursive process in which dispositions frequently serve as the catalyst for knowledge and skill development, and at other times are shaped by the processes through which candidates acquire knowledge and skill. Our collaborative leadership disposition statements emphasize this action-oriented expression of agency, identity, and quality of character. We believe that dispositions are shaped by moral attitudes and beliefs, and are committed to the position that professional programs can foster the development of practices that are congruent with particular dispositions.[1] Five years ago these positions were much more implicit. Through our ongoing work, our thinking is becoming much more visible.

Collaborative leadership dispositions are not the goal or end product of our work. They are a means of engaging preservice teachers, to empower them. The ultimate goal of our program is to grow collaborative leaders who are able and committed to reaching beyond their classrooms to sustain and improve a socially just, democratic society. By this, we don't mean democracy in a primarily governmental sense; we view democracy as an ethical stance, which carries both rights and responsibilities directed toward improving the common good.[2]

In the remainder of this chapter, we will illustrate how the faculty of three programs with decidedly different theoretical views and differing levels of commitment to any conceptual framework are working to build stronger programs that make explicit the role of collaborative leadership dispositions. We will also share some lessons learned along the way, present ongoing challenges, and describe future directions for our work.

ENACTING COLLABORATIVE LEADERSHIP DISPOSITIONS, KNOWLEDGE, AND SKILLS

Teacher education at UWEC consists of three programs: EAA/ECA (secondary education), MCEA (elementary education), and SPED (special education). Each program has its own faculty, its own curriculum structure and practices, and its own philosophy. The programs operate independently yet collaborate to provide common support courses and accommodate the needs of students seeking multiple licenses. All programs provide students with three levels of field experience, culminating in a full public school semester of student teaching.

While all three education programs agreed upon the philosophical, moral, and ethical foundations inherent within the conceptual framework of "Preparing Collaborative Leaders" each program developed its own set of priorities, taking into account the mandates and best practices of their field, organizational parameters such as time constraints within the program, and faculty philosophies. All three programs ask students to first look inward and think about themselves as leaders, and then begin looking outward to consider collaborative practices and leadership roles at the classroom, school, and community levels. In preprogram courses, students are expected to develop *awareness of collaborative practices* and their impact on student learning. Candidates observe classrooms, participate in planning sessions involving regular education and special education teachers, and coteach lessons. They are introduced to collaborative leadership dispositions, knowledge bases, and skills. Candidates are required to address their own collaborative leadership dispositions in their teacher education portfolio (used for admission to a specific program). During the education coursework phase of programs, candidates are expected to *begin to apply collaborative leadership knowledge and skills.* Leadership and followership practices are modeled and supported through collaboratively taught courses, establishing student advocacy roles in goal setting and evaluation activities, and requiring students to assume multiple leadership and followership roles in methods course projects. Candidates design and teach lessons over the three to four weeks they are in the schools, use collaborative practices in instruction and classroom management, and reflect on the effectiveness of those practices in their teaching. Candidates may also work with their cooperating teachers to assume limited leadership responsibilities for some elements of the classroom environment. During student teaching, candidates are expected to assume increased responsibility for *initiating collaborative approaches* to support student learning. Candidates are expected to identify and seek appropriate contributions from teachers, parents, coaches, and others to support student success, take some responsibilities for team planning and meetings, and assume appropriate followership and leadership roles.

Our teacher education candidates are formally evaluated at (a) application to program, (b) application to student teaching, and (c) completion of student teaching (program exit). At each point, candidates develop portfolios to present evidence of professional growth with respect to the collaborative leadership dispositions, and to document growth in knowledge and skills with respect to the WTS. Candidates are observed and evaluated by cooperating teachers and university supervisors using program-specific forms of the collaborative leadership dispositions rubric. A complete data set for one candidate typically includes artifact sets selected by the individual, evaluations by cooperating teachers, and at least two evaluation forms completed collaboratively by cooperating teachers and university supervisors. Additional student-oriented artifacts vary by program, but include reports of individual and group presentations to teachers and administrators, peer evaluations, reflective writings during courses, and lesson plans with reflections.

Program Perspectives

The following vignettes provide examples of the shared and program-specific application of the process of "Preparing Collaborative Leaders" within each program. The journeys of students in each of our programs are provided below to illustrate the commonalities and differences we have had to accommodate as we implemented the five collaborative leadership dispositions. Each vignette begins with a brief description of the program organization, faculty expertise, and programmatic involvement in the development and implementation of the dispositions.

Early Adolescence to Adolescence Program

The Early Adolescence to Adolescence/Early Childhood to Adolescence (EAA/ECA) secondary education program has three full-time education faculty and eleven part-time content methods faculty representing different majors. The program structure finds students immersed in content (major and minor) during their first two and a half years and in education coursework the last three or four semesters of their university experience, which includes several field experiences. Three program faculty members work with candidates for a maximum of two years after completion of the content majors and minors. They are strongly constructivist, have strong interpersonal relationships, and have redesigned their program around seven essential questions, using a "team-taught with student cohort" model of instruction. These program faculty members played an active role in the development of the conceptual framework and are therefore fully committed to all aspects of collaborative leadership.

A Student's Experience

Last week was tough for me and some others in our education cohort. We have a classmate who is always negative, always pointing out flaws, and basically impossible to work with—not being a collaborative leader by any stretch of the imagination. We were concerned about her teaching dispositions and how we can support her growth. We came to the realization that if we believe the teaching dispositions that we are always talking about, it was our responsibility to help her grow, and her responsibility to do the growing. So we met with some of our faculty teachers and asked for help so that we could be more helpful to our classmate. When we were talking to the facilitators, they started laughing and commenting on how much we have grown since our first education course. It has been quite a journey.

Two semesters ago I finally got into CI 210 (the first education course), after not getting in the previous semester because all the seats were already filled. I was so glad because it meant that I was finally on my "teaching" journey. CI 210 was a very different kind of course. Almost every week, my teacher started with a morning meeting, where we had to share something about our perspectives or ourselves or what made us unique. While that was different, what was really weird was that he kept trying, on purpose, to make us mad; he called it "cognitive dissonance," but we were just mad at him—at first. What was also weird was that we came to enjoy the intellectual challenge of thinking and reflecting and making clear our beliefs and values. He kept referencing these things called "collaborative leadership dispositions" as well as the ten Wisconsin Teaching Standards. Every week we would talk about what we were experiencing in our school placements, and then connect those experiences to what he called the dispositions, knowledge, and skills, of teaching. I am not sure how many times we talked about the fact that they could teach us the knowledge and skills of being an excellent teacher, but the dispositions, the "want to," were up to us. He kept talking about this thing called "choice theory" and that every choice we made was a result of what we valued and where we wanted to go. He said that focusing on the dispositions would allow us to pick certain knowledge and skills so that we could act congruently with our deepest beliefs.

At midterm, he assessed every one of us on our teaching dispositions. He used a rubric that he had given us at the beginning of the semester, and scored us where he thought we were at this point in time, and also wrote comments to each and every one of us about how to make improvements through specific actions that could be observed. I am not sure how long he spent on those forms, but I began to finally see what he had been talking about when he mentioned "dispositions." He told me I needed to consider other points of view more seriously, think more in terms of win-win instead of me win– you lose, and also that my body language was showing that I was not respecting other people's point of view. I didn't even know he was paying attention—and that he was probably right. I really worked hard on making those changes because I knew that no matter how else I did in the course, if he scored me low on my dispositions, I would not get into the education program. I knew this because it happened to this guy I knew.

It was deep stuff, but it helped me view the classroom and the teachers we observed in many different ways. I saw that lots of teachers focused on content and managing their students, that classroom management was important, and that most teachers worked in isolation. My teacher said that those were choices that teachers were making, and that we would be expected to hopefully make different choices (whatever that meant).

Anyway, I passed the class, got a passing score on my teaching portfolio (after three tries), and also met all my content area requirements for admission to the program. The very next semester when I applied, I did get in—but eighteen other people did not.

Our block semester started like nothing I have ever experienced—five faculty and thirty students, meeting every day for two hours, talking, sharing, doing team-building activities, being in charge of the classroom and our own learning. Posters in the room show what our facilitators say is most important: our teaching dispositions and our relevant essential questions. Most days, I am not sure who is going to be teaching what, but it is always challenging, and time flies by. We have these things called community meetings that happen at the end of every teaching unit—the relevant essential questions. We get to talk by ourselves first and then share with the facilitators how we think things are going. The interesting thing is that they take us seriously.

One of the very unique things we see in class is that, most of the time, they preface each teaching activity with a conversation about a teaching disposition, and then end it by talking about asking us how it connects to the teaching standards. Everything is connected. I have learned more about who I am as a person/teacher than I could have ever imagined. I am coming to believe that I am a collaborative leader and that I do possess the dispositions that I see modeled every single day. I have come to believe that there is a win-win solution, that we do know more as a group than as a collection of individuals, that I am responsible for my own learning (and that of others), that I can persevere (and others can help me do this), and that excellence is what I am all about. I am not sure how I have grown this much so fast, but I believe it today, and it makes me feel like I have never felt in school before.

Our facilitators met with a group of us earlier this week to work on some skills so that we can help our classmate. We talked about the why of doing what we were doing (they called it the knowledge thing), and then we learned some verbal skills and then practiced them doing some role-plays. We shared what we thought would be some scenarios when we met with our classmate; and when we left, we felt like we could do it. We set up a meeting with our classmate, listened first, used our verbal skills, but in the end were unsuccessful. When we debriefed with our facilitators, we had a very long and deep dialogue about the entire experience. As it turns out, our facilitators had also had the same concerns and after our unsuccessful experience, had tried an intervention of their own. Yesterday we found out that our classmate had been removed from program—due to her unwillingness to address her teaching dispositions. Wow.

In four weeks I finish my coursework and begin student teaching. As excited as I am to be done with school, I am also scared that I might fall back into what we laughingly refer to as the "dark side"—the "teach content only" way of teaching. I do have our class Facebook page to keep me connected—and our facilitators keep saying they are there for us—but I am still worried; worried that my past experiences have more power over me than I thought, worried that my cooperating teacher will not support me as I grow into a collaborative leader teacher, and worried that my students will not learn enough to enhance the quality of their lives. I guess that I am also worried about letting down my teachers and my classmates. On the other hand, like they said a thousand times in class, if not us, then who?

Discussion

This narrative illustrates that our students are seeking ways to grow into becoming exceptional teachers. As we have begun to make our expectations explicit, we have seen our candidates exceed the norm. Holding students accountable for their dispositions and knowledge and skills, at developmentally appropriate levels, provides them with opportunities for growth. Promoting the development of any set of dispositions, knowledge, and skills in our candidates is a messy undertaking; as this candidate explains, modeling is crucial. Candidates need to see what the expectations look like, sound like, and feel like—every single day—if they are to own those ideas within themselves.

Middle Childhood to Early Adolescence Program

The Middle Childhood to Early Adolescence (MCEA) elementary education program has seven full-time education faculty and several part-time instructors who work with students for three years. Students begin completing preprogram program courses as early as sophomore year and are formally admitted as sophomores or juniors. Although the MCEA program does not have a formal cohort structure, most students move through program semesters as a group based on their "block," or methods semester. The MCEA faculty bring a range of theoretical perspectives to the program. They tend to work in a cooperative but independent manner. Few faculty in this program were involved in the development of the conceptual framework, so commitment varies widely among individuals. The MCEA faculty developed assessment tools and procedures for the five collaborative dispositions that differ from the other programs by emphasizing the development of both individual and collaborative approaches as equally satisfactory. In many ways, the products reflect political as well as conceptual compromise.

A Student's Experience

I was one of the lucky ones to get into CI 203 right away. That meant I could apply to the program next semester. It was pretty tense, since there were about eighty of us and only sixty spots in the program. We learned about the ten Wisconsin Teaching Standards—I guess everyone in Wisconsin has those. We also learned about collaborative leadership. We looked at some definitions of collaborative leadership and at a rubric for collaborative leadership dispositions. I didn't see any of them as a problem. I mean, who wouldn't believe in them? It wasn't so clear to me, though, whether we were supposed to think that collaborative leadership was the only way to go, or if it was an idea that we could think about but wasn't actually required.

We looked for examples of collaboration in our schools, but mostly we did whatever our cooperating teacher assigned to us. It was pretty interesting being in a first-grade classroom! . . . I taught three lessons after they were approved by my cooperating teacher. I ended up confused, though, because we talked about collaboration, and we learned that our application to the program and the application rubric showed that we had to explain how we collaborated. On the other hand, our CI 203 evaluation form really didn't emphasize collaboration very much compared to individual attitudes. The collaborative leadership dispositions sheet was not really used at all. We talked about being professional and always putting students first and wrote about how teachers needed to work together for their students, so maybe that was where we were supposed to make the connection.

I made it into the program! I made sure that my GPA was way above 3.0, did so much volunteering in schools that they almost added me to the staff, and went to Washington, D.C., for three weeks to work in the urban schools. It paid off, though, because my application essays for the Wisconsin Teaching Standards were really great. When block began one semester later, I became part of a group of sixty people and five instructors in math, science, reading, social studies, and language arts methods courses. Everyone talked about how much work there was and how we'd better be ready to lose sleep. After the first week, it was clear that there was no "I" in "you and your partner." Almost every assignment was done with our partner or in a group. Some instructors talked about collaborating with each other and with other groups as we work, but the whole idea of collaborative leadership was still pretty fuzzy. It was defined in all our syllabi, but nobody really laid it out for us. I remember thinking that if I took some initiative, that would be counted as leadership, and if I included someone else, that made it collaborative leadership. Or was it just working together to get the assignments done?

We went to our school all of week 4 to get to know the kids, our cooperating teachers, and the school. Our class had twenty-three third graders, with three English language learner (ELL) students and two more identified with learning disabled (LD) and emotional and behavior difficulties (EBD). There was an ELL aide in the room two mornings, and the resource teacher worked with the other two students every day for reading. Some middle school students came in to read with the kids. I didn't realize there were so many people in and out of the room. How did Mr. Johnson (our cooperating teacher) keep track of it all? I began to see where this collaborative leadership stuff might make sense, but it was still really fuzzy. By week 7, we were just about ready to go back to the school for a whole month. I know we were supposed to work together to plan our units and lessons, but there was so much to manage that it didn't really work. We couldn't find time to meet, much less agree on everything. It's a good thing we have e-mail and D2L [distance learning]!

We talked more about the collaborative leadership ideas in some classes. I get the leaderful actions part, and I see where we can do some of them, but it still looks like it isn't required. We weren't evaluated on it in any assignments or during week 4.

During the last month of block, we stayed in school all day every day to teach, observe Mr. Johnson, and work with other teachers. Our lessons went really well—though the sneezing and coughing were way more than I expected. I can't believe that R____ actually licked the doorknob and thought it was funny! Mr. Johnson was amazing. He handled all the meetings, e-mails, phone calls, and letters about T_____ without ever losing it. There must have been six people trying to help her fit into the class. I never did figure out who was in charge of all that—it just seemed like lots of meetings. I never realized just how much of that stuff goes on each day. I really get the "why" part about collaborating for the sake of kids, but it seemed pretty haphazard. Nobody really seemed to be in charge, though stuff got done. Gwen (my partner) and I both got great evaluations. Mr. Johnson thought we did well in both the individual and the collaborative parts on the disposition rating form. He said there is a lot of both in teaching and that you have to be ready to go either way, depending on the situation.

There was a light at the end of the student teaching tunnel . . . but first I had nine weeks with fourth graders and nine weeks of math with seventh graders. There were many similarities between my block classroom and my fourth-grade placement. We had lots of adults in and out of the room all the time and regular grade-level meetings with our principal. She was really big on "team" meetings—one each week. Most were about curriculum, planning for the fall holiday units, and talking about the new math program (which I actually learned about in block—though the teachers didn't seem thrilled about it). I got asked to find some background materials to add to the science unit on electricity, so I brought in the motors activity from block to show how electricity and magnetism combine to produce motion. It was nice to be treated as part of the team and be able to contribute something new in a meeting. During my lead weeks, I finally got to show that I could handle the entire teaching load by myself.

The seventh graders were such great kids! I had three math sections each day and two sixth-grade reading to two groups of six graders. Our team meetings had teachers from all subjects. Most of the team time was spent talking about which kids were struggling, and how they were doing across classes. We also had department meetings for seventh-grade math—which were usually checks to see where everyone was at in the curriculum, and to plan for common assessments. All the students took the same unit tests at about the same time. There didn't seem to be much space for individual choices. My cooperating teacher said that curriculum planning was done for both middle schools using a district administration process and that each building sent representatives. Since it happened in the spring, I did not get to see it in operation.

I've gotten a lot better at anticipating things that will come up, though I was better with the material I planned than with the other curriculum stuff. It was still so new to me. My biggest sticky point in fourth grade was math, because I liked the math curriculum and my cooperating teacher did not. We were pretty good at talking about it, though I doubt she will ever change her mind. It seemed that she put in a lot of her own materials instead of using the math curriculum and didn't think it would make a difference for the kids next year. I wasn't sure how anyone could really tell since the fourth-grade tests are over early in the year. For the other subjects, though, she's great and really in line with the other teachers. I wonder what I will do if I don't like part of the curriculum when I get my own classroom? People in both my placements talked about collaborating; team time in seventh grade was labeled as a place to collaborate. But it seemed to mean different things to different people. When we looked at the collaborative leadership dispositions on my student teaching evaluation form, both my cooperating teachers gave me very positive feedback about my individual and collaborative work and told me that I would be a good team member who would have no trouble handling my own class. Why do I feel like I still don't get it?

Discussion

The student's sense of ambiguity about what collaborative leadership means in many ways mirrors the ambiguity of the faculty. Three of the full-time faculty consistently participate in teacher education activities designed to examine collaborative leadership principles; however, only one person worked on the development of the conceptual framework. As a result, students experience pockets of emphasis on collaborative leadership during their program but do not see continuity in their courses. It is encouraging that some agreement about the collaborative leadership dispositions has emerged, though, as faculty gain experience with them.

Special Education Program

The Special Education (SPED) program has seven full-time faculty and one instructional staff member. Students begin taking special education coursework early in their college experience, often enrolling in our introductory courses during their freshman year. Because of this, the department has been able to employ a developmental process to teach collaborative leadership dispositions. All of our coursework, particularly field-based experiences, includes embedded requirements that address collaborative leadership–related information and skills. Ultimately, students achieve skills in reflective application of these competencies. Our faculty consistently evaluates students' growth in these areas in order to support and shape students' dispositions.

A Student's Experience

This has been an exciting, yet challenging journey. I started this journey while I was in high school. I was a teacher's helper in a classroom for students with severe disabilities. While I was nervous at first, I learned to love working with these students! . . . So I decided to go to UWEC and declare special education as my major—specifically, learning disabilities/ cognitive disabilities . . . SPED 205 was my first opportunity to look at the field and its requirements. In addition to learning more about the broader field, I learned about what was expected of students in the SPED program. Wow, not only did we need to understand and practice the Wisconsin Teaching Standards, we needed to understand how collaborative leadership dispositions and professional behaviors play a role in our success as future teachers.

This knowledge from SPED 205 was tested when I had my first opportunity to be in a classroom for students with special needs. I was really nervous at first. This wasn't like the first classroom in my high school, where I spent time working with the teacher, two paraprofessionals, and the students on fun art activities. In this new class, the teacher was trying to teach a group of students who had very different skill levels. This made me question whether or not special education was for me. At the end of the semester, my evaluation form was filled out by the cooperating teacher. It revealed that I had actually done a pretty good job for a beginning student. My scores on the evaluation form showed that I exhibited appropriate skills—in particular, the collaborative leadership disposition of seeking beneficial solutions—because I had asked a lot of questions.

Meeting with my adviser, I developed my gate 1 portfolio to apply for admission to the program. I was so glad that my evaluation from 205 was so positive. Even though my skill level in understanding the WTS and collaborative leadership was pretty basic, I had demonstrated enough skills in each of these areas to be accepted into the program. Now that I was in the program, I wondered what they were going to expect of me!

Well, I found out! Surprisingly, the next class (SPED 301) I took did not require me to work with kids in special education. Instead, I worked with kids in general education classrooms. At first I was confused about the reasons I had to have this experience, but the more time I spent in the classroom, the more I could see how special education and general education are pretty similar. Boy, I really saw how collaboration, leadership, and good dispositions are so important. I saw my general education cooperating teacher work with all students and the special education teacher. They took responsibility for each other, worked to find common solutions, and really built a strong relationship. I never realized how much work it takes to coordinate all those students and who's going to teach what. With pull-out or inclusion, I could see how it could really get confusing for the teachers and the students if people didn't work together. You would have a difficult time finding beneficial solutions! My evaluation for this class had the same requirement areas as SPED 205. However, now that I was more actively involved in planning and teaching, everybody required me to make a lot more decisions on my own! I thought the professors were trying to make us recognize what it meant to take responsibility for ourselves. They told us that we had to reflect, which meant that I had to think about what I was doing all of the time. I did OK in the areas of WTS, but the area of collaborative leadership dispositions still scared me. Can I really be a leader? How do I show a passion for excellence? What is really meant by relationship management?

If I thought the SPED 205 and SPED 301 experiences were fulfilling and challenging, SPED 404, the elementary school experience, was even more than I imagined. Not only was I able to spend more time in the classroom, I was able to teach actual lessons. Once again, dispositions played a big role. The stakes were higher here for my performance. I was expected to be more developed in the way I used the teaching standards and showed the collaborative leadership dispositions and skills. In other words, I was actually required to apply these skills over and over. I could really feel my professors and cooperating teacher expecting me to be more mature and independent in the classroom. If we did not meet these expectations, there was a strong possibility that we would not be allowed to continue in the program. Shoot, if that doesn't make you nervous, I don't know what would!

I made it through my elementary field experience with flying colors. Well, sort of flying! There were some areas that I definitely needed to work on. I will say that the feedback from the instructor and the teachers in the school gave me a clear picture of my strengths and areas of need. I still felt clumsy at relationship management. Was I ready to face high school students? Well, I found out in SPED 416. I loved it! I can't believe I was afraid of this age group. It is true that I had to make some adjustments in my own attitude and approaches to deal effectively with this group. I got good support from my cooperating teacher and the university instructor, which made this experience work in the long run. I realized how much I have grown in my views of collaborative leadership when I observed my cooperating teacher trying to get one of her high school students with a learning disability into a history class. Before this experience, I would have said that this student had the *right* to be in this class period. However, after watching my teacher work with the general education teacher in a collaborative way by taking the supportive rather than a "pushy" role, I came to the conclusion that if I wanted to be an effective special education teacher, I had to work collaboratively with a lot of other people. Ahhh, relationship management was making more sense to me. I had to be willing to step up and take a problem-solving role at times. I think this is the leadership that my university instructors keep talking about. Collaborative leadership dispositions are as needed as knowing about curriculum. I think this is true, especially at the high school level.

Finally, I reached the end of the road, student teaching. I am so excited I have an elementary placement and a high school placement. I have been told that collaborative leadership will be evaluated in both placements by my cooperating teachers and people from the university. In my seminar course, we will be doing a self-evaluation to measure our own growth in collaborative leadership. From my earlier experience and even in my more recent experiences in the schools, it seems to me that collaboration is an area where experienced teachers may have a lot of difficulty for lots of reasons. I think the idea of collaborative leadership needs to be more planned, instead of just sort of happening in these settings. I wonder if planning collaboration and taking a leadership role to make sure it happened will help me be a more effective teacher when I have my own classroom.

Discussion

This narrative illustrates how the SPED faculty shapes the development of candidates' collaborative leadership dispositions throughout the program, especially the field-based courses, where the expectations increase as candidates move through the program sequence. Because of this process, we have become more proactive both in encouraging the development of desirable dispositions and in addressing dispositional concerns when they arise. The disposition emphasis we have incorporated has provided us with the opportunity to begin to work with candidates early in their formative experiences, allowing us to support them in their development of dispositions consistent with our professional expectations. By addressing dispositions more consistently and openly in courses and personal interactions with candidates, faculty help candidates gain a greater sense of the importance of dispositions in their professional development.

Dispositions First Approach

These three student vignettes underscore some key understandings across our programs. First, students view something as valuable when the faculty address it explicitly. The more common the message across faculty, the more powerful it becomes. When different faculty talk about the same issues from their own perspectives, candidates have more opportunities to process that information in relationship to their own thoughts and experiences. Second, connections are everything. The interrelationships between the dispositions, knowledge, and skills of teaching are complex. To simplify and fragment does not allow students to come to understand the complexity and beauty that is effective teaching. Lastly, developing dispositions requires time—time to think, time to practice, and time to grow.

These understandings have helped us rethink and review what we believe to be true about student learning and therefore effective instruction. Dispositions act like mental models. When they remain invisible, they limit one's ability to think critically and be solution oriented. They hold the learner prisoner to one way of thinking. To make those lenses visible allows the learner to improve their thinking and assumptions, which may be true but may also be incomplete. Those lenses drive the moral and ethical choices an individual makes, and also point them to certain knowledge fields and skill sets. It has also become abundantly clear that beginning with the end in mind allows for developmentally appropriate experiences and learnings. Having a clear point and end in mind allows both the student and the faculty the opportunity to connect all the learning experiences in ways that fundamentally impact the learner.

All programs have experienced significant learning and growth as a result of our emphasis upon teaching dispositions. We found that making our dispositions explicit and a fundamental part of our expectations provided a framework for cultivating student behaviors. Students' actions are referenced by the rubric, and thus the conversation becomes focused on teachable moments rather than punitive actions and faculty preference. The dispositions also provide a lens for selecting the knowledge and skill sets that the programs attempt to help students learn. When we focus on teaching the collaborative leadership dispositions, it allows us, as faculty, to work with students more as emerging colleagues than as students in our classrooms.

In addition, all programs face some common challenges, particularly the gaps in concepts and language between university and school settings. Many of our school partners are engaged in collaborative practices and leaderful actions; however, their meanings and language vary from those used in our preservice programs. In some instances, philosophical differences between teachers' views and our program goals about leadership result in limited support for the development of collaborative leadership principles in beginning teachers.

Significant differences exist between programs. The elementary and special education programs engage candidates for at least three years and thus can provide significantly more longitudinal support than is possible in the secondary education program, where faculty and students work together for less than two years. Thus, the secondary education program is more assertive at the early stages in holding students accountable for demonstrating collaborative leadership dispositions, and implements more formal remediation practices than do the other programs. The elementary education program places less emphasis on collaborative approaches as a strict requirement than the other two programs; the faculty elected to emphasize both individual and collaborative actions as evidence of successful advancement through the program. Significant variation also exists between programs with respect to the ways that the dispositions are made explicit to students. Our efforts to generate common language and understanding around the core knowledge and skills vary across programs. Such differences represent challenges in consistent implementation of collaborative leadership principles.

Another set of challenges is reflected in articulating the underlying collaborative leadership knowledge and skill base, given the implications of "beginners as leaders." Some stakeholders in our process perceive the developmental path from participant to active follower to collaborative leader as needing an intermediate level of "collaborator" as a precursor to "collaborative leader." At this point we are seeking more specific insight about participants' views of developmental trajectory. Some possibilities under consideration include students' readiness to assume more leaderful roles, the existence of knowledge gaps—and discomfort—on the part of school staffs about the shift in roles implied for educators, and mismatches between university and school cultures. The impact on their ability to contribute leaderful actions such as advocacy, solution-oriented thinking, and group facilitation to their schools as new teachers is a subject of ongoing study as our first graduates from the revised programs are only now entering classrooms as licensed professionals.[3] We will continue to track their success in fostering learning by K–12 students, as well as their contributions and professional success as measured by supervisor evaluations, professional development activities, and career paths.

CONCLUSION

We have made significant strides in our own understanding about the power of explicit dispositions that are grounded in the philosophical, moral, and ethical dimensions of a conceptual framework. When we began our journey into "Preparing Collaborative Leaders," we had a motto. What emerged from our beginning activities were a set of dispositions and descriptors that all three programs agreed upon. Those descriptors were powerful and allowed us the opportunity to seek something more: the enactment of our vision and a deeper understanding of the interplay between dispositions, knowledge, and skills. We have now made clearer a fundamental premise of all our programs: dispositions convey the deep purpose of our programs. They make explicit the moral structure of our program and help us more successfully observe and reflect on *behaviors* as indicators of *ethical choices*.

As we better understand the impact of a disposition-oriented approach, we continue to reform our programs to strengthen their impact on candidates' collaborative leadership *dispositions, knowledge, and skills*. Ordering these words differently reflects a fundamental change in our thinking, and brings us closer to a time when asking ourselves, "Are we ensuring that our program practices really reflect the deep philosophical commit-ments we value?" will be our most essential question. We understand that the process itself is ongoing. Becoming comfortable with the ever-changing nature of our programs is a challenge we continue to address as we shift from a product-oriented to a process-oriented view. We will con-tinue our efforts to provide clear models that help our students under-stand the construct of collaborative leadership and its potential for their teaching practice.

CHAPTER SEVEN

Finding a Tipping Point

John Fischetti, Scott Imig, Abdou Ndoye,
and Robert Smith

Editors' Case Introduction: University of North Carolina Wilmington

The Watson School of Education is housed on the campus of the University of North Carolina Wilmington (UNCW), a comprehensive four-year college in southeastern North Carolina with 11,500 students. The third largest provider of teachers in North Carolina, the Watson School offers multiple pathways into the classroom for its 1,556 students. Formal partnership agreements with over 100 schools support the different teacher education programs.

In 2007, the state Department of Public Instruction introduced new teaching standards and gave institutions of higher education in North Carolina two years to "revision" all teacher preparation programs and demonstrate "how [each] new program is different from the current program, and how it reflects the North Carolina Professional Teaching Standards and the 21st century knowledge, skills, and dispositions embedded in the standards."[1] That mandate served as a "tipping point," motivating the authors and their colleagues to reexamine their teacher education programs in light of the strong emphasis that the new standards placed on professional dispositions.

This chapter describes the challenges that the new state standards presented, especially because of their strong emphasis on dispositions. It details how the authors crafted a conceptual response for their institution and how their leadership at the local and state levels helped promote program changes.

MEETING NEW STANDARDS FOR PROFESSIONAL DISPOSITIONS

"It is unacceptable to speak with a country dialect."

"I will not tolerate lazy English or Ebonics."

"I don't really think achievement gaps are a teacher's responsibility."

These statements, written by college juniors in response to a chapter on language and diversity by Lisa Delpit, reflect some of the challenges we faced as teacher educators in confronting the biases and misconceptions of our teacher candidates.[2] It was the second week of block 1 in our newly revised secondary teacher preparation program. Program faculty had spent considerable time choosing readings and designing activities and field experiences that reflected the importance of preparing teachers who could successfully teach all students. The five faculty members who taught block 1 classes discussed how to respond to these students whose beliefs and imagined practices did not align with the program's new dispositional goals. We realized that none of our program descriptions, materials, or syllabi included these expectations. We were still using previous program standards that emphasized lower-level professional behaviors like punctuality and professional dress. Nowhere were we making explicit our commitment to the preparation of teachers who would serve all students.

Under our previous system of monitoring dispositions, such comments might never have caught the attention of instructors or been raised as a programwide issue. If these same candidates were later placed in honors class settings in "successful" suburban high schools for their student teaching, they would likely have gone through the program mostly unchanged.

We had spent almost two years developing a new program designed to give our candidates more direct contact with diverse learners in diverse settings and more leadership opportunities in classroom settings. But in the first week of the semester we realized that we had changed the content and pedagogy of the program without attending to the dispositional expectations required under North Carolina's new Professional Teaching Standards.[3]

This chapter describes how we came to recognize the limitations of our earlier efforts to foster professional dispositions and how we used the impetus of the new state standards to frame a new definition of teacher professionalism centered on the notion of "leadership for diverse learners." The mounting expectations of No Child Left Behind, the failure of North Carolina's schools to adequately prepare and graduate all learners, the state's new teaching standards, and the state-mandated teacher education revisions all created a tipping point that pushed us toward a more profound emphasis on leadership, serving diverse learners, and dispositions in teaching and teacher education.

Recognizing an Opportunity

We launched the project described here in car rides across the state that we made in order to respond to drafts of the new state standards, in debriefing conversations after faculty meetings, and in e-mail exchanges about the kinds of graduates we wanted to produce. The four of us work in different program areas and bring different backgrounds to this task. Abdou, our unit assessment director, assists program areas in formalizing assessment plans. Upon reviewing data from our graduates and school partners, he realized that one of the key challenges for our graduates is working with diverse learners. Scott, former director of the curriculum, instruction, and supervision graduate program, recently became associate dean for outreach. His interests lie in building programs that prepare candidates for the challenges of diverse classrooms and communities. Robert brings a strong social justice framework to his work as director of secondary education and a commitment to imbedding dispositional characteristics and challenges into program designs. John teaches in the undergraduate and graduate secondary programs. He is interested in rethinking the role of formal teacher education in light of the pressing needs of young people and their families, given the low high school graduation rate in the United States and an increasingly diverse, global environment.

When we used to talk about the success of our program, we often ended up telling stories about our "shining stars"—former students who teach in challenging schools with diverse student populations yet manage to succeed right from the start. Not only do these former students implement the pedagogies we espouse in our classes, they also serve as strong role models, motivating students to do their best work. Strong leaders who advocate for their students, they have a deep sense of caring for all students and know how to engage them in meaningful learning.

When we asked ourselves whether our shining stars excelled because of the program or because of the prior experiences and dispositional traits they brought to the program, we had to admit that the program was probably not the main factor in their success. While these students gave us an image of the possible, they represented only a small number of our total graduates, most of whom perform "well enough" to survive their first year but quickly become teachers who perpetuate the status quo of public schools.

When North Carolina's Department of Public Instruction released drafts of the twenty-first-century teacher standards for feedback, we realized that the new standards placed a huge emphasis on professional dispositions, much more than we anticipated. This seemed like a golden opportunity to rethink our programs so that success with all students and leadership could become the norm, not the exception. The new state mandates also gave us an opportunity to influence other faculty members and programs in our institution and to work with colleagues in the Department of Public Instruction to promote the development of professional dispositions as part of teacher education reform across the state.

Earlier Approaches to Dispositions

Before the new state standards were released, our institution's dispositional processes were largely based upon the National Council for Accreditation of Teacher Education's (NCATE's) recommended practices. These processes served us well through NCATE and state reviews in the past. In 2002, our faculty drafted the Watson School's Standards of Professional Conduct that describe the general behaviors and ethical standards we expect of our students. For example, under "commitment to students," we have the following expectations in relation to diversity: (1) supports, acknowledges and respects diversity among individuals in all educational settings and (2) sets high expectations for all students and provides various methods and opportunities for students to achieve goals.

Besides developing this written statement of expectations, we created a plan of action. The first step toward greater accountability involved making sure that students were aware of the standards. So we identified particular times (admission) and places (specific courses) when the standards of professional conduct would be distributed and discussed with students. Next we worked on infusing professional standards into courses by creating problem-based learning scenarios and case studies to support reflective decision making. The third step involved establishing a process for remediation, advisement, and retention decisions in situations where a documented pattern emerged of a candidate not meeting a standard.

A committee developed a plan for implementation, but most faculty members did not participate in discussions about appropriate or inappropriate behaviors. There was little faculty support, especially for changing syllabi. Some faculty made some modifications. For example, a self-assessment of dispositions was piloted at the beginning and end of the introductory course Teacher, School, and Society, and the results were discussed with students. But there was insufficient faculty interest and administrative support to integrate this assessment across the curriculum, and it was dropped after a few semesters. A social identity paper assignment in the same course asked students to examine their beliefs about diversity by exploring "the development of your own social identity as a way to better understand how race, class, and gender affect people's lives." While this assignment is still used, faculty teaching subsequent courses rarely draw on the original self-assessment framework.

Without significant faculty buy-in, most of the changes were piecemeal, often the result of an individual faculty initiative. The standards were mainly used to identify dispositional "problems," with only minor new emphasis on the development of candidates' dispositional traits. At any point in a candidate's program, a faculty member could complete a performance review form for any candidate whose behavior raised concerns. This process focused attention on the following professional behavior: "behaviors and skills related to becoming a professional educator, such as preparation for field-based assignments (e.g., having lesson plans completed); punctuality and attendance; appropriate attire; development of positive rapport with children, parents, teachers, and administrators; professional demeanor; professional interactions with university students, faculty, staff, and administrators; use of standard English in oral and written communications; and adherence to school rules and ethical standards." When such a form was submitted to the associate dean's office, the administration decided whether or not to meet with the candidate. A faculty member might also decide to meet individually with a candidate instead of completing a performance review form or to ignore the behavior completely. Fear of retribution from the candidate on course evaluations may have influenced some faculty members to let such matters drop.

In short, our institution's earlier approach to dispositions was largely a gatekeeping process designed to help "red flag" individual problem students. While there were some shared understandings among faculty related to professionalism—punctuality, respect for teachers and students, and appropriate attire—there was little common understanding of or focus on broader dispositions. When the development of broader dispositions occurred in courses or supervised fieldwork, it was usually the result of individual faculty members, not a programmatic effort.

Besides our Standards of Professional Conduct, the Watson School of Education has a conceptual framework that helps define who we are as an institution. Developed in 2004, this framework includes dispositional qualities such as respect for diversity, but there was little discussion of this framework. Without elaborating what *respect for diversity* meant, faculty viewed the conceptual framework as an affirmation of what we were already doing or a vague vision toward which we could aspire.

The absence of significant conversations in and across programs about our purpose as a school, our identity, and our shared beliefs made it difficult to develop a shared statement of dispositional expectations. Courses and programs focused mainly on developing content knowledge and pedagogy, with only minimal attention to the development of dispositions. The following quote from a middle-class, white, female, social studies student teacher reflects the inadequacies and failures of our earlier efforts to address important dispositions in our teacher candidates:

> What I did always feel guilty about was the amount that race, class, and gender influenced the way that I interacted with my students. My favorite students typically were the middle-class white males. It wasn't that I didn't like students that were different from me; I just tended to relate to those who were more similar to me as an individual. I did struggle with the fact that lower-income students, who were typically minorities, had such great disregard for the authority of the school, and they seemed to have no concern about how they did in their classes . . . Why couldn't all students be a little more like me?[4]

While we could appreciate this student teacher's honesty about her "favorite students," we had to face the fact that her preparation had failed to challenge her beliefs about poor students or provide her with the kinds of experiences that may have enabled her to relate to all students, not just those like herself.

The failure of our programs to foster such dispositions stemmed from the absence of clear and shared expectations regarding the dispositions of an effective teacher. Without such agreement, we did not offer the kinds of coherent programs likely to foster a passionate, caring nature in our students and prepare them to teach all students successfully.

Impetus for Change

In 2007, with the introduction of the North Carolina Professional Teaching Standards, institutions of higher education had two years to "revision" all teacher preparation programs and demonstrate "how [each] new program is different from the current program, and how it reflects the North Carolina Professional Teaching Standards and the 21st century knowledge, skills, and dispositions embedded in the standards."[5] The new standards replaced the Interstate New Teacher Assessment and Support Consortium (INTASC) standards that institutions in North Carolina had used for almost twenty years. Programs that failed to make significant changes would be "turned around and sent back" by the state board of education.[6]

The state mandates motivated us, the authors of this chapter, to take some institutional leadership. Our overlapping interests in equity, school reform, the influence of race and class on teaching, and leadership development compelled us to view these mandates as challenges to improve our programs. As parents of children in the public school system, we supported the need to rethink public education in ways that increase the supply of caring teachers committed to equal educational opportunities for all young people and to working toward proactive change. Given our previous work together in responding to the new standards and our common vision for teacher education, we took on the role of advocates within our institution. We encouraged programs at UNCW to develop a common set of clearly defined dispositions based on our analysis of the new state standards.

OUR "NEW" PROGRAMS

Recently, colleagues in our school of education submitted twenty-three revised programs for approval. The type and scope of the revisions vary widely across programs. Some are minor changes—for example, increasing field experiences hours—while others involve more extensive reforms, including developing new courses and requiring fewer credit hours. This process has sparked discussion by some about the process the state used to generate change, but it has also caused others to revisit the fundamental questions that guide our work. Do we have the obligation to develop teachers who are good practitioners and good professionals who see the importance of being change agents in the classroom, school, and community? Can we help candidates develop leadership dispositions to support diverse learners and their families? Can we expand school and community-based experiences in the preservice years? What changes would we have to make to our teacher education programs to realize these outcomes?

When we did a content analysis of the elements that make up North Carolina's Professional Teaching Standards, we found that 68 percent related to professional dispositions. Table 7.1 summarizes the importance of dispositions in each of the five standards.

Leadership and diversity are the first two standards, and elements of leadership and diversity are imbedded throughout all five standards in significant ways. Still, the state's charge to revision all initial licensure programs did not include a specific request to emphasize these dispositions. Since *these* two areas are important to us, we advocated for dispositions in these areas.

We asked ourselves how we could redesign our teacher education programs so that the shining stars became the norm rather than the exception. We started by developing a new definition of professionalism that emphasizes the dispositions of leadership and caring for diverse learners. We grounded our thinking in a large body of writing on teacher dispositions, caring educators, multicultural education, and global education. Below we share a brief sample of the professional literature that informs our work.

Many writers highlight the importance of teacher leadership. Mary Diez challenges teacher educators "to develop practitioners whose knowledge goes well beyond the content of the discipline to an understanding of the social context and who can collaborate with others—fellow professionals and parents, students and the broader community—to make a difference in the lives of children."[7] Charlotte Danielson states, "Today more than ever, a number of interconnected factors argue for the necessity of teacher leadership in schools."[8] She notes, "In every good school there are teachers whose vision extends beyond their own classroom . . . who want to influence change." Linda Darling-Hammond and Diane Friedlaender identify teacher leadership as a significant factor in successful school reform.[9]

Caring is a prominent theme in professional writing about teachers who succeed in helping all students learn. Nel Noddings analyzes an ethic of caring and the challenges and necessity of fostering care in schools.[10] She argues that the main aim of education should be a moral one, that of nurturing the growth of competent, caring, loving, and lovable per-

TABLE 7.1 Importance of dispositions in teaching standards

North Carolina Professional Teaching Standards	Percentage of elements relating to dispositions
1. Teachers demonstrate leadership.	100 (20 out of 20 elements)
2. Teachers establish a respectful environment for a diverse population of students.	100 (12 out of 12 elements)
3. Teachers know the content they teach.	30 (3 out of 10 elements)
4. Teachers facilitate learning for their students.	38 (9 out of 24 elements)
5. Teachers reflect on their practice.	100 (3 out of 3 elements)

sons. She proposes "that education might best be organized around centers of care."[11]

Sonia Nieto identifies "key attitudes and sensibilities" of caring teachers.[12] These are a sense of mission; solidarity with, and empathy for, students; the courage to challenge mainstream knowledge; improvisation; and a passion for social justice.[13] Nieto and Nodding both stress the importance of caring and committed teachers within the school and the larger society.

In terms of advocacy on behalf of all children, Jonathan Kozol offers a strong statement. In *Savage Inequalities* he writes, "One searches for some way to understand why a society as rich and, frequently, as generous as ours would leave these children in their penury and squalor for so long—and with so little public indignation."[14] Kozol questions our lack of care as a society when it comes to the education provided for "other people's children."

Multicultural educators also advocate for an effective school environment that serves all children well. James Banks defines the goal of multicultural education as "creating equal educational opportunities for all students by changing the total school environment so that it will reflect the diverse cultures and groups within a society and within the nation's classrooms."[15] He proposes five dimensions of multicultural education: content integration, knowledge construction, prejudice reduction, equity pedagogy, and empowering school culture. The first four dimensions focus on the classroom and overlap with Nieto's attitudes and sensibilities. The fifth dimension, empowering school culture, refers to the total environment of the school, including the attitudes, beliefs, and actions of teachers and administrators.

Our preparation of leaders for diverse learners occurs within a global context, which calls for a new kind of awareness on the part of teachers. In *Five Minds for the Future*, Howard Gardner discusses the impact of science and technology and the inexorability of globalization.[16] He argues that we must learn to examine our contribution in work or in our community by asking, "What is my responsibility in bringing such a world into being?" From his "look into the future," Gardner identifies the intellectual dispositions we will need and our schools will have to help develop for the success of our society and our planet.

This literature informed our thinking and our discussions about the dispositions required for leadership on behalf of diverse learners. One outcome of our revising process was a new framework aligned with the state standards and organized around five pillars.

The Five Pillars

Our new framework provides a more comprehensive overview of dispositions than previous institutional documents. It rests on a definition of *professionalism* as leadership to support diverse learners and their families. The framework also provides a way of thinking about dispositions development that moves from a concrete focus on self to an expanding sense of self as a change agent in a dynamic community, region, nation, and world. Each element, described below, is crucial for the successful professional to be an effective leader.

The foundation of professional dispositions consists of basic *attitudes and ethics*. We contend that candidates must first have a sound ethical compass and a willing attitude toward personal growth before they are capable of looking beyond themselves and effecting change in the lives of those they serve. In our framework, attitudes and ethics relate to professional qualities such as promptness, professional dress, courtesy, appropriate conduct, effective people skills, honesty, acceptance of feedback from others, following rules, maintaining a clear criminal background check, and adhering to the approved code of ethics. These compliance-oriented dispositions ensure that teacher candidates will adhere to the professional standards and cultural norms expected by the school community.

As candidates embrace attitudinal and ethical standards, they do so on multiple levels: classroom, school, and community. Characteristics associated with *cultural awareness and learner differences* include caring, thoughtfulness, respect, consideration, concern, self-reflection, self-direction, flexibility, and recognizing differences. We want our teacher candidates to show awareness of and respect for learner differences.

Candidates stretch beyond knowledge of self as they develop *cultural sensitivity and connections to families*. This element is demonstrated by candidates' using awareness of learner differences to modify curriculum; seeking out connections with colleagues to help understand how students learn; exhibiting effective collaboration and teamwork skills; initiating experiences with families; showing sensitivity to adapt and modify practice; demonstrating compassion, sympathy, and helpfulness; accommodating to special situations faced by students and families; and exhibiting cultural sensitivity and recognizing and respecting differences.

Another aspect of teacher professionalism is *classroom leadership to support diverse learners*. This includes advocacy on behalf of all students in one's class, commitment to overcoming bias, helping to eliminate prejudice, engaging in active leadership for self-improvement, modeling for students, demonstrating resourcefulness, and incorporating community resources to benefit students and families. Here candidates act on their knowledge and resources from the previous pillar to influence positive change. They seek resources and opportunities for students to appreciate their culture and the culture of others. Candidates use knowledge of learners, culture, and diversity to reduce bias and prejudice and to make modifications that enhance student learning and the quality of school experiences. They incorporate community resources to benefit students and their families. This pillar emphasizes action, while the previous pillars highlight awareness and sensitivity to differences.

School leadership to support diverse learners includes advocating on behalf of all students, demonstrating schoolwide responsibility, promoting fairness, facilitating a team or professional learning community on behalf of all students, and modeling best practices for the school. As candidates are exposed to the importance of leadership for diversity, they become aware of the imperative to connect the curriculum to the student's family, culture, learning needs, educational history, and story. This requires teacher advocacy on behalf of students at the school level. Being a member of a strong professional learning community involves modeling best practices and contributing to the school's leadership process with honesty, responsibility, and fairness. School leadership includes active participation in all phases of the curriculum across grade levels and subject areas as appropriate, participating in research-based data collection, and practice in building support for the school with parents and the community. It involves home visits and incorporating community resources to support students.

The pillar of *community leadership to support diverse learners and their families* involves reaching beyond the school. Actions and attributes of teacher leaders who embrace this pillar include advocating on behalf of equity issues in the community, promoting social responsibility, striving for social justice, exhibiting self-accountability, demonstrating personal responsibility, and contributing as a community-wide leader for the betterment of schools and society. Community leaders demonstrate modeling for society, seeking solutions to overcome obstacles that prevent family and community involvement, and helping to build partnerships between the school and the community. Candidates incorporating this element influence change beyond the classroom. They understand that the actions they take in the classroom cannot result in long-term change unless the school system supports and facilitates those changes. Candidates attempt to influence school policies, to facilitate student learning outside of school, and to make school change sustainable. Candidates expand their initiatives beyond the school by reaching out to the community and society as a whole. They participate as change agents in the community for the betterment of schools and society. Candidates use community resources to provide a bridge between what is happening in school and what is happening in the community. This element is best demonstrated in apprenticeships with other teachers or leaders of the school, community, or university who are attempting to make change and forge partnerships to support young people and their families.

Figure 7.1 describes the foundation and pillars of our framework. The pillars represent five key areas related to dispositions that a teacher education program should seek to foster. Each pillar is vitally important. The pillars rest on the foundation of attitudes and ethics and hold up the tenets of a revised definition of teacher professionalism—leadership to support diverse learners and their families. The framework may help teacher educators embed experiences in programs that help preservice teachers develop traits such as caring, respect, and commitment to improving student learning. Our responsibility as teacher educators is to weave profound experiences into our programs across the pillars so that candidates have exposure to each area.

Table 7.2 lists potential experiences and sample evidence that teacher educators can use to embed opportunities for candidates to demonstrate dispositional prowess throughout programs. The table also lists indicators and attributes for each dispositional element.

FIGURE 7.1 Five pillars of the new framework

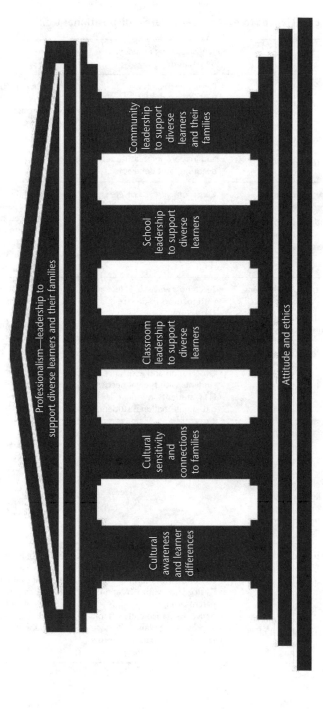

Professionalism—leadership to support diverse learners and their families

Cultural awareness and learner differences

Cultural sensitivity and connections to families

Classroom leadership to support diverse learners

School leadership to support diverse learners

Community leadership to support diverse learners and their families

Attitude and ethics

TABLE 7.2 **Experiences to expand candidates' dispositional traits**

Dispositional framework	Potential learning experiences in TE programs	Sample evidence
Attitude and ethics Promptness, professional dress, courtesy, respect, consideration, effective people skills, acceptance of feedback from others, follows rules, clear criminal background check, adheres to code of ethics	• Formal discussion of professionalism • Exposure to code of ethics • Parent conference to discuss decorum • Specific examples of appropriate and inappropriate attitudes, decorum, and behaviors	• Positive performance review • Daily observations by supervisor/faculty
Cultural awareness and learner differences Caring, thoughtfulness, concern, self-reflection, self-direction, recognizes differences	• Classroom visits to diverse classrooms, shadowing students, visits with exemplary teachers in multiple schools live and virtual • Visits and tutoring in afterschool programs and community centers	• Observations note that teacher recognizes differences, holds students to high standards, exhibits caring and concern for students' progress
Cultural sensitivity and connections to families Uses awareness to modify curriculum, connections with colleagues, experiences with families, adaptive sensitivity, compassionate, sympathetic, helpful, accommodating	• Teaching minilessons, lessons with mentors in diverse classrooms • Video reflection on content, pedagogy, and dispositions with mentors • Parent contact • Observation and assistance with students with special needs, ELLs, students identified as gifted, international students	• Modified curriculum, lesson plans • Collaboration with colleagues and families, phone call log to families
Classroom leadership to support diverse learners Commitment to overcoming bias, eliminating prejudice, active leadership for self-improvement, models for students, resourceful, incorporating community resources to benefit students and families	• Community tour • Home visits to selected students • Volunteering/service to community agencies	• Home visits • Invited guest speakers • Trips to cultural sites • Incorporating community resources
School leadership to support diverse learners Advocacy on behalf of all students, honesty, responsibility, fairness, classroom, team, professional learning community, school leadership on behalf of all students, models for school	• Active participation in schoolwide committees and meetings with mentors • Participation with PTA and other parent groups • Active assistance with school improvement plan • Formal use of data to improve teaching and learning	• School improvement team leader promoting significant change • Advocacy on behalf of students through PTA and other established groups

TABLE 7.2   Experiences to expand candidates' dispositional traits, *continued*

Dispositional framework	*Potential learning experiences in TE programs*	*Sample evidence*
Community leadership to support diverse learners and their families Equity, social responsibility, social justice, self-accountability, personal responsibility, schoolwide/systemwide/community-wide leadership that results in change for the betterment of schools and society, models for society, seeks solutions to overcome obstacles that prevent family and community involvement, builds partnerships with school and community	• Active participation with teachers, teacher educators, and community leaders in policy reform efforts • Presentation to school board and other school-related forum • Active participation and presentation at professional and community conferences • Mentor-led seminars on social change and school reform • Self-reflection and guided coaching meetings related to dispositional strengths and areas for growth	• Proactive change agent to benefit children and families • Presents to school board or other agencies • Incorporates community resources into curriculum • Studies issues of school and society • Models exemplary citizenship and stewardship • Promotes prejudice reduction

This framework serves several key purposes for teacher preparation programs. First, it presents a range of dispositions that are important in preparing effective teachers. It also provides some guidance in sequencing courses and experiences designed to cultivate important dispositions. For example, before they can demonstrate cultural sensitivity and connections to families and communities, students need field experiences and/or coursework that help them understand their own cultural background and relate to diverse learners. Beyond a linear sequence, the framework invites a weaving of experiences that allow teacher candidates to grasp the multiple roles of a teacher and to acquire and develop relevant content knowledge, pedagogical skills, and related dispositions.

CHANGING DISPOSITIONAL PROCESSES IN OUR SCHOOL OF EDUCATION

As program coordinators and the assessment director for the unit, we shared our initial ideas about the new state standards and their implications for the redesign of our programs. Faculty were interested in the changes required by the state, but the state education department provided little guidance about how to proceed. Because we believed in the importance of the new standards with their emphasis on diversity and leadership, we began to consider how we could engage our colleagues at UNCW and around the state. We identified committees and meetings in our institution and asked to be included on the agenda. We made presentations to the program coordinators, to the school's diversity committee, to specific program areas and course development committees, to the lead staff member for the North Carolina Department of Public Instruction and the state board of education, and, through a webinar, to teacher education colleagues across the state.

Mobilizing Our Colleagues

In talking with our colleagues, we shared our perspectives on the state mandate, our content analysis of the new standards, our pillar graphic and framework. We pointed out that dispositions extended beyond the traditional assessments of professional conduct that had been part of our programs. We invited people to consider the implications of the new emphasis on dispositions compared with the familiar focus on content knowledge and pedagogical skill. We discussed the importance of providing early community experiences in conjunction with early school experiences. We suggested that the new focus on leadership for diverse learners challenged programs to integrate profound experiences that would expand the dispositional traits of candidates. In most cases, programs kept the previous dispositional processes intact.

Throughout the program meetings and follow-up conversations, the dispositional framework helped build support for integrating additional experiences that enable candidates to participate in more proactive change processes and to apprentice with faculty as we model change efforts with our public school colleagues. For example, in the elementary education program, one faculty member now integrates tutoring and assistance at the local homeless shelter into his literacy class. That example has motivated other programs to consider planning intensive experiences that guide candidates across the framework.

While program areas have submitted drafts of their revised programs, conversations about dispositions are still in the early stages. We made three recommendations to our associate dean. First, we called for an overarching school framework regarding professionalism. Second, we suggested expanding our office of professional experiences to include community outreach and service learning. Third, we proposed revising the school's conceptual framework to reflect more clearly the need for teachers to develop dispositions related to serving young people and their families. The associate dean agreed to incorporate these matters into the rollout of the new programs this year.

TABLE 7.3   A sample of program changes reflecting increased emphasis on leadership to serve diverse learners and their families

Elementary education	Required community service opportunities and increased diverse field experiences
Special education	Home visits and enhanced field experiences with diverse learners
Secondary Education	Focused tutoring and teaching in high-need schools, revamped introductory course, new diversity course, and community experiences
Middle grades education	Stronger emphasis on leadership roles during internship, with special focus on promoting interdisciplinary teaming, parent/school/community partnerships
	Stronger focus of field experiences on community literacy through tutoring at-risk students in their specialty area
	Opportunities to complete a portion of the internship abroad in order to foster global awareness
Master's in curriculum, instruction, and assessment	Revised dispositional framework in program
	Developing and embedding opportunities for student advocacy within the program

While we still need agreement on an overarching vision for teacher education as a unit, the main challenge for initial licensure programs is increasing dynamic classroom, school, and community experiences; guiding candidates through these experiences; and reflecting with them about their growth and the opportunities to raise achievement and promote school success. Table 7.3 presents early examples of changes proposed by various programs that increase candidates' opportunities to grow in the areas of our framework.

Working at the State Level

As one of sixteen campuses in the University of North Carolina (UNC) system, our school works inside multiple layers of bureaucracy. We report to the UNC general administration that houses the university president. We also report at the state level to the North Carolina Department of Public Instruction and the state board of education. Our programs operate as part of both state systems. Because individual programs cannot invent in a vacuum, we shared our ideas related to the new standards and dispositions with Kathy Sullivan, the chief liaison for teacher education from the state board of education.

With Sullivan's assistance, we sponsored a webinar for all teacher education programs in North Carolina where we shared our content analysis, rationale and framework and invited colleagues to see the new standards as a tipping point moving us to integrate dispositions into the fabric of our programs. We pointed out that most of the indicators and elements in standards 1, 2, and 5 are dispositional and that dispositions are also a prominent part of standards 3 and 4. We made clear that standards 1 and 2 give priority to leadership for serving diverse students and their families. Instead of treating dispositions as a separate category alongside knowledge and skills, the new standards invite us to treat dispositions as integrally connected to content and pedagogy. This challenges us to provide enhanced experiences early on in programs in and beyond the classroom.

One hundred fifty participants, including associate deans of education from most of North Carolina's forty-eight public and private teacher education institutions, joined the webinar. Follow-up meetings reinforced the integrated nature of dispositions. Hopefully, our work has assisted the state in promoting teacher education programs to look very different from current practice. The major differences will be demonstrated in how candidates are prepared to teach diverse learners and to serve as proactive advocates for students and their families at the classroom, school, and community levels. These activities at the state level helped us gain traction inside our own building.

Impact on the Secondary Program

In response to the new state standards, the secondary education faculty has created a new, cohort-based program specifically for future high school teachers. This increases the influence of the secondary faculty on candidates' development. In the past, we were frustrated that candidates enrolling in their final semester before their internship often displayed inappropriate beliefs about students, like the ones quoted at the start of this chapter. Since the new program began, the five faculty members teaching the block 1 courses have been in frequent communication regarding our dispositional expectations of candidates.

This kind of collaboration is key to refining and sharing our views regarding candidate dispositions. Our next step is to engage the entire secondary faculty in developing a clear programwide statement about our purposes, our identity as a faculty, and our expectations about desirable knowledge, skills, and dispositions and how to develop them. We recognize the need to monitor candidates' development from the beginning of the program through guided field experiences so that we can help candidates grow beyond the traditional, race-, class-, and gender-biased environments in which they were raised and schooled. Our aim is not to weed candidates out but to assist them in understanding their own biases, ignorance, and prejudices and to use our shared high school classroom and community experiences to facilitate their growth into caring and competent teacher leaders. When necessary, we must also be able to encourage or require candidates to withdraw from the program, and we are still working on that process.

Developing and Assessing Dispositions

As with all programmatic change, we are keenly aware of the need to measure our influence. How will we know whether we have adequately nurtured and guided candidates who do not enter the program as shining stars? For the pre–student teacher who is reluctant to see her role in closing achievement gaps or the intern who wishes all of his students were like him, we are attempting to design a dispositional assessment plan that will (1) identify evidence of teacher candidates' dispositional growth or struggles in relation to the different pillars of our framework; (2) analyze teacher candidates' needs in terms of dispositional development; and (3) provide the readings, reflections, guidance, and other experiences necessary to assist teacher candidates in moving forward as leaders for diverse learners.

The successful implementation of this assessment process will depend on our faculty's readiness and preparation to identify teacher candidates' needs and to take the first steps in providing necessary help and support. Therefore, our proposed assessment plan will incorporate training of education school faculty members and cooperating teachers to use and analyze assessment results and, more importantly, to provide candidates with necessary support to address dispositional concerns that arise. We see our assessment of dispositions following a six-phase, formative process that spans the program from recruitment to induction.

First, we will push for a clear articulation of what we expect of our graduates in terms of knowledge, skills and dispositions, given our framework and the new standards. If potential candidates are aware of our dispositional expectations prior to admission, we may create a culture of leadership for diverse learners from the start and rightly dissuade some from even applying. The other obvious benefit of a clear articulation of beliefs is a formative metric by which to nudge and support candidate growth and readiness for field placements, internships, and graduation.

Second, we plan to develop new dispositional tools and modify existing instruments (e.g., self-assessments, observation instruments) to capture data on our candidates. These assessments will include a teacher candidate self-assessment, a candidate assessment completed by education faculty, and a candidate assessment completed by a cooperating teacher. Faculty members from all teacher education programs and representatives from our public school partners will participate in developing these assessments.

Completing a self-assessment can raise candidates' awareness of their own dispositional characteristics and fosters self-reflection. It can also reinforce bias and prejudice if responses are not discussed. We plan to use self-assessments as checkpoints to guide reflection about course assignments and about school and community experiences that challenge biases and prejudices, and to provide opportunities for increasing open-mindedness and willingness to use the program experiences to prepare to become a caring, passionate teacher for all students. Further, conferences with faculty and teacher candidates about self-assessment results combined with observations will help minimize the limitations of self-reported data.

Adding field experiences and service learning opportunities to the programs should help improve candidates' understandings of their students' lives. Field experience conferences with cooperating teachers will take on a coaching format in which candidates are challenged to reflect on their teaching practices, content knowledge, and dispositions. We will also provide opportunities for interactions with community organizations and families to promote growth in leadership and understanding of diversity.

We also plan to revise the way we currently assess candidates during the student teaching semester. Using a scaffolding process, candidates discuss information with partnership teachers at multiple stages during the semester. These coaching cycles allow us to assess candidates' dispositions while providing them with opportunities to reflect on their dispositional aptitudes. Using cognitive coaching as a foundation, our school currently trains cooperating teachers in the coaching process.[21] We will embed specific training and examples related to the dispositional frameworks into these training sessions. Candidate work products, such as lesson plans, and data from intern evaluations will serve as evidence in the assessment of candidates' dispositions. At the end of the internship, teacher candidates are assessed using an Intern Performance Scale linked to the North Carolina Professional Teaching Standards that focuses on content knowledge, pedagogical skill, and dispositional success as emerging leaders to serve diverse learners.

After completing the internship successfully, teacher candidates will fill out another version of the self-assessment they completed in the third stage. Results of this post-self-assessment can then be compared with results of the preassessment and with mentors' rankings, and candidates will be given a chance to reflect on their growth with their mentors. Those recommended for licensure will leave our programs with specific goals for continuing to refine their content, pedagogy, and dispositions.

CONCLUSION

During our state and NCATE accreditation team visits in 2005, our programs were highlighted as strengths. Our systems were in place, our processes of gathering evidence were clear, and our use of data for program improvement was obvious. However, the recent experience of revising our programs in light of new standards, No Child Left Behind, and our professional understandings revealed that we lacked a common vision for teacher education centered on teacher leadership and student advocacy. We had not thought hard enough about our major purposes as teacher educators. The four of us continue to work with colleagues in evolving, enacting, and assessing our dispositions framework. And we continue to advocate for change within our programs, across our school of education, and at the state level in order to prepare teachers with the knowledge, skills, and dispositions they need to be effective leaders for diverse learners—indeed, for all learners.

CHAPTER EIGHT

Making the Path by Walking

Eleni Katsarou

Editors' Case Introdution: University of Illinois at Chicago

The University of Illinois at Chicago (UIC) is a state-funded public research university located in Chicago, Illinois. Part of the University of Illinois system, UIC is the largest university in the Chicago area, serving approximately 26,000 students in 15 colleges, including the nation's larges medical school, with research expenditures exceeding $340 million and consistently in the top 50 U.S. institutions for research expenditures.

The UIC College of Education (COE) offers baccalaureate, master's, and doctoral programs to students seeking to become certified teachers, principals, and other school personnel, and to students seeking to become researchers, policy makers, or community-based organizational leaders. The COE teacher preparation program operates in partnership with the Chicago Public Schools, placing students in four semesters of intensive, school-based fieldwork in urban sites.

"Making the Path by Walking" is the story of how one faculty member, working collaboratively with a group of long-term cooperating teachers, created, piloted, and revised a formative assessment tool directly focused on a set of dispositional domains and teaching practices. The tool, the Development of Ethical and Caring Actions in Urban Teaching (DECA-UT), became a vehicle for articulating a shared vision of good urban teaching for the undergraduate and graduate initial teacher preparation programs in elementary education at UIC.

This formative assessment tool ensures that each teacher candidate is provided with opportunities to engage in critical self-reflection about his or her own skills, knowledge, and dispositions in the urban teaching context. The tool also structures conversations in the mentor/candidate dyad, focused on nurtur-

ing and monitoring the teacher candidate's knowledge, skills, and dispositions. The figures provide a clear and useful picture, for one of the dispositions, of the definition, self-reflection prompts, and rating forms.

• • • • •

> Selection and retention of potential teachers who are committed to all students is a key issue, but we must also be clear and direct about the knowledge, skills, and dispositions that we expect of our candidates.[1]

TEACHER PREPARATION AND THE DEVELOPMENT OF URBAN TEACHERS

At UIC, a major aim across all the school personnel preparation programs is to graduate committed, knowledgeable, and effective educators. In our College of Education (COE), we expect our candidates to dedicate themselves to the continuing development of their own abilities to educate all students in the face of social and educational inequalities rooted in race, class, language, gender, disability, and other social differences. In addition to this, we want our teacher candidates to commit to the democratic ideal of developing all students' potential and seek remedies to such inequalities, take appropriate action, and motivate students to do the same. And finally, we expect our candidates to dedicate themselves to understanding and valuing the cultural and linguistic wealth of each student's community, and to collaborate with other professionals and community members to support student success.

These expectations are a tall order, especially in light of recent changes in our institution. Unlike in years past when our pool of entering students was predominantly white and female, we now have a far more diverse student body. Concomitant with this change, we have also have begun deliberately exploring how to promote candidates' *willingness* to teach in underserved urban schools. This emanates from our explicit and well-publicized commitment to developing *urban educators*—professionals deeply knowledgeable about how culture, language, and poverty shape and influence students' lives, and how to use cultural and linguistic diversity as assets in the classroom.

Like many colleges of education with a similar commitment to urban education, we have looked to specify *dispositions* crucial to successful preparation of teachers for urban schools. A group of cooperating teachers and I, a clinical professor in the teacher preparation programs, have been engaged in this work for a few years. Most recently, in a joint effort with the Chicago Public Schools (CPS), we have been creating, piloting, and revising a formative assessment tool directly focused on a set of dispositional domains and teaching practice, named the Development of Ethical and Caring Actions in Urban Teaching (DECA-UT). This case will examine the development of effective and caring urban teachers in our program by describing our process of the enactment of dispositions using the formative assessment tool to develop our desired dispositions in field-based practice.

The Emergence of a Relationship: Fieldwork and Mentorship Conceptualizations

In my role as field instructor, I typically work with twenty to thirty teacher candidates each academic year, which includes setting up their fieldwork placements in urban classrooms. This approach to teacher preparation takes place in the two elementary programs (baccalaureate and graduate) at UIC, not in the other seventeen programs at UIC; rather, it is idiosyncratic and more common in the two elementary education programs in the COE. In my role as field instructor, I have formed deep relationships with numerous CPS elementary schools and a selected number of teachers at each site. In total, I have worked with approximately fifty cooperating teachers and in approximately fifteen schools. Attrition rarely happens, and most of these teachers have mentored candidates from our elementary education programs for many consecutive years.

Of the fifty or so cooperating teachers, my closest school partners number around thirty and are practicing in seven schools. My relationship with this tighter group of thirty teachers includes members of a *second generation* of mentors, folks who graduated from our teacher education program and are now mentoring candidates. Indeed, this relationship with the thirty or so teachers has become stronger and deeper as the academic years accrue and the number of candidates that we collectively mentor increases. Clearly, these relationships, perhaps as all good relationships go, rest partly on good fortune, but in fact, they are not entirely happenstance. My working relationship with these cooperating teachers is dependent on three connections: (1) our common understanding and deep caring for urban students; (2) our similar perceptions of good teaching practice, especially as this relates to teacher candidates' learning and development; and (3) our commitment to, and investment in, learning from the practices of collaborating in the field instruction of our candidates. This means that, in order to develop dispositions of caring and effective practice in urban contexts, we have to *live* the dispositions we espouse throughout the collaborative professional work of our field practice.

Much of what we would consider opportunities for "dispositional work" occurs in the settings of practica. During student teaching especially, candidates spend the majority of their time in the fieldwork placements at schools where they are observed and assessed on a daily basis by their mentor teachers. As field instructors, we observe the developing practice of our candidates teaching in front of live students, four to six times during their student teaching practicum, for about an hour each time, and with an equal amount of time holding a pre- as well as a postobservation conference. It is not unusual for me, as a field instructor, to conduct three-way, postobservation conferences with the critical *triad* of candidate, mentor, and myself. Much depends on how carefully we are able to collectively reflect upon the important dispositions for caring and effective practice in the course of our interactions in field-based instruction.

In looking back over hundreds of such conversations, the comments that related to classroom practice were sometimes captured in the documentation of our candidates' evolving practice, and at other times they were not. Thus, while we always made use of observation forms printed in triplicate—a copy for each member of the important triad—this process often left some of the expert mentors and myself wanting a more thorough, consistent, and developmental approach to the assessment of the teacher candidates. In fact, it was this perceived missing aspect of our work with the candidates that provided the impetus for undertaking the development of a formative assessment tool—the DECA-UT.

As I recall many postobservation conferences, I remember making such cryptic comments as "We need you to be a bit more *culturally responsive* here" or "How about being more *resourceful* in this lesson?" Although I might have had a particular practice or action in mind when providing feedback on an observed lesson, as time went on, I realized that such comments were vague and quite possibly inconsequential. I asked myself, "How could I more systematically animate the dispositions of 'cultural responsiveness' and 'pedagogical resourcefulness?'" I assumed that by virtue of my established relationships with the cooperating teachers and the volume of observed lessons they conducted in an academic year's time, my partners would be able to further shape and reinforce the development of these dispositions in candidates in their formative comments to the candidates over time. Was this too much to expect? Could we depend on the quality of two-way and three-way interactions to sufficiently develop dispositions?

Besides the uncertainty about whether we were making a considerable difference with our comments, the larger assessment aspect of the candidates became especially troublesome and raised the following questions for all of us, both the experienced mentors and me, as the field instructor: What might we use as *evidence* so that we could see how and to what extent each teacher candidate was thoughtfully addressing our guidance? How could we ensure that each teacher candidate was provided with opportunities to engage in *critical self-reflection* about his or her own *skills, knowledge and dispositions* in the teaching context in which he or she was placed? In what ways could we understand and assess the willingness and sophistication of teacher candidates' sensibilities, and how would we determine whether they would be *amenable to development*? If there were candidates who entered the program at different levels of *willingness* and *understandings, how* could we differentiate between developmental levels for the purpose of developing candidates?

The Design of the DECA-UT: Phase 1

With support from a teacher quality grant that our college dean had procured, we began exploring what our candidates brought with them as they entered the COE and in what ways we could monitor their development during their time they spent with us. We began an inquiry to identify what knowledge, skills, and dispositions were needed in order to become thoughtful urban teachers. Moreover, assuming that all these skills and sensibilities could be adequately identified, we were also interested in developing ways to make these apparent and tangible to the teacher candidates. During this deliberative period, I also realized that I needed to turn to the field and approach a group of my closest collaborators in teacher education—the cooperating teachers with whom I had worked successfully for a number of years. I was interested in finding out what assessment tool we could design together that would allow for *conversations to take place* in the mentor/candidate dyad, and that would also have a sharp focus on how these knowledge/dispositions could be nurtured and monitored. As mentioned earlier, the relationship between a particular set of mentor teachers and myself had developed fully, and in retrospect, it was precisely because of the *nature* of our existing relationship that the teacher candidate assessment void became prominent. As I examine the journey, I can say with confidence that our collaborative work was motivated by a desire to formalize and actualize the rich and deep conversations we were having together about the skills, practice, sensibilities, and dispositions of urban teaching. We recognized the need to concretize what we collectively deemed as critical attributes in an urban teacher candidate and ensure that our candidates would have opportunities to observe and practice caring and ethical actions in classrooms. On that basis we could trust that with particular and explicit pathways, they would grow and develop over the course of their time with us.

The first working version of the DECA-UT emerged at the end of the school year in 2005. After some recrafting and editing, we piloted it during the 2005–2006 academic year, with twenty mentor/candidate dyads in the elementary education program. Two meetings were held with a subgroup of these twenty mentors to examine the instrument's utility. Both meetings were recorded, transcribed, and analyzed. For the following two academic years, 2006–2008, as the DECA-UT was being refined and finalized, the Council on Teacher Education (CTE), which oversees and supports all nineteen teacher education programs at UIC, made mandatory the inclusion of dispositions in the assessment of all teacher and educator candidates. Thus, the DECA-UT became widely available to all the program coordinators when we instituted a number of training sessions on its use and implementation. Numerous programs adopted the DECA-UT during this two-year period, albeit with slight modifications to the original.

The DECA-UT in Its Current Form: Final Design and Implementation

During the last two years of this project and while the DECA-UT was still in its pilot phase, an additional relationship pattern and version of the tool emerged. Eight cooperating teachers were also my former students, having matriculated from the same program, and were mentoring teacher candidates using the DECA-UT. This new community of eight folks is a configuration of participants that includes two members from the original Ithaca School group while including six new cooperating teachers. Having met twice during the summer of 2007 and in several monthly meetings in 2008, this group made its impact by sharpening the DECA-UT.

In its current form, it is certain that the tool is reflecting changes based on both the original and the second group's deep understanding of the university programs and our urban schools' mission. While the major aim of this recrafting was identical to the first group's intent of preparing effective urban teachers, the final form of the DECA-UT is well expanded and includes a wider range of skills and dispositional domains. Lastly, in its current form, the DECA-UT's adoption is much wider than ever before: both the undergraduate and the graduate elementary education programs are using it as the main formative and summative assessment tool and at earlier times during the candidates' educational journey; and numerous Liberal Arts and Sciences (LAS) teacher preparation programs are now implementing it as it has become readily available as an online tool on the CTE Web site.

The DECA-UT as Tool to Good Practice: Structure and Use

By using the DECA-UT in the last few years, we have accomplished the operationalization and translation of the six identified dispositional domains into viable actions, in particular settings, and under certain conditions. The six dispositional domains and paths into practice are cultural and contextual understanding, adaptation and flexibility, initiative and risk taking, dedication and personal investment, resourcefulness and organizational development, and awareness and thoughtfulness about teaching.

Each dispositional domain is considered in terms of a succinct *definition* and three *developmental levels*—initial, developing, and advancing. At least one *performance indicator* is tied to each developmental level. For every performance indicator and its adjoining developmental level, there are a number of *possible actions* that exemplify and concretize the performance indicator and larger domain. All of the above components constitute the Understanding and Practice Opportunities section of the DECA-UT. To illustrate, the domain cultural and contextual understanding can be viewed in figure 8.1.

It is in the explicitness of the definitions, performance indicators, and possible actions that the structured conversations materialize between the cooperating teacher and the teacher candidate, as well as with the university instructor. Across the critical student teaching semester, it has been our experience that the suggested actions in particular, which are clear and unambiguous, become the major tool with which we continually discuss how theory relates to practice and with which we docu-

FIGURE 8.1   Cultural and contextual understanding dispositional domain: Disposition #1   Cultural and Contextual Understanding

Section I: Understanding/Practice Opportunities

Definition: TC recognizes and appreciates diverse cultures, languages, and ethnic heritages, particularly as they intersect with race, social class, and gender. The TC also seeks to understand the social, political, and economic contexts of the school and the community and seeks to understand how these affect both teaching and learning in the classroom.

The performance indicators for this disposition are presented here.
Actions serve as examples and are not an exhaustive list of possible actions.
These are referenced in the weekly seminar.

PERFORMANCE INDICATORS (1–4):

1) *Initial Level: Embraces the students' communities through word, deed, and personal connections.* Demonstrates this orientation with the following *actions* or their equivalents:

Possible Actions
   • Writes a letter of introduction to the students' parents and communicates own availability for conversations—as negotiated with CT and/or principal.
   • Attends a community event (e.g., service at worship center, makes purchases at neighborhood store, participates in community recreational experience).
   • Does a "community walk" either in the immediate surrounding of school or in its "feeder community."
   • Recognizes that kindergarten or sixth-grade students have a culture and age/specific artifacts and significant events that impact teaching and learning.
   • Gathers school information and asks students to do an autobiography and provides opportunities for all to share.

2) *Developing Level: Understands the difference between the neighborhood school and selective enrollment schools (e.g., magnet, voluntary transfer), including the difference in the ideological, political, and economic origins of each.* Demonstrates this orientation with the following *actions* or their equivalents:

Possible Actions
   • Revisits the premises of the (junior-year/ED 350) *School and Community Project*—and conducts interviews, observes, acts as "ethnographer" in the school/community.
   • Arranges for a visit in another school within the immediate surrounding of the FW site.

3) *Advancing Level: Recognizes the education of all children as a moral endeavor, with ethical and sociopolitical significance, and appreciates parents' aspirations and fears about their children.* Demonstrates this orientation with the following *actions* or their equivalents:

Possible Actions
   • Seeks ways to connect with a parent by sharing a success or concern via a telephone call, note, or home visit.
   • Approaches students' communication styles and ways of being with respect and intellectual curiosity.
   • Incorporates a cultural component to design a lesson (e.g., reads books aloud by authors of the school community culture).

- Selects literature with an urban or multicultural theme (e.g., *Felita, Bronx Masquerade*) and integrates into existing grade-level curriculum.
- Highlights contributions of those representing other cultures, classes, linguistic groups, genders, especially as these relate to the specific content areas (e.g., designs an integrated thematic unit on the *Harlem Renaissance*).
- Incorporates local views/*funds of knowledge* by suggesting or organizing resources, events, topics as ways to enrich the existing curriculum.
- Collaborates with local/community organization(s) to better understand students and parents. For example, working with a local health facility and having students engage in a new sport activity or arranging with the local *Boys and Girls Club* for an event/ activity.

4) *Advancing Level: Has a vision of equity and the courage to be an advocate for all children by adopting an antiracist/antioppressive stance.*

   Possible Actions
- Creates and implements consistently and consciously the perspective of the cultural or ideological "other" in many areas of the curriculum. E.g., provides students with opportunities to conduct inquiries (via surveying and interviewing) into the community on the topic of *nutrition*. On the topic of *genetics* and in an all-Latino school, TC has students understand the definitions related to racial characteristics.
- Plans literacy events and conducts in-class discussions that expose the educational, social, and political injustices by historicizing particular groups' literary and lore traditions.
- Seeks local artists and community folks to visit the classroom as primary sources, or organizes a field trip that is tightly related to a socially relevant topic.

ment and are able to rate the teacher candidates' progress. Nonetheless, at three distinct intervals of the student teaching semester, at weeks 3, 6, and 12, the cooperating teacher/teacher candidate dyad has formal sit-down conversations. These constitute the Critical Self-Reflection section of the DECA-UT and can be seen in figure 8.2.

At week 3, both the teacher candidate and the cooperating teacher come to the meeting prepared by having thought about, or written in the case of the candidate, their respective answers to *guiding questions*, which are intended as invitations and entrées for the dyad's initial conversation. Essentially, the teacher candidate brings to the table as a form of introduction her or his essays/responses to the questions for each of the six domains. At the sit-down conversations for weeks 6 and 12, the teacher candidate/cooperating teacher dyad uses this time to document the individual candidate's actions in the internship site; to provide the teacher candidate with an opportunity to self-reflect by bringing to the meeting journal entries and other forms of documentation; and to jointly assign a rating of the teacher candidate's growth by developmental level (initial,

**FIGURE 8.2   Critical Self-Reflection section of the DECA-UT
Disposition #1 Cultural and Contextual Understanding: Week 2 Guiding Questions**

Section II: Critical Self-Reflection

Guiding/Essential Questions for the Teacher Candidate (TC): Define your sense of
the term *culture*. Refer to your *own* cultural identity from the perspective of your self-
perceptions/memberships to various subgroups within the larger culture. Based on these
reflections and the recommended actions above, what is your stance about *cultural teaching*
and how do you hope to enact this in your classroom?

Guiding Questions for the Cooperating Teacher (CT): How have I illustrated the
importance of my own culture to my TC and classroom students? What have I done to learn
about my students' culture? How have the larger community perspectives and concerns
entered my classroom curriculum?

developing, or advancing). It is important to point out that although the notion of "critical self-reflection," as the term itself denotes, is primarily a *self*-reflection for the teacher candidate to be checking herself or himself, it has been our experience that the ways in which the all-important conversations in the dyad are instantiated determine the candidate's development, as indicated in figure 8.3 for week 6; an identical documentation/rating is used for week 12.

To illustrate how the DECA-UT approach works in concretizing candidates' theoretical understanding into viable and tangible actions by having them critically reflect on their classroom practice, I will offer two excerpts from the Critical Self-Reflection section of the tool.

The first excerpt is from a teacher candidate's week 6 documentation and journal entry, which prompted the teacher candidate/cooperating teacher dyad to rate this candidate with a *developing* level rating, on initiative and risk taking, based on the DECA-UT's suggested actions.

Teacher candidate's reflection—rating of developing stage, week 6:

(1) [I wrote an] Introductory letter to parents; (2) [I became] Widely available to parents; (3) [I initiated] Contact with parents, thought mostly about behavioral issues; (4) [I related with the students' pain and recovery and visited after school the] Murder site visitation/support [NOTE: a 14-year-old boy from the school was shot and killed during this time, and the teacher candidate made some major decisions as to how to acknowledge this event and honor the pupils' voices]; (5) Coached football after school and raised [own] funds to purchase uniforms.[1]

FIGURE 8.3   Disposition #1   Cultural and contextual understanding: Week 6 documentation/rating

Please document the TC's actions in the developmental column that best fits the action. For your convenience, the performance indicators for each developmental level are listed.

Definition: TC recognizes and appreciates diverse cultures, languages, and ethnic heritages, particularly as they intersect with race, social class, and gender. The TC also seeks to understand the social, political, and economic contexts of the school and the community and seeks to understand how these affect both teaching and learning in the classroom.

Initial	Developing	Advancing
Embraces the students' cultures through word, deed, and personal connections.	Understands the difference between neighborhood school and selective enrollment schools (e.g., magnet, voluntary transfer), including the difference in the ideological, political, and economic origins of each.	Recognizes the education of all children as a moral endeavor with ethical and sociopolitical significance, and appreciates parents' aspirations and fears about their children. Has a vision of equity and the courage to be an advocate for all children by adopting an antiracist/antioppressive stance.

RATING

(Please place an X at the point that best indicates the TC's current *overall* development)

←—————————————————————————————————→

The second excerpt is from week 12, and in this instance, the agreed-upon developmental level rating for this teacher candidate at week 12 is *advancing*. Here is the teacher candidate's entry at week 12, in which he articulates how his topic of study with his students mirrors the suggested actions in the DECA-UT:

With this unit "Our World and Our Place In It" students saw how work done or studied in school applies to the real world . . . When students see what they are learning is important not only in school but in the world in which they live, they begin to develop an interest in learning. Another intention of this unit was for my students to become "aware." . . . Also, once my students are able to become aware of certain things (i.e., inequalities in America) I hope that this unit will teach them to act on this knowledge . . . Even though my students are only 10 or 11 [years of age], they will learn how to become activists, whether that is in school, at home, in their community, their city, their nation, or someone else's situation . . . This unit is personal and meaningful to me because I am strong advocate of equality [in the US] and [making] African-American history [known] . . . I embraced the students' culture through tangible experiences and personal connections, [such as having students] survey the local community and family members about issues affecting gun violence, [providing the students with opportunities to engage in] organizing and anti-gun/violence assembly and bringing in [local community member/author of Our America] LeAlan Jones to speak to the students.

The last excerpt here is the cooperating teacher's feedback on the week 12 conversation and documentation.

Cooperating teacher feedback, week 12:
[TC] fully understands the community of learners both within the class [grade 5] and within the entire school and its community. Though he sometimes feels and shows frustration at the systemic problems, he empowers our students by giving them the chance to read and write powerfully and in socially relevant ways.

It is important to note that because the development of each teacher candidate is monitored and rated at two intervals (at weeks 6 and 12), the university seminar is yet another space in which we discuss and deepen the teacher candidate's understandings and knowledge of practice by revisiting the dispositional domains and by closely examining and discussing the individual teacher candidate enactments of these. In fact, by engaging in this intentionally recursive manner (i.e., in the Understanding and Practice Opportunities and Critical Self-Reflection sections/phases), we are in a better position to assess the candidate's own willingness to accept ideas and suggestions, and therefore gauge their level of development. During the course of this project, we remained certain that the range of the developmental levels among our teacher candidates necessitates that the performance indicators and their respective actions be concretely developmental and both reflect our high expectations and, at the same time, offer a classification of the suggested actions by difficulty level and sophistication. This approach is based in our inherent belief that our approach and tool are mainly designed to support and nurture our teacher candidates across the dispositional domains and skills of practice.

LESSONS LEARNED

We have come to understand that the tool itself, as well as this approach to teacher preparation and assessment, is useful because we have been able to provide our teacher candidates with the following explicit ways of teaching and learning. First, the *actions* that define and describe each dispositional domain constitute an entrée for deep discussion and conceptual development at the university seminar and as such build candidates' necessary knowledge and understandings prior to entering the field. Second, as the actions are observed in the fieldwork classroom, candidates are provided with opportunities to *practice* these under the aegis of their mentors. Third, teacher candidates engage in *conversations* with their mentors that enable the candidates' critical *self-reflection* and an occasion to be formatively assessed by the mentor on the observed performances or actions. Eventually, of course, the extent to which the actions are the perceived embodiments of the dispositions, a summative evaluation of the teacher candidates both at the seminar and in the fieldwork classroom is additionally formulated.

There are two key elements in the development of the desired dispositions: namely, in the concepts of the identified *actions* and in the practice of the *dialogic conversations*. The actions are mere demonstrations and are not meant to be an exhaustive list of possible fieldwork events. In fact, our assumption is that the dispositions can be nurtured in very particular, explicit, and developmental ways, and as many of the suggested actions are framed actions within content area teaching (e.g., science, social studies), they help candidates concretize a particular disposition within a content domain.

It has been our experience that the ways in which a candidate realizes some or all of the illustrative actions determine that person's willingness to embrace all that was theorized or understood at the university setting. That is, teacher candidates who see that their actions can embody a disposition within a concrete teaching event are more likely to continue to develop the disposition.

The second sacred aspect of the DECA-UT is the conversations between the candidate and the mentor that provide the dyad with guiding questions around each dispositional domain. Sustained efforts of the mentor to advance the candidate's dispositional knowledge are evidenced in the two formal sit-down conversations and at more regular intervals through informal discussions. The more formal conversations occur at weeks 6 and 12 of a 15-week student teaching practicum.

As we examine the past five years' practices and the ways in which we have reconceptualized the development and assessment of teacher candidates who are preparing to become urban teachers, we are clear about what we believe are important considerations for all teacher education programs, but especially those in urban environments. Consistent with the important contributions of scholars on the key notions about effective and transformative urban teaching, our approach to teacher preparation addresses and synthesizes three key "learnings."

First, we are well convinced that the route to desirable and sound *practice* is in the introduction, specificity, and elaboration of the major dispositions and sensibilities in situ. That is, we believe that the dispositions and sensibilities we are looking for in our teacher candidates—toward becoming effective, nourishing, and culturally responsive urban teachers—are those we should be enacting daily in the course of our work. The formative assessment tool has helped us focus on those dispositions in a systematic way. The six identified domains are presented to the candidates with a clarity and transparency that also adhere to Lisa Delpit's insistence that, as teacher educators, we need to inspire and transform teachers with explicit, tangible examples that can be accessed with ease.[2] Our contribution is in deciphering for teacher candidates the rather abstract notions about teaching into viable actions in practice.

Second, our structured approach of presenting our candidates with definitions, performance indicators, and possible actions is aligned with developmental levels. We begin where each candidate is developmentally, and aim to support them in their growth via deliberate and guided conversations and critical self-reflection. Our trust in our students' development is in concert with the necessary aspect reflection of self-assessment in teacher preparation.

Third, the collaboration that has evolved between the university and the partnering teachers is defined precisely and expressly for the interrogation of what constitutes caring and ethical practice in urban sites. With every end of the academic year as a new cohort of graduates exits our program and enters the teaching profession, we have found it necessary to keep refining our tool, the DECA-UT. In doing so, we have discovered new ways to become even clearer and more explicit. Peter Murrell's central ideas of community teacher and circle of practice have been an inspiration for this community of teacher educators as we deliberated on the construction of the DECA-UT and we brought it to fruition.[3]

CHAPTER NINE

Defining, Developing, and Assessing Dispositions: A Cross-Case Analysis

Sharon Feiman-Nemser and Deborah L. Schussler

How can these seven cases help teacher educators think more clearly about the role of dispositions in teaching and teacher education? What can we learn from these narratives about what it means and what it takes to conceptualize, develop, and assess professional dispositions for teaching? To answer these questions, we conducted a cross-case analysis of the institutional narratives, probing for patterns, insights, and lessons for the field. In this chapter, we share what we found in order to help readers see more clearly what we can learn from those teacher educators whose work and thinking are represented in this book. Hopefully, this will advance our collective efforts to help teacher candidates integrate ways of thinking, knowing, caring, and acting into a principled teaching practice that promotes ambitious learning for all students.

CONCEPTUALIZING DISPOSITIONS

Conceptualizing dispositions is as much about a process as it is about an end product. When taken seriously, conceptualization includes the relational and intellectual work of developing a shared, moral vision within and across programs.[1] The work is intellectual when faculty grapple with the question of "how life ought to be lived in the unit."[2] The work is relational when faculty proceed not from "authoritative fiat but from a sense of belonging."[3] The work of conceptualization also creates a vital foundation; how teacher educators conceptualize dispositions has implications for how they choose to develop and then assess dispositions in their programs. Conceptualization consists of the following processes: (1) *defining*—delineating what the educators mean when they use the term *disposition*; (2) *enumerating*—determining the specific dispositions that the faculty of the unit wish to espouse; and (3) *justifying*—rationalizing the moral imperative the faculty of the unit possess for developing particular commitments and inclinations in their teacher candidates.

Defining

A number of educators treat the lack of a shared definition of dispositions as one reason why dispositions should not be used as a viable construct in teacher education.[4] While achieving complete consensus is appealing, it may prove unnecessary, as our case writers demonstrate. Despite the absence of a shared definition, we found commonalities in how these institutions define dispositions. Since the units did their work, including the writing of their cases, independently of each other, the commonalities suggest that teacher educators believe dispositions embrace similar concepts. The field has not reached consensus on the construct, but if the comparable definitions offered by our case writers are an accurate representation of the field, the range of definitions is less extensive than critics like to claim.

The first pattern we noticed is that five of the seven cases provide a formal definition of *disposition,* and these five definitions include a reference to actions or behaviors. The University of Southern Maine (USM) and the University of Wisconsin-Eau Claire (UWEC) employ definitions that echo the early definition (1985) of Lilian Katz and James Raths, who define dispositions as "the trend of a teacher's actions in particular contexts."[5] According to USM, dispositions are the "tendency to act or react in characteristic ways in certain situations." UWEC uses the same definition but replaces the word *tendency* with *choice* to highlight the teacher's agency (see Hollon, Kolis, McIntyre, Stephens, and Battalio, chapter 6 this volume). Several institutions extend the definition beyond patterned actions to include the idea of predictive behavior based on beliefs.[6] Although their definition lacks any cause-effect implications, the definition adopted by Winthrop University aligns with Villegas's idea that teachers' dispositions involve not just their behaviors, but also their professional judgments. Winthrop states that dispositions are a "trend in judgments, behaviors, and reflections over time" (see Johnson, Evers, and Vare, chapter 3 this volume).

The University of North Carolina Wilmington (UNCW) also relates dispositions to something other than just behaviors, though they are less specific about what this additional component means. They state that dispositions can be defined as "who we are and how we behave," implying that a teacher's actions are related to his or her identity (see Fischetti, Imig, Ndoye, and Smith, chapter 7 this volume). While the University of Cincinnati's definition does not initially include behaviors, their analysis of their candidate vignettes revealed that "dispositions are composed of multifaceted skills, understandings and attitudes which need serious cultivation" (see Laine, Bauer, Johnson, Kroeger, Troup, and Meyer, chapter 4 this volume). By including skills, understandings, and attitudes in their definition of dispositions, they underscore the complexity and interrelatedness of the construct. It should also be noted that the two case narratives that do not offer a formal definition of dispositions—the University of Illinois at Chicago (UIC) and the Boettcher Teachers Program at the University of Denver—nonetheless incorporate behaviors with commitments in the specific dispositions they enumerate.

Although none of these definitions are exactly the same, by folding behaviors, actions, or skills into the meaning of dispositions, the case writers acknowledge that dispositions entail what teachers have the ability to put into practice. In other words, dispositions are interrelated with knowledge and skills and cannot be separated.[7] Teaching, like any professional practice, combines habits of mind, hand, and heart, or the knowledge, skills, and commitments of the teacher.[8] The construct of dispositions provides a means to demonstrate the interrelationship among these. Acknowledgment of this interrelationship serves more than just an analytical purpose. If, conceptually, dispositions are interrelated with knowledge and skills, then it is misguided to separate them in practice. By conceptualizing dispositions in this way, the case writers imply that teacher educators seeking to develop and assess dispositions cannot do so by disentangling them from knowledge and skills. Rather, teacher educators must address them together.

The other three patterns evident in the conceptualizations offered by the case writers are less prevalent. The second pattern involves context. Half of the definitions indicate the importance of context, though there is little elaboration as to what this means. If the social context influences the teacher's ability to enact dispositions, as argued by Mary Diez and Peter Murrell (in chapter 1, this volume), it stands to reason that some professional contexts will enable the teacher's enactment of particular dispositions, while others will constrain them. This idea is not new. In describing what it means to be a caring teacher, Nel Noddings states, "The caring teacher . . . is not best construed as one who possesses certain stable, desirable traits that might be identified before she steps into a classroom. Rather a caring teacher is someone who has demonstrated that she can establish, more or less regularly, relations of care in a wide variety of situations. This approach reminds us, too, that a teacher who fails in one situation may succeed in another and vice versa."[9] If dispositions are conceptualized as how a teacher will act under certain circumstances and how these behaviors and judgments develop over time, then teacher educators must be purposeful about the experiences they create for their candidates and whether these experiences help or hinder their candidates' efforts to enact the dispositions embraced by the institution.

The third pattern we noted in the case writers' definitions of *disposition* is the inclusion of an underlying moral aspect. Two of the case writers specifically use the terms *moral* or *ethical*, explicitly denoting that dispositions include a moral component (see Johnson, Evers, and Vare, chapter 3 this volume; Hollon, Kolis, McIntyre, Stephens, and Battalio, chapter 6 this volume). Other case writers do not use the terms *moral* or *ethical*, but they imply an underlying moral component in their conceptualization through the dispositions they enumerate or in their justification for this dispositions. For example, UWEC explicitly defines dispositions as what "drives the moral choices that an individual makes." They go on to say, "These choices are enacted—and thus evidenced—through the individual's ethical behavior" (see Hollon et al., chapter 6 this volume). The University of Cincinnati, like a number of the case writers, indicates moral underpinnings by conceptualizing dispositions in terms of particular commitments and values they want to instill in their candidates: "Educators must be committed to their students' learning and to issues of social justice . . . We wanted our candidates to care about their students and their profession" (see Laine, Bauer, Johnson, Kroeger, Troup, and Meyer, chapter 4 this volume). These definitions reinforce a view of teaching as more than just a technical-rational activity; it is a moral activity.[10] The knowledge and skills teachers possess are valuable because they are used to achieve worthwhile ends. Dispositions entail both the intellectual and the moral work of teaching.

The final pattern is the least prevalent. At two institutions, case writers espoused a definition that points to personality traits: UNCW says dispositions include *who we are*, and the University of Cincinnati includes *predispositions* as part of their definition. Defining dispositions as consisting of personality traits or elements of character can easily lead to what Diez and Murrell in this volume refer to as an *entity view*. However, the institutions represented in this volume do not address dispositions as static traits, resistant to change. Because they all address the development of dispositions at least to some extent, they acknowledge that dispositions are malleable, capable of being cultivated within a teacher education program dependent on the learning opportunities that are provided.

Enumerating

When a unit undertakes the process of enumerating dispositions, the complex nature of teaching is revealed—specifically, the intellectual, moral, and relational aspects that teaching entails. Because dispositions combine actions with moral commitments, they operate as an explanatory adhesive showing how the habits of mind, hand, and heart operate synergistically. The specific dispositions our case writers enumerate demonstrate this synergy in a variety of ways. Furthermore, most case writers encapsulate their dispositions into an overarching theme (e.g., collaborative leadership, humanizing dispositions, and leadership for diverse learners), which signifies the kinds of teachers they want to engender.

When we conducted a content analysis of the dispositions that the seven institutions identified, we found that the case writers often expressed similar ideas but used different language to convey these ideas. The most obvious example has to do with issues related to teaching diverse learners. As they enumerated specific dispositions, all the case writers tried to express the import of teachers possessing the commitment and capacity to teach all children. Across the cases, there is an emphasis on cultural sensitivity, the belief in the potential of all students, and a commitment to high expectations for all students. Given that the overarching themes each institution derived predominantly focused on teaching diverse learners, we did not find this pattern surprising. As our case writers illustrate, having the commitment and capacity to teach all learners is at the heart of the moral responsibilities of all teachers. Choosing a program focus like "teaching so all children can learn" is only the first step. Figuring out what understandings and skills are required to engender dispositions toward this end entails moving beyond mere rhetoric to operational specificity. In other words, the language and content of the dispositions enumerated must provide clarity without being too constricting.

For example, the case writers of the Boettcher Teachers Program at the University of Denver demonstrate how a unit can operationalize what it means to teach so all children can learn, by unpacking specific dispositions around a broad concept: *humanizing dispositions*. The Boettcher Teachers Program faculty identified humanization as the crux of what they wanted to engender in their candidates. They broadly conceptualized humanization as "promoting the notion that students' cultural, linguistic, and familial roots are essential to their academic achievement." The five humanizing dispositions they articulated contain language that is clearly dispositional in nature. Words like *commitment, relentless belief, conviction, willingness,* and *persistence* illustrate habits of heart (see Salazar, Lowenstein, and Brill, chapter 2 this volume). These dispositions also indicate the moral commitments that the teacher must enact. For example, the third disposition, "Conviction to coconstruct knowledge with students and families," requires the commitment to collaborate with students and families as well as the ability to do so. Having formulated five humanizing dispositions, the faculty translated each into a set of *conceptual indicators* and *behavioral indicators*. The conceptual indicators include teacher beliefs and understandings, while the behavioral indicators include specific actions the teacher will take to enact the humanizing disposition. By operationalizing each humanizing disposition in terms of commitments, understandings, and actions, this formulation highlights how dispositions combine habits of mind, hand, and heart.

Another major pattern that emerged from our content analysis had to do with collaboration. Some institutions focused on collaboration as a critical, professional disposition to a greater extent than others. The University of Wisconsin-Eau Claire is the most evident example. Faculty, teacher candidates, and educators in the field worked collaboratively, embodying the spirit of the motto they developed: "Preparing Collaborative Leaders." Although the overarching theme involved collaboration, and the overarching theme of Denver involved humanization, case writers at both institutions highlight that dispositions are a means to integrate habits of mind, hand, and heart. In fact, the UWEC case writers claim that the process of enumerating and operationalizing their dispositions helped them articulate the relationship among knowledge, skills, and dispositions:

> We now view the development of dispositions, knowledge, and skills as a complex recursive process in which dispositions frequently serve as the catalyst for knowledge and skill development, and at other times are shaped by the processes through which candidates acquire knowledge and skill. Our collaborative leadership disposition statements emphasize this action-oriented expression of agency, identity, and quality of character. We believe that dispositions are shaped by moral attitudes

and beliefs and are committed to the position that professional programs can foster the development of practices that are congruent with particular dispositions.[11]

In describing dispositions as both influencing and being influenced by knowledge and skills, the UWEC case writers suggest what Lee Shulman proposes as two key attributes of the teaching profession: theoretical understanding and professional practice. "While the theoretical is the foundation for the entitlement to practice, professional practice itself is the end to which all the knowledge is directed," Shulman says.[12] In other words, the enactment of what the teacher knows, is able to do, and, furthermore, is committed to do, is what matters most in teaching.

The formulation that the University of Cincinnati devised also illustrates how knowledge, skills, and dispositions operate synergistically. By enumerating dispositions under the broad categories of commitment, caring, and competence, the case writers integrate knowledge, skills, and dispositions all under the umbrella of dispositions. On the surface, the words *commitment* and *caring* connote the moral and relational work of teaching, or habits of heart. The language is dispositional. Similarly, the word *competence* indicates the intellectual as well as the practical, a confluence of habits of mind and hand. The language signifies knowledge and skills. However, when we examine the dispositions enumerated under each of these categories, it is clear that knowledge, skills, and dispositions are dependent on each other for the enactment of the dispositions enumerated. For example, one of the dispositions under the commitment category is, "responsibility to promote effort and excellence in all learners." This disposition indicates a moral commitment, a commitment one cannot enact unless one possesses particular knowledge (such as knowledge of human motivation and subject matter knowledge) and skills (to motivate learners and bring out their best effort) such as pedagogical competencies. Interestingly enough, "competence in a discipline or multiple disciplines and accompanying pedagogy," is a disposition under their category of competence. This disposition seems less dispositional in language, but it exemplifies what is necessary for candidates to enact some of the other dispositions. Although this integration of knowledge, skills, and dispositions makes it difficult to delineate between them, it helps to illustrate their interrelatedness when translated into practice.

Justifying

In order for the overarching themes and specific dispositions that programs enumerate to operate as more than just rhetorically appealing phrases that impress policy makers or accrediting agencies, it is important for teacher educators to justify the rationale behind these conceptualizations. Where did these ideas originate? What is the moral imperative that teacher educators have to society? What does this mean for the kinds of candidates a program envisions and how the faculty undertakes cultivating the dispositions set forth?

The case writers at some of these programs were more specific than others about their justification for the dispositions they enumerated. At least two units (Winthrop and the University of Southern Maine) were purposeful about aligning their dispositional frameworks with the mission of their department, college, and/or university. Case writers at a number of institutions justified the dispositions they enumerated by explaining that they had a moral imperative as teacher educators. For example, to explain their focus on collaborative leadership dispositions, the University of Wisconsin-Eau Claire invoked John Dewey's call for sustaining a socially just democratic society and improving the common good. Other case writers were similarly consistent with the overarching themes for their dispositional frameworks, expressing a moral or ethical obligation to prepare teachers to educate all students. Two units, the University of Illinois at Chicago and the University of North Carolina Wilmington, extended this moral imperative beyond the classroom to broader societal structures, stating that teacher education must prepare candidates who will "seek remedies to inequalities" (UIC) and work to close the achievement gap (UNCW).

We have two recommendations/cautions for units striving to be purposeful in justifying their dispositional frameworks. First, we want to highlight the necessity of clear, shared language around both the enumeration and the justification of dispositions. As UNCW identified in one of their initial attempts to craft a disposition framework, lack of specificity in how the framework was operationalized or justified meant that "faculty viewed the conceptual framework as either largely affirming what we were already doing or else providing some vague vision of which to aspire" (see Fischetti, Imig, Ndoye, and Smith, chapter 7 this volume). Specificity from the conceptual level to actual teaching practice is necessary. Raths provides an example of how such specificity can operate in a teacher education program: "A teacher education program could adopt the goal of strengthening candidates' dispositions to be interactive. This decision indentifies a goal at a reasonable conceptual level. In clarifying the goal for candidates, specific instances that reflect the goal could be identified as well as instances that appear to be counterindicators of the goal."[13] Second, we caution teacher educators to be realistic about the expectations placed on beginning teachers. Ameliorating ingrained, systemic, educational inequities is a laudable, societal goal. But is it a reasonable goal for an individual, beginning teacher? Research on expertise and concerns of teachers indicates that beginning teachers do not possess the capacity to enact commitments to solve macro-level problems.[14] If they are not careful, teacher educators who adopt this moral imperative may be setting their candidates up to fail. That's not to say that beginning teachers cannot recognize how their actions may contribute to the problem or the solution of social change. In the Boettcher Teachers Program example of JH, his action research project in his second year of teaching targeted the macro-level problem of building access to higher-level math for Latino students. JH started where he was, in his own classroom, building relationships with his students so that he could individualize support for their learning. These classroom practices were responsive to his awareness of the larger social context that he wished to affect. Teacher educators must purposefully create a realistic scaffolding of commitments that beginning teachers can translate into enacted practice.

DEVELOPING DISPOSITIONS

We have already said that dispositions are an integral component of effective teaching and that they develop in relation to knowledge and skills. In order to provide the conditions and learning opportunities that foster desirable professional dispositions in teacher candidates, the field of teacher education needs a theory of dispositions development. Since the 1980s, researchers have been studying how people learn to teach and get better at teaching over time, drawing insights from theories of learning, training, and development to inform their thinking about teacher learning.[16] If we think of learning to teach as a process of coming to know, think, feel, and act like a teacher, then dispositions focus our attention on how teachers put it all together—how they integrate their knowledge, skills, and commitments into a coherent professional identity and practice.[17]

As we analyzed the seven cases that make up this book, it seemed that the writers devoted less attention to the process of dispositions development than to the conceptualization and assessment of dispositions. Of course, they describe specific courses, field experiences, and assignments designed to foster dispositions, but overall there is less explicit discussion of how teacher candidates develop particular habits of thought and action and what teacher educators do to enable that learning. At the same time, there is intriguing evidence that some of the case writers do have implicit theories of dispositions development. We believe that making these ideas explicit can help build such theories. There are also some instructive examples of efforts to link specific interventions with the cultivation of particular dispositions.

In research on teacher learning, three problems have been widely documented that bear directly on the matter of developing dispositions.[18] The first concerns the problem of *preconceptions* and the need to help teacher candidates develop defensible visions of the possible and the desirable in teaching and learning. The second concerns the problem of *enactment* and the need to help teacher candidates develop a beginning repertoire of practice so that they can act on their convictions and beliefs.[19] The third concerns the problem of *complexity* and the need to help teacher candidates maintain their moral compass as they contend with the complexities and uncertainties of classroom teaching without abandoning their values and commitments. We use this problems framework to organize our discussion of dispositions development, drawing relevant examples from the cases.

The Problem of Preconceptions

Teacher candidates come to their preservice preparation with ingrained views about teaching, learning, and subject matter. Dan Lortie refers to this as an "apprenticeship of observation" whereby future teachers watch what teachers do during their own elementary and secondary schooling and begin to form images and ideas about what they will do and be like when they become teachers.[20] Through their upbringing and life experience, teacher candidates also build up attitudes and beliefs about people who are different from themselves in terms of race, class, culture, and approaches to learning. If left unexamined, these preconceptions will influence teacher candidates' learning and their teaching in ways inconsistent with the mission and values of the unit. A central task of preservice preparation is helping teacher candidates surface, examine, and, if necessary, revise these preconceptions in light of new possibilities and understandings.[21]

Several case writers acknowledge this problem of teacher candidates' preconceptions and describe how they sought to address this problem through the design of new program structures (e.g., revised courses and field experiences) as well as through specific interventions with particular teacher candidates. The two examples below reveal how teacher educators from the University of Cincinnati and from the Boettcher Teachers Program in Denver think about the problem of preconceptions and what they are doing to address it. Both examples also underscore the importance of working on this problem with teacher candidates whose backgrounds differ from those of the students they will be teaching, so that they will be disposed to see all students as capable learners.

After scrutinizing the cases of Ruth, Henry, and Brady, student teachers who did not demonstrate an adequate "commitment to teach all students," the University of Cincinnati team wondered whether their program had done enough to "disrupt candidates' notions of who would be in their classes and what it means to be a teacher" (see Laine, Bauer, Johnson, Kroeger, Troup, and Meyer, in chapter 4 of this volume). They thought about the need for early field experiences where "our predominantly white, middle-class candidates confront and address their biases and misconceptions about students unlike themselves" (see Laine, et al., in chapter 4 of this volume). They also wondered how the foundations courses, where teacher candidates first encounter issues of race, class, gender, and culture, could be redesigned to help foster the professional disposition of caring: "These courses, prior to candidates' entry into a professional cohort, should provide time to work through the misconceptions or biases they may bring to the classroom about urban teaching, young people unlike themselves, what it means to be a teacher, and that all children learn. Exposure, reflection, and guidance with situations and populations unlike their own may increase candidates' knowledge and comfort in working with students who differ from themselves in race, class, learning challenges. This sense of comfort then becomes *caring about individuals* in their classroom" (see Laine, et al., in chapter 4 of this volume).

Having learned that some of their teacher candidates reach student teaching without acquiring or developing appropriate dispositions, these teacher educators consider two changes in their program: early opportunities for "exposure, reflection, and guidance" in situations with learners whose background differs from the teacher candidates' own backgrounds, and an early opportunity to work through misconceptions and biases about diverse learners. We wonder what these experiences must be like to foster the disposition of caring. Also, we wanted to know what assumptions are being made about the relationship of comfort, knowledge, and caring. Answers to such questions would contribute to our understanding of dispositions development.

An example of what it means to work on the problem of preconceptions at the level of the individual teacher candidate comes from the chapter about the Boettcher Teachers Program at Denver. This example also shows how formative assessments can serve as learning opportunities. For their first assessment in the program, residents write a personal education history in which they explore their identity and the key educational experiences that have shaped their beliefs about teaching, learning, and the purposes of education. Reading one candidate's assignment, the faculty noticed that JH, a white, middle-class, musician-mathematician, framed his accomplishments solely in individual terms, without recognizing his membership in a privileged group. They also realized that JH needed help in looking at the experience of urban schooling through the eyes of a learner different from himself. The next performance assessment in the program provided an opportunity to work on that because it required JH to study one child in the contexts of the classroom, school, and family and come up with ways to improve that child's academic achievement. After reading the first draft of JH's child study, the faculty challenged him to probe Jose's experiences more deeply in order to uncover his strengths and struggles. A revised child study revealed that JH was beginning to see that Jose's struggles in learning arose not so much from his individual qualities and capacities, but from the disconnect between the content of his life and the content of his schooling. "When magnifying the lens of analysis on Jose," JH wrote, "I found that when he wasn't always showing success, it was usually because he needed reinforcement of traits he already possessed" (see Salazar, Lowenstein, and Brill, chapter 2 this volume). Through targeted and individualized interventions around each performance assessment, the faculty charted JH's progress while helping him move toward the humanizing dispositions that animate the program.

In both these examples, faculty create learning opportunities for teacher candidates to examine the preconceptions they bring to teacher preparation and to develop new interpretive lenses. Without such interventions, teacher candidates are subject to the influence of their taken-for-granted attitudes and beliefs, which can prevent them from seeing students in context, feeling responsible for their achievements, and persisting in finding effective ways to help them learn. These examples also illustrate that dispositions develop over time as teacher candidates gain knowledge of themselves and others and learn to act on their commitments.

The Problem of Enactment

We know that dispositions do not stand alone, isolated from the understandings and skills that make their enactment possible. When we talk about developing professional dispositions, we have to think about cultivating particular commitments in relation to knowledge, judgments, repertoire, and stance so that teacher candidates learn to enact their values in practice. This means helping teacher candidates acquire and learn to implement a beginning repertoire of curricular, instructional, and management strategies. It also means helping them develop the capacity to think on their feet and come up with appropriate responses in keeping with the program's dispositional commitments.

Learning to manage the routine aspects of teaching and learning to improvise are tall orders for beginning teachers, but the nature of teaching demands it. Teacher educators must consider how to prepare teacher candidates for both aspects of teaching, the routine and the unexpected, as they shape strong dispositions toward students, teaching, and ongoing learning. This means addressing the disconnect between what teachers say and what they do.

The problem of enactment surfaced in several chapters. Writers from Winthrop University, the University of Southern Maine, and the University of Cincinnati all wrote vividly about encountering teacher candidates who expressed moral imperatives aligned with the program's dispositional goals but could not or did not act on them in their field placements. The phenomenon of "candidates being able to say but not do what we had identified as important dispositions" often provided the impetus to rethink different parts of the teacher education program in order to help teacher candidates become the kinds of teachers the program aims to produce (see Laine, et al., in chapter 4 of this volume). The writers (and the editors) speculated whether the reported problems of enactment stemmed from a lack of conviction on the part of the teacher candidate, an inadequate set of conceptual and practical tools for interpreting and responding to particular situations, or insufficient opportunities to observe and practice enacting the desired dispositions and reflect on the consequences for students and their learning.

The chapter from the University of Cincinnati illustrates this kind of diagnostic thinking on the part of teacher educators as they try to figure out why competent teacher candidates fail to demonstrate desirable dispositions. Analyzing the cases of Ruth, Henry, and Brady, the case writers realize that "some of our teacher candidates were challenged by the fundamental moral claim that all children can learn and that teachers must persist in helping every student achieve success (see Laine, et al., in chapter 4 of this volume). Instead of seeing this as a reflection of some inadequacy on the part of the teacher candidates, the teacher educators realize that "dispositions are composed of multi-faceted skills, understandings and attitudes which need serious cultivation" (see Laine, et al., in chapter 4 of this volume). If they want teacher candidates to enact particular dispositions in their work with students, families, and colleagues, they must help them acquire the requisite understandings, skills, and commitments that enable such enactments. It is easier to persist in helping an ELL student learn to read if you have a repertoire of conceptual and practical tools to draw on. Without such a repertoire, the tendency to blame the student for not caring or not trying becomes understandable, though not commendable.

To communicate confidence in the learning potential of all students and to persist in finding ways to support each student's learning, teacher candidates need connected courses and field experiences, which help them acquire specific strategies and understandings to make this belief a reality. This includes opportunities to see how experienced teachers support the learning of individual students and to get inside their thinking as they diagnose student needs and identify appropriate materials and learning tasks. It also includes opportunities for guided practice in analyzing student work, assessing learning needs, devising appropriate interventions, and studying their effects on student engagement and learning. Without such focused learning opportunities, teacher candidates are unlikely to develop sufficient confidence in their own and their students' efficacy.

In traditional teacher education programs, teacher candidates are expected to acquire new knowledge and skills in education courses and then apply what they learn in student teaching. This linear structure ignores the contextualized nature of learning and the related problem of transfer. Contemporary theories of learning suggest that new understandings and skills are acquired most effectively if they are situated in the contexts of their use. This has implications for the design of clinical experiences. It also highlights the value of pedagogies, which situate teacher candidates' learning in "artifacts of practice" such as classroom videotapes, copies of student work, and curricular materials.[22] These pedagogies offer sheltered opportunities to practice the intellectual work of teaching—analysis, diagnosis, assessment, planning—in the service of student learning so that teacher candidates develop the skills and habits they need to act on their commitments.

Several cases provide examples of teacher educators working for better alignments between the dispositions they want teacher candidates to enact and the learning opportunities they provide. We mentioned above that teacher educators from the University of Cincinnati thought about redesigning an early foundations course to provide students with a deeper and more personal encounter with issues of class, race, and gender. They also reconceptualized the roles of mentor teacher and university supervisors to enable more productive learning in the field and began experimenting with methods courses cotaught by a subject matter and a special education specialist to help teacher candidates connect strategies for teaching subject matter concepts with the needs of diverse learners. In such examples, we see teacher educators thinking about how particular learning opportunities build capacity over time for teaching practices that, in turn, form professional identities that reflect particular dispositions.

The Problem of Complexity

The problem of complexity relates to the problem of enactment. Stories of teacher candidates coping with the day-to-day demands of teaching highlight the extent to which teaching is a complex, multidimensional, uncertain practice. Teachers rarely do one thing at a time. They must attend to the needs of individuals while attending to the needs of the group. They must manage the development of ideas while managing the behavior of students. Teachers are constantly absorbing new information and figuring out what to do next. Moreover, the embedded contexts of classroom, school, and community add layers of complexity as teachers interact with colleagues and families, and consider the implications of external policies for their practice.

Dealing with these complexities without losing their moral compass is particularly daunting for beginners who have limited experience and a modest repertoire. The problem of complexity challenges teacher educators to consider what core competencies and commitments teacher candidates need to develop during the preservice stage of learning to teach so that they are prepared to begin teaching and to continue developing as teachers. What foundation will enable beginning teachers to embrace the complexities of teaching with a sense of agency and moral clarity and continue growing into capable and effective teachers?

In formulating a response to the problem of complexity, several institutions identify collaborative skills and dispositions as a critical resource in teacher candidates' development and effectiveness. Embracing collaboration as a core disposition builds on decades of research that demonstrates the power of teachers working together to strengthen their teaching and improve their students' learning.[23] While collaboration is commonplace in other professions, teaching is largely viewed as an individual undertaking. So teacher candidates must experience the benefits and acquire the skills of serious collaboration in order to internalize this disposition.

What distinguishes a professional learning community from a support group, where teachers share ideas and offer encouragement, is their critical stance and commitment to inquiry.[24] In professional learning communities, teachers exercise what Brian Lord calls "critical colleagueship" as they ask probing questions, invite colleagues to observe and review their teaching, and present ideas for discussion and debate.[25] Learning to participate in this kind of professional interaction with peers and mentors requires a willingness to raise questions and concerns, an openness to constructive criticism, and a sense of trust and mutuality. These qualities must be cultivated, presumably in the contexts of their use with appropriate coaching and incentives. Three cases shed some light on this process.

Placing interns in cohorts is a "bedrock commitment" of the USM program, as the case writers explain: "We want our teacher candidates to have 'colleagues with whom they can talk, argue, invent, discover and weave their craft.'"[26] The faculty depends on the cohort to become a community "guided by a strong moral contract," where values can be openly explored and critical reflection developed (see Fallona and Canniff , chapter 5 this volume). The cohort serves as the main setting for cultivating and assessing the disposition of collegiality. We get some picture of what this involves mainly through the story of George, a teacher candidate who resists becoming a constructive member of the group.

Collaboration is the central commitment at UWEC, where "collaborative leadership" provides a unifying focus for three programs, enabling teachers to "succeed individually while accomplishing collective goals." The rubric for assessing collaborative leadership dispositions projects an image of a teacher who "actively seeks assistance from others to meet identified needs," "considers other's ideas and perspectives to generate possible solutions," "acknowledges all participants' contributions, concerns and ideas," to name a few of the behavioral indicators (Hollon, Kolis, McIntyre, Stephens, and Battalio , in chapter 6 of this volume).

The chapter from the University of Illinois at Chicago features another context of collaboration in the form of structured conversations between teacher candidate and mentor. These "sacred" conversations, organized around guiding questions, create openings for mentors to assess and advance teacher candidates' dispositions as they reflect together on the candidates' decisions and actions. While we do not get a clear picture of the conversations themselves, we share the conviction that focused and purposeful talk between a more and a less experienced educator can serve as a miniapprenticeship in dispositions and skills of critical colleagueship.

In these three examples, teacher educators recognize the need to teach the dispositions and skills of collaboration, rather than assuming that teacher candidates already know how to collaborate or will spontaneously learn through interactions with peers and mentors. They embrace collaboration to mediate the complexities of teaching and enhance teachers' learning and effectiveness. While the accounts lack sufficient detail to build a grounded theory of dispositions development in teacher preparation, they do contain some intriguing clues about a "developmental" progression.

"Developmental" Progressions

None of the chapters puts forward an explicit theory of dispositions development, but there are hints that several case writers have images of what teacher candidates look like (or should look like) as their commitments and capacities grow over time. The use of terms like *developmental path* (UWEC), *developmental levels* (UIC) and *developmental milestones* (Denver) suggest that these teacher educators can picture, and in some cases describe, general patterns of growth in preservice teachers. Similarly, the repeated use of a phrase like, "at this point in the program, we expect teacher candidates to . . ." implies that the teacher educators have some fairly clear notions about what teacher candidates typically look and sound like at different points in the program and what they need to work on. These linguistic clues signal an opportunity for further probing and elaboration so that the implicit theories of experienced teacher educators can become an explicit resource in understanding something about the sequence of dispositions development under particular conditions.

The University of Wisconsin-Eau Claire chapter outlines a prescriptive path that teacher candidates are supposed to follow as they move toward collaborative practices and leadership roles. Across three programs, faculty help candidates progress from "thinking about themselves as leaders" to "awareness of collaborative practices" to "application of collaborative leadership knowledge and skills" to "initiation of collaborative approaches to support student learning" (see Hollon, Kolis, McIntyre, Stephens, and Battalio, in chapter 6 of this volume). This progression, from knowing about to knowing how, fits the structure of the program in which coursework precedes student teaching. It is also built into a rubric that provides *behavioral anchors* for different levels of each disposition from "understanding" to "independent practice" to "collaborative practice." What we need is a clearer account of how candidates develop these dispositions and what enables them to move from one level to the next.

A different kind of developmental framework can be found in the chapter on the Boettcher Teachers Program in Denver. Here the case writers present a more descriptive trajectory as they trace the progress of one teacher candidate across the program, claiming that his "developmental flow" parallels the experiences of many other teacher candidates they have worked with. The case writers describe JH at different points in the program in relation to their expectations about what teacher candidates are usually capable of seeing, thinking, doing, and feeling over time. In this "developmental" conceptualization, discrepancies between what teacher candidates can say and what they can do are treated as expected signs of ongoing development and data to guide the faculty's interventions, not evidence of any deficiency in the teacher candidates.

For instance, the faculty expect that midway through their first year of the program, students will express "a growing sophistication in their vision of themselves as teachers" but will still be grappling with "the immediacy of planning, assessment, and classroom management" (see Salazar, Lowenstein, and Brill, in chapter 2 of this volume). By the end of the year, faculty "expect teacher candidates to envision equity as a compass that guides their instructional decisions" (see Salazar, Lowenstein, and Brill, in chapter 2 of this volume). The case writers point to evidence that JH has reached this developmental milestone: "He [JH] articulated strong beliefs in the potential of all learners . . . he identified instructional strategies to help his students succeed" (see Salazar, Lowenstein, and Brill, in chapter 2 of this volume). The final assessment reveals that JH has moved beyond "focusing on what students and their families lack" to consider "his own role in supporting students' achievement and well-being." (see Salazar, Lowenstein, and Brill, in chapter 2 of this volume)." While the chapter paints a picture of how JH changes over time, we still need more detail about what learning opportunities enabled his development.

In general, the case writers were clearer about the dispositions they wanted to develop than they were about what and how particular learning opportunities contribute to that development. We have highlighted examples where such connections were drawn, and tried to indicate what kind of elaborations would provide a fuller account of how particular dispositions grow in the context of particular learning opportunities. We do not necessarily expect a one-to-one correspondence between disposition and learning opportunity since dispositions evolve over time in relation to increased knowledge and skill. Rather, we want to encourage thoughtful teacher educators to theorize their efforts at dispositions development so that the field can learn from the wisdom of their practice.

ASSESSING DISPOSITIONS

The assessments described in the seven cases include tools (summative, diagnostic, and formative) and processes that serve a variety of functions—screening, program improvement, and development of individual candidates' dispositions. Because a goal of teacher education is to produce competent and caring teachers, capable of integrating habits of mind, hand, and heart, assessment should work toward the purpose of developing these capacities. Therefore, we sought evidence in the case narratives for assessments that serve the primary purpose of candidate development. We also looked specifically for how case writers are asking the central question, "What counts as evidence?" noting that this question is most robust when programs are purposeful and systematic about aligning assessments and evidence with the dispositions they seek to engender in their candidates.

Programs that use summative assessments for screening purposes, such as program admission, typically adopt an *entity view*, in which dispositions are seen as fixed traits (see Diez and Murrell, chapter 1 of this volume). None of the cases in this book adopt such a rigid stance. One discussion of assessment for screening purposes can be found in the University of Southern Maine narrative, where the case writers describe how information they gleaned in initial assessments of two candidates provided "clues . . . that these individuals might not possess the moral dispositions to be good teachers" (Fallona and Canniff, in chapter 5 of this volume). Although such assessments might seem like an efficient means of gatekeeping, USM is moving toward thinking about their initial screening as a diagnostic assessment. Reflecting on the challenges they experienced with Patrick and George, USM initiated some programmatic changes, including being more explicit about the dispositions candidates were expected to exhibit throughout the program and adopting a uniform action plan to support candidates, like Patrick and George, who were struggling. USM can also capitalize on their reflections of Patrick and George to consider how they can work at the individual level to provide interventions and learning opportunities to cultivate their four core dispositions in these struggling candidates.

The case writers at Winthrop University also used summative assessments, but for the purpose of program improvement. To determine what was not working in their program, they used two instruments, the Defining Issues Test (DIT-2) and the self-created equity matrix, both grounded in Lawrence Kohlberg's theory of moral development. By measuring candidates' moral

cognition on multiple assignments, the case writers identified a key disconnect between candidates' espoused moral imperatives and their tendency to
enact these moral commitments in practice. The measures also suggested a
problem faced by many teacher educators: candidates likely responded to
course assignments using ideas they thought their professors wanted to hear.
Armed with empirical data, the case writers at Winthrop used the information gleaned from these assessments to make programmatic changes. The
Winthrop case writers also demonstrate how assessment measures can be
used diagnostically to consider the strengths and weaknesses of a program.
A constructive next step would be to take this same information to diagnose the strengths and areas of growth for the individual candidates, considering the mechanisms necessary for engaging candidates in dialogue and
reflection.

Lisa Stooksberry says the main question we should ask about assessment
related to dispositions is, "How does the assessment of candidates' dispositions provide evidence of strengths, weaknesses, and growth over time?"[27]
This question serves as a reminder that assessing candidates' dispositions
involves looking beyond single snapshots. Rather, it involves building capacity over time, as we mention in the previous section. Because formative
assessment serves an educative function, teacher educators who adopt this
approach will reap the largest benefits for developing their candidates' professional dispositions. Formative assessment is assessment *for* learning rather
than assessment *of* learning.[28] Teacher educators interested in addressing the
problem of enactment and moving their candidates from knowing about
to knowing how should use formative assessments that open up important
instructional opportunities.

With their collaboratively designed DECA-UT assessment, the University
of Illinois at Chicago offers guideposts to how teacher educators can consider using formative assessments as instructional opportunities in their programs. Some key components of this assessment tool include its progression
of four different levels of performance, a list of potential actions that count
as evidence for placing candidates at a particular level, guiding questions
that form the basis for discussions between the candidate and the cooperating teacher, and opportunities for candidates to reflect on their beliefs and
commitments and on how they enact them in practice.

This approach has a number of promising aspects that may inform other
programs. First, a flexible structure is in place. The program is structured in
that it both enumerates and defines the dispositions expected of the candidates; this structure is flexible in that it allows for instructional conversations

to take place at an appropriate level for each candidate. Second, each disposition includes the candidates' commitments and corresponding actions. Furthermore, candidates' must reflect on both their beliefs/commitments and their teaching practice and how these align with each other. Third, a rubric sets the expectation for a developmental trajectory. Fourth, the instrument originated out of collaboration between teacher educators and practicing teachers, and the instrument is used as a collaborative tool among supervisors, cooperating teachers, and the teacher candidates. Such collaboration not only helps with program cohesion by ensuring that candidates' field placements echo the goals of the teacher preparation program, it also helps candidates to bridge the divide between theory and practice. While this case narrative offers a number of promising guideposts, further explication about the learning opportunities that enable candidates' development would really further the field.

The case writers at the University of Southern Maine present different formative assessments, though with some of the same qualities as at UIC, especially collaboration. The USM case writers describe how their shared vision enables them to "identify, assess, and foster teacher candidates' dispositions from the time of a candidate's admission through program completion" (Fallona and Canniff, in chapter 5 of this volume). The assessment of core dispositions—inquiry, responsiveness, opportunity to learn/high expectations, and collegiality—takes place through a set of common tasks that provide valuable opportunities for candidates to practice connecting their developing understandings, skills, and commitments. The assessments include (a) a study of learners, (b) a teaching philosophy, (c) reflective journals and videotape analyses, (d) a classroom management system, (e) a disciplinary or interdisciplinary unit, and (f) a final internship portfolio. Such tasks not only serve assessment purposes, they have the potential to offer rich opportunities for individualized intervention and for learning. How, then, can teacher educators best capitalize on this potential?

Teacher educators who have worked hard to conceptualize dispositions may be inclined to develop assessments to be used at strategic points throughout a program or in conjunction with specific courses, and assume that they are finished. But they still must consider the kind of evidence that each assessment produces and how this evidence relates to candidates' enactment of moral commitments in practice. They also must consider the developmental appropriateness of each assessment and how it can contribute to the development of candidates' dispositions. An assessment that shows a candidate is not meeting some expectation at a given point in time serves a limited function if it does not provide any guidance to help the candidate improve. In sum, teacher educators must be purposeful about showing how their assessments relate to candidates' habits of thought and action; this process must be visible.

The case writers at the Boettcher Teachers Program at Denver were transparent about how their assessments relate to the habits of thought and action espoused by the unit. They showed how they aligned their "humanizing dispositions" with specific conceptual and behavioral indicators that corresponded to particular assessments. Using JH as an example, they articulated where this candidate was meeting their expectations and where he was falling short. They then undertook a critical next step: they began to describe the interventions, namely the conversations and the feedback, they used to guide JH to where they thought he needed to be, demonstrating how they fostered the development of the humanizing dispositions the program wanted to engender in teacher candidates.

To illustrate, the faculty recognized that after his first assignment, writing a personal education history, JH clearly viewed himself as an individual, not as a member of a group. The faculty knew they wanted to help JH contrast his own experiences with those of learners unlike himself, an intervention the faculty pursued in the next assessment, the child study. The faculty challenged JH to "probe deeply into the strengths and struggles" of one student (Salazar, Lowenstein, and Brill, chapter 2 this volume). Although JH's first attempt at the assignment showed his nascent awareness of the importance of a student's background, the faculty asked increasingly penetrating questions to bring JH to "a greater understanding of the complexity of Jose's experiences" (see Salazar, Lowenstein, and Brill, in chapter 2 of this volume). Some of the questions the faculty asked of JH were, "How do you know the student is living a successful bicultural life? What indicators can you identify that led you to state your observation as fact? How do the student's experiences with his classmates either support or limit his engagement?" (see Salazar, Lowenstein, and Brill, in chapter 2 of this volume). JH then revised the assignment.

The Boettcher Teachers Program at Denver was like programs at USM, UIC, and in some of the other case narratives found in this volume in that the faculty identified common assessments for their candidates that were to be used at particular points during the program. Many of the programs identified similar assessments, like a child study, an analysis of one's teaching, and a portfolio. Identifying these assessments and attaining a shared understanding of all faculty members in a program to use common assessments can be challenging work. This is especially true for larger programs. However, it is not the assessment, per se, that provides the necessary guidance for development of candidates' dispositions. Rather, it is how the assessment is used. Unfortunately, teacher educators frequently neglect to explicitly articulate the nuanced technicalities of how their assessments are used as interventions for candidates' development. Moving toward more articulated transparency is what the Boettcher Teachers Program offered; they explained in detail how their assessments showed the status of JH at various points throughout his program and, most importantly, how they worked with JH, through feedback and dialogue, to develop his humanizing dispositions.

An assessment by itself holds little value. Assessments possess value when they measure something meaningful. Assessments for dispositions are meaningful when they are used as tools for development. If other teacher educators would share their wisdom, making their methods of using assessments for the purposes of development more visible, it would not only benefit teacher candidates who are in the process of forging their professional identities, it could also serve as a resource to the field. Teacher educators are in many ways an untapped resource, as we are lacking the structures to take advantage of our collective wisdom regarding assessing for the purpose of developing dispositions. To capitalize on our collective wisdom and move toward a theory of disposition development, we suggest adopting a culture of critical colleagueship.

PROBING PRACTICE

After numerous drafts and revisions were exchanged, the editors made one final request of the case writers: to add an epilogue reflecting on the process of producing their chapters. We were curious about how the process of collaborative writing and critical feedback over two years had influenced people's thinking and practice. These final reflections highlight several themes about the work of conceptualizing, developing, and assessing dispositions. They also underscore the value of shared understandings, the power of evidence, and the importance of critical colleagueship.

Because the concept of dispositions is fuzzy, it invites abstractions and generalizations. Such language may be inspiring, but it does not offer a clear basis for program design or candidate assessment. The Winthrop team expressed the point with honesty and eloquence: "The process of writing this chapter was all about examining the foundations for the (conceptual) castles we had carefully constructed over the past ten years related to professional dispositions" (Johnson, Evers, and Vare, in research for chapter 3 of this volume). Identifying shared commitments and figuring out what they mean and what they could look like in practice is difficult and time-consuming intellectual work, but without it, programs and units have no firm foundation for program development and candidate assessment.

The work of unpacking dispositions and translating them into concrete sensibilities and observable actions strengthened teacher educators' commitments to "equitable and engaged learning," to "serving culturally and linguistically diverse students and their families," to "effective and transformative urban teaching," to name some of the aspirations mentioned in the epilogues (Johnson, Evers, and Vare, chapter 3 this volume). Several units and programs got to the work through a critical review of evidence about teacher candidates' learning and discussions of what is and is not working in their programs. This process pointed the direction for change, often motivated by the need to address the demographic imperative in schools. As the Cincinnati team put it, "If our candidates are not demonstrating the dispositions we have identified, we must find ways to develop those dispositions. We must be concerned with the quality of the teachers, and how they impact the students they will serve" (see Laine, et al., in research for chapter 4 of this volume).

For many of the case writers, the impetus to examine how they were addressing dispositions in their programs originated outside the unit, most often as a result of an National Council for Accreditation of Teacher Education (NCATE) accreditation review or changes in state requirements. Although these external agencies helped bring dispositions to the foreground in discussions about teacher preparation, they have also contributed to conceptual confusion and superficial compliance. If policy makers mandate programmatic changes without acknowledging the conceptual and practical complexities that accompany them, they may inadvertently promote a compliance mentality. In response to what seems like a straightforward request, units may pursue a response that misrepresents the complex nature of the task and masks the moral decision making involved.

When teacher educators only ask what needs to be done to meet the accreditation standards, they miss an opportunity for serious and productive discussion with colleagues about the kind of teachers the unit wants to prepare. Such discussions are possible when a culture of inquiry and critical colleagueship exists that welcomes thoughtful and honest examination of goals and practices in light of evidence. In such a culture, critique is valued and disagreements are opportunities to probe different perspectives, possibilities, and evidence.[29] Since this is the same culture that some programs seek to create with and for their teacher candidates, the exercise of critical colleagueship among faculty serves the dual purposes of building professional culture and improving the quality of teacher education.

The process of working with colleagues to reach consensus about how to conceptualize, develop, and assess dispositions might be more streamlined in a small program, like the Boettcher Teachers Program with three faculty, than at a large institution like the University of North Carolina Wilmington, where the education unit has twenty-three programs. But the size of the unit is less important than the leadership of those within the unit to create the space for critical conversations that lead to shared purposes and understandings. Developing shared purposes and the means to achieve them cannot be mandated externally. It is a form of "covenant building" that derives from the moral imperatives of the work itself—preparing teachers with the qualities and capabilities to help all students be successful and engaged learners.[31]

The institutions represented in this book took the time to inquire into their own practice and to grapple with the challenges of defining, specifying, developing, and assessing dispositions for teaching. The process continued as they accepted the invitation to tell some important aspect of their story. Some admitted to passing their external reviews without feeling that they were doing justice to their mission. Others discovered through the analysis of data that candidates were unable to enact their knowledge and skills in practice or failed to see how their values and beliefs connected to their classroom practice. This led to revisions in programs and/or to refined assessments.

This book is the result of a collective inquiry on the part of the case writers, their colleagues, and the editors into the meaning, development, and assessment of professional dispositions. By making their thinking and practice public, the case writers model what it means to articulate and clarify dispositional goals for teacher education, design learning opportunities to foster these outcomes, and create assessments that align with the goals, document progress, and give direction to continued learning. The book is also an invitation to other teacher educators to probe their own thinking and practice in light of the moral imperatives of teaching and learning in the twenty-first century.

Notes

Preface

1. George Will, "The Truth About Teaching," *Newsweek*, January 16, 2006, 98.
2. Hilda Borko, Dan Liston, and Jennifer A. Whitcomb, "Apples and Fishes: The Debate over Dispositions in Teacher Education," *Journal of Teacher Education, 58* (2007): 359–364; and Hugh Sockett, "Dispositions as Virtues: The Complexity of the Construct," *Journal of Teacher Education* 60 (May 2009): 291–303.

Introduction

1. Lilian G. Katz and James D. Raths, "Dispositions as Goals for Teacher Education," *Teaching and Teacher Education* 1 (1985): 301–307.
2. Ibid., 304.
3. Alverno College Faculty, Student Assessment as Learning at Alverno College (Milwaukee, WI: Alverno College Institute, 1994), 9.
4. Mary E. Diez, "Looking Back and Moving Forward: Three Tensions in the Teacher Dispositions Discourse," *Journal of Teacher Education 58*, no. 5 (2007): 388–396.
5. Interstate New Teacher Assessment and Support Consortium, "Model Standards for Beginning Teacher Licensure and Development: A Resource for State Dialogue," (Washington, DC: Council of Chief State School Officers, 1992).
6. Mary E. Diez, "Looking Back and Moving Forward," p. 389.
7. See William Damon, "Personality Test: The Dispositional Dispute in Teacher Preparation Today, and What to Do About It," 2005, http://edexcellence.net/detail/news.cfm?id=343; Jacob Gershman, "'Disposition' Emerges as an Issue at Brooklyn College," 2005, http://www.nysun.com/new-york/disposition-emerges-as-issue-at-brooklyn-college/14604; John Leo, "Class(room) Warriors," *U.S. News and World Report,* October 24, 2005, http://www.usnews.com/usnews/opinion/articles/151024/24john.htm; and Arthur Wise, response to George Will's column "The Truth About Teaching," *Newsweek*, January 16, 2006, NCATE News, http//www.ncate.org/public/0124_truthAboutTeaching.asp?ch=150.
8. For example, Ana Maria Villegas, "Dispositions in Teacher Education: A Look at Social Justice" *Journal of Teacher Education* 58, no. 5 (2007): 370–380.

Chapter One

1. See Rachel Swords, "Teaching Standard English in Urban Classrooms" (forum, Harvard Graduate School of Education, Cambridge, MA, November 7, 2007). The event was recorded by National Public Radio: http://forum-network.org/lecture/teaching-standard-english-urban-classrooms.

2. Steven Covey, *The Seven Habits of Highly Effective People* (New York: Simon & Schuster, 1989), 47.
3. Lilian G. Katz, "Reflections on Respecting the Learner," *Inside Gateways*, June 2006, 1, http://www.ilgateways.com/newsletter/archives/lkatz062006.aspx.
4. Hilda Borko, Dan Liston, and Jennifer A. Whitcomb, "Apples and Fishes: The Debate over Dispositions in Teacher Education," *Journal of Teacher Education* 58, no. 359 (2007): 359–364.
5. Jean P. Anyon, *Radical Possibilities: Public Policy, Urban Education, and a New Social Movement* (New York: Routledge, 2005); and John Dewey, *Democracy and Education: An Introduction to the Philosophy of Education* (New York: Free Press, 1916/1944).
6. www.nea.org/home/30442.htm
7. Lisa M. Stooksberry, Deborah L. Schussler, and Lynne A. Bercaw, "Conceptualizing Dispositions: Intellectual, Cultural and Moral Domains of Teaching," *Teachers and Teaching: Theory and Practice* 15, no. 6 (2009): 729.
8. Peter C. Murrell Jr., *Race, Culture, and Schooling: Identities of Achievement in Multicultural Urban Schools* (Mahwah, NJ: Lawrence Erlbaum Associates, 2007).
9. Peterhans Kolvenbach, "The Service of Faith and the Promotion of Justice in American Jesuit Higher Education" (paper presented at the Commitment to Justice in Jesuit Higher Education Conference, Santa Clara, CA, October 6, 2000).
10. Urie Bronfenbrenner, "Toward an Experimental Ecology of Human Development," *American Psychologist* 32, no. 7 (1977): 513-531.
11. Peter C. Murrell Jr., "Identity, Agency, and Culture: Black Achievement and Educational Attainment," in *Handbook of African American Education*, ed. Linda C. Tillman (Thousand Oaks, CA: Sage Publications, 2009; Peter C. Murrell Jr., "Community Action and Agency in the Education of Urban Youth," in *Handbook of Educational Action Research*, eds. Susan E. Noffke and Bridget Somekh (Thousand Oaks, CA: Sage Publications, 2009).
12. Richard J. Stiggins, "Assessment Crisis: The Absence of Assessment for Learning," *Phi Delta Kappan* 83, no. 10 (2002): 758-765.
13. Mary E. Diez, "Looking Back and Moving Forward: Three Tensions in the Teacher Dispositions Discourse," *Journal of Teacher Education* 58, no. 5 (2007): 388–396; and Mary E. Diez, "The Heart of the Matter: Teacher Dispositions' Role in Building Learning Communities" (paper presented at Florida A&M University Induction Symposium, 2009).
14. Carol S. Dweck, "Motivation," in *Foundations for a Psychology of Education*, eds. Alan Lesgold and Robert Glaser (Hillsdale, NJ: Erlbaum, 1989).
15. M. Mark Wasicsko, "The Perceptual Approach to Teacher Dispositions: The Effective Teacher as an Effective Person," in *Dispositions in Teacher Education*, eds. Mary E. Diez and James D. Raths (Charlotte, NC: Information Age Publishing, 2007).
16. Patrick C. Kyllonen, Alyssa M. Walters, and James C. Kaufman, "Non-cognitive Constructs and Their Assessment in Graduate Education: A Review," in "Assessment of Noncognitive Influences in Learning," eds. J. Abedi and H. O'Neil, special issue, *Educational Assessment* 10, no. 3 (2005): 147–152.
17. Sharon N. Oja and Alan J. Reiman, "A Constructivist-Developmental Perspective," in *Dispositions in Teacher Education*, eds. Mary E. Diez and James D. Raths (Charlotte, NC: Information Age Publishing, 2007), 91–115.

18. Judith R. Wilkerson, "Measuring Teacher Dispositions: Standards-Based or Morality-Based?" *Teachers College Record*, 2006, http://www.tcrecord.org.

19. Stooksberry, Schussler, and Bercaw, "Conceptualizing Dispositions," 719 – 736.

20. William Damon, "Personality Test: The Dispositional Dispute in Teacher Preparation Today, and What to Do About It," 2005, http://edexcellence.net/detail/news.cfm?id=343; Jacob Gershman, "'Disposition' Emerges as an Issue at Brooklyn College," 2005, http://www.nysun.com/new-york/disposition-emerges-as-issue-at-brooklyn-college/14604; John Leo, "Class(room) Warriors," *U.S. News and World Report*, October 24, 2005, http://www.usnews.com/usnews/opinion/articles/151024/24john.htm; and Arthur Wise, response to George Will's column "The Truth About Teaching," *Newsweek*, January 16, 2006, NCATE News, http//www.ncate.org/public/0124_truthAboutTeaching.asp?ch=150.

21. Erskine S. Dottin, "A Deweyan Approach to the Development of Moral Dispositions in Professional Teacher Education Communities: Using a Conceptual Framework," in *Teacher Dispositions: Building a Teacher Education Framework of Moral Standards*, ed. Hugh Sockett (Washington, DC: American Association of Colleges for Teacher Education, 2006), 27–47.

22. John Leo, "Class(room) Warriors," *U.S. News and World Report*, October 24, 2005, http://www.usnews.com/usnews/opinion/articles/051024/24john_2.htm.

23. Stephen Milam, "Understanding the Institutional Context: Legal Implications of Decisions About Individual Candidates" (presentation at the annual meeting of the American Association of Colleges for Teacher Education, San Diego, CA, January 2006).

24. Mary E. Diez, "Assessing Dispositions: Five Principles to Guide Practice," in *Teacher Dispositions: Building a Teacher Education Framework of Moral Standards*, ed. Hugh Sockett (Washington, DC: American Association of Colleges for Teacher Education, 2006), 51

25. Richard D. Osguthorpe, (2009) AACTE Webinar "Lessons From Practice in Teacher Education: Toward a Professional Consensus around Dispositions," October 15, 2009.

26. Erskine S. Dottin, (2009). AACTE Webinar "Lessons From Practice in Teacher Education: Toward a Professional Consensus around Dispositions," October 15, 2009

27. National Council for Accreditation of Teacher Education, *Professional Standards for the Accreditation of Schools, Colleges, and Departments of Education,* 2006 ed. (Washington, DC: NCATE, 2006), 23.

28. Raymond L. Pecheone and Ruth R. Chung, "Evidence in Teacher Education: The Performance Assessment for California Teachers (PACT)," *Journal of Teacher Education* 57, no. 1 (2006): 22–36.

29. Stiggins, "Assessment Crisis"; and W. James Popham, "Common and Day-to-Day Classroom Assessment: Fostering Formative Uses by Teachers and Students" (paper presented at AERA Conference, San Diego, CA, April 12–18, 2009).

Chapter Two

1. Sonia Nieto and Patty Bode, *Affirming Diversity: The Sociopolitical Context of Multicultural Education*, 5th ed. (Boston: Allyn & Bacon, 2007), 84.

2. Ana Maria Villegas and Tamara Lucas, "Preparing Culturally Responsive Teachers: Rethinking the Curriculum," *Journal of Teacher Education* 53 (2002): 20–32.

3. Zulmara Cline and Juan Necochea, "Teacher Dispositions for Effective Education in the Borderlands," *Educational Forum* 70, no. 3 (2006): 268–282.

4. Nieto and Bode, *Affirming Diversity,* 101–102.

5. Geneva Gay, *Culturally Responsive Teaching: Theory, Research, and Practice* (New York: Teachers College Press, 2000).

6. Sonia Nieto, *Why We Teach* (New York: Teachers College Press, 2005).

7. Eugene E. Garcia, "Effective Instruction for Language Minority Students: The Teacher," in *Latinos and Education*, ed. Antonia Darder (New York: Routledge Press, 1997), 362–372.

8. Franita Ware, "Warm Demander Pedagogy: Culturally Responsive Teaching That Supports a Culture of Achievement for African American Students," *Urban Education* 41, no. 4 (2006): 427–456.

9. Lee S. Schulman, "Pedagogies of Uncertainty," *Journal of Liberal Education* 91, no. 2 (2005): 18–26.

10. María Salazar et al., *The State of Latinos 2008: Defining an Agenda for the Future* (Denver, CO: University of Denver, DULCCES, 2008).

11. Nieto, *Why We Teach*, 52–53.

12. National Board for Professional Teaching Standards, *What Teachers Should Know and Be Able to Do*, http://www.nbpts.org/UserFiles/File/what_teachers.pdf, 10.

13. Gloria Ladson-Billings, "Liberatory Consequences of Literacy: A Case of Culturally Relevant Instruction for African American Students," *Journal of Negro Education* 61, no. 3 (1992): 385.

14. National Board for Professional Teaching Standards, *What Teachers Should Know and Be Able to Do.*

15. Paulo Freire, *Pedagogy of the Oppressed* (New York: Seabury Press, 1970): 34.

16. The Education Trust, *Latina/o Achievement in America*, http://www.edtrust.org/dc/publication/latino-achievement-in-america.

17. Freire, *Pedagogy of the Oppressed*, 28.

18. This and all quoted material from "John Henry" (pseudonym) are taken from program performance assessments from August 2005 to May 2007.

Chapter Three

1. Gary Fenstermacher, "Agenda for Education in a Democracy," in *Leadership for Educational Renewal*, eds. Wilma Smith and Gary Fenstermacher (San Francisco: Jossey-Bass Publishers, 1999).

2. Jonatha Vare and Rebecca Evers, "From Missionary to Transformative Intellectual: Cultivating Dispositions of Social Justice" (presentation at the annual meeting of the American Association for Colleges of Teacher Education (AACTE), Washington, DC, 2005).

3. Rebecca Evers and Sandra Wilson, "The Society Essay" (Unpublished teaching materials, 2005).

4. Ibid.

5. Ibid.

6. Vare and Evers, "From Missionary to Transformative," 2.

7. Lisa Delpit, "Lessons from Teachers," *Journal of Teacher Education* 57, no. 3 (2006): 220–232.
8. Professional Standards for Accreditation of Teacher Institutions (Washington, DC: NCATE, 2008).
9. Paul Witty, "An Analysis of the Personality Traits of the Effective Teacher," *Journal of Educational Research* 40, no. 9 (1947): 662–671; David E. Hunt, "Teachers' Adaptation: 'Reading' and 'Flexing' to Students," *Journal of Teacher Education* 27, no. 3 (1976): 268–275; Richard L. Percy, "The Effects of Teacher Effectiveness Training on the Attitudes and Behaviors of Classroom Teachers," *Educational Research Quarterly* 14, no. 1 (1990): 15–20; Patricia K. Arlin, "Wisdom and Expertise in Teaching: An Integration of Perspectives," *Learning and Individual Differences* 5, no. 4 (1993): 341–349; and Alan J. Reiman and Lois Thies-Sprinthall, *Mentoring and Supervision for Teacher Development* (New York: Addison Wesley Longman, Inc., 1998).
10. William Damon, "Dispositions and Teacher Assessment," *Journal of Teacher Education* 58, no. 5 (2007): 365–369; Lilian G. Katz and James D. Raths, "Dispositions as Goals for Teacher Education," *Teaching and Teacher Education* 1, no. 4 (1985): 301–307; and Alan J. Reiman, and Lisa E. Johnson, "Teacher Professional Judgment," *Journal of Research in Education* 13, no. 1 (2004): 4–17.
11. Robert Bergman, "John Dewey on Educating the Moral Self," *Studies in Philosophy and Education* 24, no. 1 (2005): 39–62.
12. Rebecca Evers, Jonatha Vare, and Sandra Wilson, "Assessing Undergraduate Teacher Education Candidates' Conceptions of Educational Equity and Social Justice" (paper presented at the annual meeting of the American Educational Research Association, Chicago, IL, 2007).
13. James Rest et al., *Postconventional Moral Thinking: A Neo-Kohlbergian Approach* (Mahwah, NJ: Lawrence Erlbaum Associates, 1999).
14. Jonathan Vare, Rebecca Evers, and Maria Mensik, "Conceptions of Equity and Social Justice: Developing a Rubric to Assess Teacher Candidates' Dispositions" (paper presented at the annual meeting of the American Educational Research Association, New York, 2008).
15. David T. Campbell, "Degrees of Freedom and the Case Study," *Comparative Political Studies* 8 (1975); and William M. Trochim, "Outcome Pattern Matching and Program Theory," *Evaluation and Program Planning* 12 (1989): 355–366.
16. Linda Winter et al., "We Taught. We Saw. We Read" (presentation at annual meeting of the American Educational Research Association, Chicago, IL, 2007).
17. James R. Rest and Darcia Narvaez, *Guide for the DIT-2* (Minneapolis, MN: Center for the Study of Ethical Development, 1998); and Muriel Bebeau and Stephen Thoma, *Guide for DIT-2* (Minneapolis, MN: Center for Ethical Development, 2003), 1–28.
18. Rest et al., *Postconventional Moral Thinking*.
19. Lisa E. Johnson, "Ethical Judgment as Teacher Disposition" (research presented at the annual meeting of the Association of Moral Education, South Bend, IN, 2008); and Lisa E. Johnson, "Teacher Candidate Disposition: Moral Judgment or Regurgitation?" *Journal of Moral Education* 37, no. 4 (2008): 429–444.
20. Rebecca Evers and Lisa Johnson, "Assessing Teacher Candidate Growth as Moral and Ethical Educators" (unpublished data from a self-study completed with funds from the institutional research grants at Winthrop University, Rock Hill, SC, 2008).

21. Ibid.
22. Ibid.
23. Ibid.
24. National Council for Accreditation of Teacher Education, *Professional Standards for the Accreditation of Schools, Colleges, and Departments of Education,* 2006 ed. (Washington, DC: NCATE, 2006).
25. Damon, "Dispositions and Teacher Assessment," 365–369; Mary E. Diez, "Assessing Dispositions: Five Principles to Guide Practice," in *Teacher Dispositions: Building a Teacher Education Framework of Moral Standards,* ed. Hugh Sockett (Washington, DC: American Association of Colleges for Teacher Education, 2006), 49–68; Erskine S. Dottin, "A Deweyan Approach to the Development of Moral Dispositions in Professional Teacher Education Communities: Using a Conceptual Framework," in *Teacher Dispositions: Building a Teacher Education Framework of Moral Standards,* ed. Hugh Sockett (Washington, DC: American Association of Colleges for Teacher Education, 2006), 27–47; Erskine S. Dottin, "Professional Judgment and Dispositions in Teacher Education," *Teaching and Teacher Education* 25, no. 1 (2009): 83–88; Katz and Raths, "Dispositions as Goals for Teacher Education," 301–307; and Reiman and Johnson, "Teacher Professional Judgment," 4–17.
26. John I. Goodlad, *Teachers for Our Nation's Schools* (San Francisco: Jossey-Bass Publishers, 1990).
27. Kids Count Data Center, *South Carolina* (Baltimore, MD: Annie E. Casey Foundation), http://datacenter.kidscount.org/data/bystate/StateLanding.aspx?state=SC.
28. National Center for Educational Statistics, *Table 52, Number and Percentage of Children Served Under Individuals with Disabilities Education Act, Part B, by Age Group and State or Jurisdiction: Selected Years, 1990–91 Through 2006–07* (Washington, DC: U.S. Department of Education, 2008), http://nces.ed.gov/programs/digest/d08/tables/dt08_052.asp; and Rose M. Payan and Maria T. Nettles, *Current State of English Language Learners in K–12 Student Population* (Princeton, NJ: Educational Testing Service, 2009).
29. Diez, "Assessing Dispositions."
30. Delpit, "Lessons from Teachers," 232.
31. Ibid., 222.
32. Alan J. Reiman, "The Evolution of Social Role Taking and Guided Reflection Framework in Teacher Education: Recent Theory and Quantitative Synthesis of Research," *Teaching and Teacher Education* 15 (1999): 597–612.

Chapter Four
1. University of Cincinnati Educator Preparation Programs (2002). *Conceptual Framework.* Retrieved from http://www.cech.uc.edu.
2. Parker J. Palmer, *The Courage to Teach: Exploring the Inner Landscape of a Teacher's Life* (San Francisco: Jossey-Bass, 1998).
3. Catherine Cornbleth, *Diversity and the New Teacher: Learning from Experience in Urban Schools* (New York: Teachers College Press, 2008).
4. Deborah Shifter and Catherine T. Fosnot, *Reconstructing Mathematics Education: Stories of Teachers Meeting the Challenge of Reform* (New York: Teachers College Press, 1993).

5. Etta R. Hollins and Maria T. Guzman, "Research on Preparing Teachers for Diverse Populations," in *Studying Teacher Education: The Report of the AERA Panel on Research and Teacher Education*, eds. Marilyn Cochran-Smith and Kenneth M. Zeichner (Washington, DC: American Educational Research Association, 2005), 482.
6. Denise Da Ros-Voseles and Linda Moss, "The Role of Dispositions in the Education of Future Teachers," *Young Children* 62, no. 5 (2007): 90–96.
7. Sharon Feiman-Nemser, "From Preparation to Practice: Designing a Continuum to Strengthen and Sustain Teaching," *Teachers College Record* 103, no. 6 (2001): 1016.
8. Gunilla Härnsten, *The Research Circle: Building Knowledge on Equal Terms* (Stockholm: Swedish Trade Union Confederation, 1994).
9. Marlene Pugach and Linda Blanton, "A Framework for Conducting Research on Collaborative Teacher Education," *Teaching and Teacher Education* 25, no. 4 (2009): 575–582; Grant Wiggins and Jay McTighe, *Understanding by Design* (Washington, DC: ASCD, 2005); and Paula Kluth and Diana Straut, "Do as We Say and as We Do: Co-Teaching in the University Classroom," *Journal of Teacher Education* 54 (2003): 228–240.
10. Carol Tomlinson, *Differentiating Instruction* (Washington, DC: ASCD, 2003); David A. Rose and Anne Meyer, *Teaching Every Student in the Digital Age: Universal Design for Learning* (Washington, DC: ASCD, 2002); and Peter Smagorinsky, *Teaching by Design: How to Create and Carry Out Instructional Units* (Portsmouth, NH: Heinemann, 2008).
11. Judith W. Little, "The Cooperating Teacher Phenomenon and the Social Organization of Teaching," *Review of Research in Education* 16 (1990): 297–351; Lee S. Shulman, "Those Who Understand: Knowledge Growth in Teaching," *Educational Researcher* 15, no. 4 (1986): 4–12; Randi N. Stanulis, "Fading to a Whisper: One Cooperating Teacher's Story of Sharing Her Wisdom Without Telling Answers," *Journal of Teacher Education* 45, no. 1 (1994): 31–38; and Kenneth Zeichner and B. Robert Tabachnik, "Are the Effects of University Teacher Education Washed Out by School Experience?" *Journal of Teacher Education* 32 (1981): 7–11.
12. Sharon Feiman-Nemser, "Helping Novices Learn to Teach," *Journal of Teacher Education* 52 (2001): 17–30.
13. New Teacher Center, *Continuum of Teacher Development* (Santa Cruz, CA: New Teacher Center, 2002).

Chapter Five
1. Robert Audi, "Dispositions," *The Cambridge Dictionary of Philosophy* (Cambridge: Cambridge University Press, 1995), 206.
2. Alan Tom, *Teaching as a Moral Craft* (New York: Longman, 1984).
3. Philip W. Jackson, Robert E. Boostrom, and David T. Hansen, *The Moral Life of Schools* (San Francisco: Jossey-Bass, 1993); and Gary D. Fenstermacher, "Method, Style, and Manner in Classroom Teaching" (paper presented at the annual meeting of the American Educational Research Association, Montreal, Quebec, Canada, April 1999).
4. Gary D. Fenstermacher, "Some Moral Considerations on Teaching as a Profession," in *The Moral Dimensions of Teaching*, eds. John I. Goodlad, Roger Soder, and Kenneth Sirotnik (San Francisco: Jossey-Bass, 1990), 133.

5. Catherine Fallona and Virginia Richardson, "Classroom Management as Moral Activity," in *Handbook of Classroom Management*, eds. Carolyn Evertson and Carol S. Weinstein (Mahwah, NJ: Lawrence Erlbaum, 2006), 1041–1061.
6. Jackson, Boostrom, and Hansen, *The Moral Life of Schools*; and Catherine Fallona, "Manner in Teaching: A Study in Observing and Interpreting Teachers' Moral Virtues," *Teaching and Teacher Education* 16, no. 7 (2000): 681–695.
7. http://www.usm.maine.edu/cehd/About-Us/mission.htm
8. Marilyn Cochran-Smith and Susan Lytle, *Inquiry as Stance: Practitioner Research for the Next Generation* (New York: Teachers College Press, 2009).
9. Hugh Sockett, "Dispositions as Virtues: The Complexity of the Construct," *Journal of Teacher Education* 60, no. 3 (2009), 298.
10. Ana Maria Villegas and Tamara Lucas, *Educating Culturally Responsive Teachers* (Albany: State University of New York Press, 2002); Geneva Gay, *Culturally Responsive Teaching: Theory, Research and Practice* (New York: Teachers College Press, 2000); Gloria Ladson-Billings, "But That's Just Good Teaching! The Case for Culturally Relevant Pedagogy," *Theory into Practice* 34, no. 3 (1995a, 1995b, 2006); and David A. Rose and Anne Meyer, *Teaching Every Student in the Digital Age: Universal Design for Learning* (Washington, DC: ASCD, 2002).
11. Gloria Ladson-Billings, "Toward a Theory of Culturally Relevant Pedagogy," in *The Curriculum: Problems, Politics and Possibilities*, eds. Landon Beyer and Michael W. Apple (Albany: State University of New York Press, 1995), 201–229; and Gay, *Culturally Responsive Teaching*, 201-229.
12. Sharon Feiman-Nemser, "Helping Novices Learn to Teach," *Journal of Teacher Education* 52 (2001): 17–30.
13. Sharon Feiman-Nemser, "From Preparation to Practice," 1042
14. Robert V. Bullough Jr. and Andrew D. Gitlin, *Becoming a Student of Teaching: Linking Knowledge Production and Practice*, 2nd ed. (New York and London: Routledge Falmer, 2001), 90.
15. Robert V. Bullough Jr., J. Gary Knowles, and Nedra A. Crow, *Emerging as a Teacher* (New York and London: Routledge, 1992), 194.

Chapter Six

1. Anne Edwards and Carmen D'arcy, "Relational Agency and Disposition in Sociocultural Accounts of Learning to Teach," *Educational Review* 56, no. 2 (2004): 147–155.
2. John Dewey, "Ethics," in *John Dewey: The Later Works, 1925–1953*, vol. 17, ed. Jo Ann Boydston (Carbondale: Southern Illinois University Press, 1932/1985).
3. Stephen McKibben, "The Power of Student Voice," *Education Leadership* 61, no. 7 (2004): 79–81; and Rubin, *Collaborative Leadership*.

Chapter Seven

1. North Carolina Professional Teaching Standards Commission (2007). North Carolina professional teacher standards. Retrieved March 3, 2008 from: http://www.ncptsc.org/ Final%20Standards%20Document.pdf
2. Lisa Delpit, *Other People's Children* (New York: New Press, 1995).
3. North Carolina Professional Teaching Standards, http://www.ncptsc.org/.
4. Student Teacher A, personal communication with R. Smith, March, 14, 2005.

5. K. Sullivan, DPI presentation at NC Teacher Education Forum, September 20, 2008

6. Kathy Sullivan, personal communication with North Carolina Department of Public Instruction, February 4, 2009.

7. Mary E. Diez, "Looking Back and Moving Forward: Three Tensions in the Teacher Dispositions Discourse," *Journal of Teacher Education* 58, no. 5 (2007): 395.

8. Charlotte Danielson, "The Many Faces of Leadership," *Educational Leadership* 65, no.1 (2007): 14–19.

9. Linda Darling-Hammond and Diane Friedlaender, "Creating Excellent and Equitable Schools," *Educational Leadership* 65, no. 8 (2008): 14–21.

10. Nel Noddings, *Caring: A Feminine Approach to Ethics and Moral Education* (Berkeley: University of California Press, 1984); Nel Noddings, "An Ethic of Caring and Its Implications for Instructional Arrangements," *American Journal of Education* 96 (1988): 215–230; Nel Noddings, *The Challenge to Care in Schools* (New York: Teachers College Press, 1992); and Nel Noddings, *Educating Moral People: A Caring Alternative to Character Education* (New York: Teachers College Press, 2002).

11. Noddings, *Educating Moral People*, xiii.

12. Sonia Nieto, *Why We Teach* (New York: Teachers College Press, 2005).

13. Ibid., 204.

14. Jonathan Kozol, *Savage Inequalities: Children in America's Schools* (New York: Harper Perennial, 1992), 40.

15. James A. Banks, *Cultural Diversity and Education: Foundations, Curriculum, and Teaching*, 4th ed. (Boston: Allyn & Bacon, 2001), 2.

16. Howard Gardner, *Five Minds for the Future* (Boston: Harvard Business School Press, 2007).

Chapter Eight

1. Carl A. Grant and Maureen Gillette, "A Candid Talk to Teacher Educators About Effectively Preparing Teachers Who Can Teach Everyone's Children," *Journal of Teacher Education* 57, no. 3 (2006): 293.

2. Lisa Delpit, "Lessons from Teachers," *Journal of Teacher Education* 57, no. 3 (2006): 220–231.

3. Peter C. Murrell Jr., *The Community Teacher: A New Framework for Effective Urban Teaching* (New York: Teachers College Press, 2001), 51–53.

Chapter Nine

1. Erskine S. Dottin, "A Deweyan Approach to the Development of Moral Dispositions in Professional Teacher Education Communities: Using a Conceptual Framework," in *Teacher Dispositions: Building a Teacher Education Framework of Moral Standards*, ed. Hugh Sockett (Washington, DC: AACTE Publications, 2006), 27–48; and Thomas J. Sergiovanni, *Moral Leadership: Getting to the Heart of School Improvement* (San Francisco: Jossey-Bass Publishers, 1992).

2. Dottin, "A Deweyan Approach," 27.

3. Ibid., 33.

4. Hilda Borko, Dan Liston, and Jennifer A. Whitcomb, "Apples and Fishes: The Debate over Dispositions in Teacher Education," *Journal of Teacher Education* 58, no. 5 (2007): 359–364; and William Damon, "Dispositions and Teacher Assessment: The

Need for a More Rigorous Definition," *Journal of Teacher Education* 58, no. 5 (2007): 365–369.

5. Lilian G. Katz and James Raths, "Dispositions as Goals for Teacher Education," *Teaching and Teacher Education* 1, no. 4 (1985): 301.

6. Ana Maria Villegas, "Dispositions in Teacher Education: A Look at Social Justice," *Journal of Teacher Education* 58, no. 5 (2007): 370–380.

7. Mary E. Diez, "Looking Back and Moving Forward: Three Tensions in the Teacher Dispositions Discourse," *Journal of Teacher Education* 58, no. 5 (2007): 388–396.

8. Lee S. Shulman, "Signature Pedagogies in the Professions," *Daedalus* 134, no. 3 (2005): 52–59.

9. Nel Noddings, "The Caring Teacher," in *Handbook of Research on Teaching*, 4th ed., ed. Virginia Richardson (Washington, DC: American Educational Research Association, 2001), 101.

10. Gary Fenstermacher and Virginia Richardson, "On Making Determinations of Quality in Teaching," *Teachers College Record* 107, no. 1 (2005): 186–213; David T. Hansen, "Teaching as a Moral Activity," in *Handbook of Research on Teaching*, ed. Virginia Richardson (Washington, DC: American Educational Research Association, 2001), 826–857; and Richard Osguthorpe, "On the Reasons We Want Teachers of Good Dispositions and Moral Character," *Journal of Teacher Education* 59, no. 4 (2008): 288–299.

11. Anne Edwards and Carmen D'arcy, "Relational Agency and Disposition in Sociocultural Accounts of Learning to Teach," *Educational Review* 56, no. 2 (2004): 147–155.

12. Lee S. Shulman, "Theory, Practice, and the Education of Professionals," *Elementary School Journal* 98, no. 5 (1998): 518.

13. James Raths, "Experiences with Dispositions in Teacher Education," in *Dispositions in Teacher Education*, eds. Mary E. Diez and James Raths (Charlotte, NC: Information Age Publishing, 2007), 159.

14. David Berliner, "Expertise: The Wonder of Exemplary Performances," in *Creating Powerful Thinking in Teachers and Students: Diverse Perspectives*, eds. John Mangieri and Cathy Block (Fort Worth, TX: Harcourt Brace, 1994), 161–186; David Berliner, "Describing the Behavior and Documenting the Accomplishments of Expert Teachers," *Bulletin of Science, Technology & Society* 24, no. 3 (2004): 200–212; and Francis F. Fuller, "Concerns of Teachers: A Developmental Conceptualization," *American Educational Research Journal* 6, no. 2 (1969): 207–226.

16. For a recent synthesis of this work and its implications for the goals, curriculum, and pedagogy of teacher education, see Linda Darling-Hammond and John Bransford, eds., *Preparing Teachers for a Changing World: What Teachers Should Learn and Be Able to Do* (San Francisco: Jossey-Bass, 2005).

17. Sharon Feiman-Nemser, "How Do Teachers Learn to Teach?" in *Handbook of Research on Teacher Education: Enduring Questions in Changing Contexts*, eds. Marilyn Cochran-Smith, Sharon Feiman-Nemser, D. John McIntyre, and Kelly Demers (New York: Routledge/Taylor & Francis Group and the Association of Teacher Educators, 2008), 698–705.

18. Karen Hammerness, Linda Darling-Hammond, and John Bransford, "How Teachers Learn and Develop," in *Preparing Teachers for a Changing World: What Teachers Should*

Learn and Be Able to Do, eds. Linda Darling-Hammond and John Bransford (San Francisco: Jossey-Bass, 2005), 358–389.

19. Mary Kennedy, "The Role of Preservice Teacher Education," in *Teaching as the Learning Profession: Handbook of Policy and Practice*, eds. Linda Darling-Hammond and Gary Sykes (San Francisco: Jossey-Bass, 1999), 54–85.

20. Dan Lortie, *Schoolteacher: A Sociological Study* (Chicago: University of Chicago Press, 1975).

21. Sharon Feiman-Nemser, "From Preparation to Practice: Designing a Continuum to Strengthen and Sustain Teaching," *Teachers College Record* 103, no. 6 (2001): 1013–1055.

22. Deborah Ball and David Cohen, "Developing Practice, Developing Practitioners: Toward a Practice-Based Theory of Professional Development," in *Teaching as the Learning Profession: Handbook of Policy and Practice*, eds. Linda Darling-Hammond and Gary Sykes (San Francisco: Jossey-Bass, 1999), 3–32.

23. For a recent review, see Joel Westheimer, "Learning Among Colleagues: Teacher Community and the Shared Enterprise of Education," in *Handbook of Research on Teacher Education: Enduring Questions in Changing Contexts*, 3rd ed., eds. Marilyn Cochran-Smith, Sharon Feiman-Nemser, D. John McIntyre, and Kelly Demers (New York: Routledge/Taylor & Francis Group, 2008), 756–783.

24. Ball and Cohen, "Developing Practice, Developing Practitioners."

25. Brian T. Lord, "Teachers' Professional Development: Critical Colleagueship and the Role of Professional Communities," in *The Future of Education: Perspective on National Standards in Education*, ed. Nina Cobb (New York: College Entrance Examination, 1994), 175–204.

26. Robert V. Bullough and Andrew Gitlin, *Becoming a Student of Teaching: Methodologies for Exploring Self and School Context* (New York: Garland, 1995).

27. Lisa M. Stooksberry, "Dispositions as a Dialogue in Teacher Education," in *Dispositions in Teacher Education*, eds. Mary E. Diez and James Raths (Charlotte, NC: Information Age Publishing, 2007), 219–232.

28. Richard J. Stiggins, "Assessment Crisis: The Absence of Assessment for Learning," *Phi Delta Kappan* 83, no. 10 (2002): 758–765.

29. Lord, "Teachers' Professional Development," 175–204; and Ball and Cohen, "Developing Practice, Developing Practitioners," 3–32.

31. Sergiovanni, *Moral Leadership*, 102.

About the Editors

Mary E. Diez, PhD, a founding member of the American Association of Colleges for Teacher Education's Task Force on Teacher Education as a Moral Community, Diez now serves as chair of the group. She is professor of education and dean of graduate studies at Alverno College in Milwaukee, Wisconsin. A 1995 winner of the Harold W. McGraw Jr. Prize in Education, Diez has served as president of AACTE, on the National Board for Professional Teaching Standards, and on both the Board of Examiners and the Unit Accreditation Board of the National Council for the Accreditation of Teacher Education. She currently cochairs the Standards Revision Committee for the Interstate New Teacher Assessment and Support Consortium. Diez's writing focuses on standards and assessment in both teacher education and K–12 school reform. She coedited the book *Dispositions in Teacher Education* with James Raths. With colleagues at Alverno, she edited *Changing the Practice of Teacher Education: Standards and Assessment as a Lever for Change*, which reported on a number of institutions engaged in the process of reconceptualizing their teacher education programs.

Sharon Feiman-Nemser, EdD, is the Mandel Professor of Jewish Education at Brandeis University and director of the Mandel Center for Studies in Jewish Education. Before coming to Brandeis in 2001, she served on the faculties of the University of Chicago and Michigan State University, where she directed innovative teacher education programs. A scholar of teacher education and learning to teach, she has written extensively about mentoring, new teacher induction, teacher centers, and the curriculum and pedagogy of teacher education. She recently coedited the third edition of the *Handbook of Research on Teacher Education* and also a book with colleagues at Michigan State, *Transforming Teacher Education*.

Peter C. Murrell Jr., PhD, is currently the founding dean of the School of Education and professor of educational psychology at Loyola University in Maryland, where he recently inaugurated the Center for Innovation in Urban Education. Murrell's research focuses upon the relationships between social identity and academic performance and scholastic achievement, and investigates the development of academic identity and racial/cultural identity in the varied social contexts in urban schools and communities. He has authored numerous articles and book chapters on building culturally centered learning communities for teachers and students. His books include *The Community Teacher, African Centered Peda-*

gogy, and *Like Stone Soup.* His most recent book addresses the dynamic of identity, learning, and teaching: *Race, Culture and Schooling.* He is a member of the American Association of Colleges of Teacher Education TEAMC (Teacher Education as a Moral Community).

Deborah L. Schussler, EdD, is a former high school English teacher and currently an associate professor in the Department of Education and Human Services at Villanova University. She teaches in the graduate and undergraduate teacher certification programs. Deborah's research interests include exploring how prospective teachers acquire the necessary dispositions to meet the needs of all learners. Specifically, Deborah has examined the epistemological nature of dispositions and how teacher education fosters awareness of dispositions to enhance prospective teachers' knowledge, skills, and moral sensibilities. Deborah also explores how schools function as learning communities to meet the social and moral development of learners. Recent articles appear in *Teachers College Record, Theory into Practice, Action in Teacher Education, Teaching and Teacher Education, and Teachers and Teaching: Theory and Practice.* Deborah has been a member of the American Association of Colleges of Teacher Education TEAMC task force since 2009. Deborah presents regularly at the AACTE and American Educational Research Association (AERA) conferences and is an active member of the Moral Development SIG.

About the Contributors

Rosemary L. Battalio, PhD., is an associate professor and chair of the Department of Special Education at the University of Wisconsin-Eau Claire. Her expertise emphasizes emotional/behavioral disorders, behavior management, transition and career development, and classroom interactions. Battalio teaches undergraduate and graduate courses in emotional/behavioral disorders and coordinates collaborative activities linking the special education and regular education preservice programs. Battalio's scholarly activities emphasize social skills training, functional behavior assessment, gender roles and inclusion for students with emotional disturbance in the school environment.

Anne M. Bauer, EdD, is a professor of special education at the University of Cincinnati. Her teaching experience is with urban students with intense educational and behavioral issues, and graduate and undergraduate courses in special education teacher preparation. Bauer has published articles in the *Journal of Special Education, School Psychology Quarterly, Focus on Special Education*, and many others. Her textbooks are widely used, and her coauthored text on behavior management is entering its tenth edition. Her research is currently on educator preparation and systems change.

Andra Brill, PhD, is codirector of the Boettcher Teachers Program and has been a part of the program since its inception in 2004. Before coming to Boettcher, Andra completed a doctorate in educational leadership and innovation at the University of Colorado at Denver (UCD) while teaching in the Denver Public Schools. Prior to her doctoral work, Andra obtained a master's degree in language, literacy, and culture from UCD and has spent more than fifteen years working in bilingual elementary classrooms. She believes passionately in working to make public schools safe and nurturing places for children and adults to learn together. Her current interests include educational leadership, culturally responsive pedagogy, and instructional technology.

Julie Canniff, is an assistant professor in the Teacher Education Department at the University of Southern Maine. She coordinates, teaches, and supervises graduate interns in the Extended Teacher Education Program—a university–school partnership based in three rural public school districts. Her research is centered in the field of cultural ecology and is currently focused on the dimensions of teacher resilience.

Rebecca Evers, EdD, is an associate professor in the Center for Pedagogy at the Richard W. Riley College of Education at Winthrop University. She holds a doctorate in special education from Northern Illinois University. Her professional experiences include teaching Braille and Activities of Daily Living at Hines Veterans Administration Hospital during the Vietnam War era, and teaching special education in the inner-city public schools of Chicago from 1973 to 1995. At present, she teaches courses in assistive technology, classroom management, and effective teaching practices for diverse and exceptional students. She is actively involved in researching methods to determine and assess the quality of teacher candidate dispositions. Her primary focus is dispositions for providing equitable access to learning for students with disabilities and other exceptional needs.

Catherine Fallona, PhD, is the associate dean and director of teacher education in the College of Education and Human Development at the University of Southern Maine. She also coordinates and teaches courses in the undergraduate teacher education pathway, Teachers for Elementary and Middle Schools. The focus of her scholarship is on studying novice and expert teachers' actions, intentions, and ways of thinking about teaching and learning related to the moral missions of schooling, particularly with regard to better understanding teachers' manner in terms of their expression of moral and intellectual virtue and the ways the classroom environment serves as a moral curriculum.

John Fischetti, EdD is a professor of secondary education. His interest is in rethinking the role of formal teacher education in light of America's low high school graduation rates and an increasingly diverse, global environment in which our young people must thrive. John most recently coordinated the planning and implementation of the Watson School's doctoral program in educational leadership. He also teaches in the undergraduate and graduate secondary programs. Other current scholarship includes a study of the Early College High School Initiative and building community capacity to support public schools.

Robert E. Hollon, PhD, is a professor and elementary education coordinator in the Department of Education Studies at the University of Wisconsin-Eau Claire. He served as a founding codirector of the former Center for Collaborative Leadership in the College of Education and Human Sciences. In addition to his role as a science educator, Hollon teaches undergraduate and graduate courses in leadership development, provides professional development in science education and leadership to schools in Wisconsin, and consults with schools and public agencies to infuse collaborative leadership dispositions, knowledge, and skills into the everyday practices of their members. Hollon has coauthored multiple publications and leadership development grants and is a frequent presenter at national and regional conferences. He serves on a variety of state and national teacher education and leadership committees.

Scott Imig, PhD, is an assistant professor and the interim associate dean for Outreach Alliances in the Watson School of Education. Scott directs the Watson School's partnership with thirteen school districts and manages collaborative grants. His research centers on the future of teacher education and supporting quality teaching. Scott has written extensively on the opportunities and challenges of teacher education. While at the University of Virginia, he directed a Teacher Quality Enhancement grant from the Carnegie Corporation.

Lisa E. Johnson, PhD, serves as senior associate to the dean in the Richard W. Riley College of Education at Winthrop University. She holds a doctorate in curriculum and instruction from North Carolina State University. As project director for Network of Sustained, Collaborative, Ongoing Preparation for Educators (NetSCOPE), a federal Teacher Quality Partnership grant, Johnson is currently working to enhance student achievement in South Carolina schools by preparing teachers to work with diverse learners. She is the author of *Developing Dispositions: Examining Mentors and Beginning Teachers* and other publications studying the judgments and actions of preservice, inservice, and mentor teachers. Her current research involves designing longitudinal measures of teacher candidate disposition and measuring the impact of university–school partnerships.

Holly Johnson, PhD, is currently the director of the School of Education at the University of Cincinnati. She served as program coordinator of the Middle Childhood Education Program prior to her current appointment, and teaches graduate and undergraduate courses in content area literacy, literacy foundations, and children's literature. She received her doctorate from the Department of Language, Reading, and Culture at the University of Arizona in 1997. She was a middle school language arts teacher in Kentucky and Arizona, and served as a U.S. Peace Corps volunteer in Botswana, where she taught industrial arts and mathematics. Her areas of research include adolescent literacy, content area literacy, and reader response. She has published four books addressing adolescent literacy, including *Developing Critical Awareness at the Middle Level, Building Reading Confidence in Adolescents*, and *Inquiry, Literacy, and Learning in the Middle Grades*.

Eleni Katsarou, PhD, is currently director of urban education and elementary education and a clinical associate professor of curriculum and instruction in the College of Education at the University of Illinois at Chicago. She teaches teacher candidates in the elementary education concentration and works most closely with senior teacher candidates as they conduct their student teaching in urban public school sites. Her work includes collaborations with teachers and leaders of schools as they jointly attempt to understand what constitutes caring and ethical teaching. The partnerships she has formed for more than fourteen years have given rise to the ways in which professional communities are enacted in pursuing common understandings about urban teaching. She also teaches literacy graduate courses.

Michael W. Kolis, EdD, is an associate professor and preadmission coordinator for the middle–secondary education program in the Department of Education Studies at the University of Wisconsin-Eau Claire. His expertise emphasizes adult education, critical and creative thinking, and systems approaches to education. Kolis currently cofacilitates a cohort-based preservice program that integrates collaborative leadership dispositions, knowledge, and skills into a set of thematic experiences for future 6–12 teachers. He has coauthored multiple publications and professional development grants in science and leadership development, has designed successful professional development and graduate programs, and is a frequent presenter at regional and national conferences in the area of collaborative practices for school and university faculty.

Stephen D. Kroeger is the special education program coordinator at the University of Cincinnati. His teaching includes work in St. Lucia, Peru, Detroit, Michigan, and Cincinnati, Ohio. His research focus is student voice and schoolwide systems change, including coteaching at the K–12 and higher-ed levels. He has published articles related to teacher preparation in *Assessment for Effective Intervention, Educational Action Research, International Journal of Applied Educational Studies, Psychology in the Schools, Qualitative Research Journal, Teacher Education and Special Education, and Teaching Exceptional Children.* Recent projects include the use of evidence-based instructional practices, and a five-year federal grant aimed at program restructuring to support preservice teachers in their work to become highly qualified teachers.

Chester Laine, PhD, is an associate professor of literacy and chair of the Licensure Council in the School of Education at the University of Cincinnati. He earned his PhD in language education from the Pennsylvania State University in 1980. His teaching experience includes high school English and developmental reading and graduate and undergraduate courses in literacy theory and pedagogy. He has published articles related to adolescent literacy—especially struggling readers and writers—in *Research in the Teaching of English, English Education, Written Communication, College Composition and Communication, Journal of Teaching and Writing, Australian Journal of Teacher Education, The Volta Review, Reading Research and Instruction, Research and Teaching in Developmental Education,* and *Educational Research Quarterly.* His research interests include adolescent literacy and teacher preparation. His grants, particularly those funded by the Ohio Board of Regents, focus on helping urban teachers become more strategic in their approach to writing assessment and instruction.

Karen L. Lowenstein, PhD, serves as codirector of the Boettcher Teachers Program. Her research, teaching, and leadership focus on culturally responsive pedagogy and the creation of health and compassionate group spaces in education. She is grateful for the collaboration she has had with her coauthors because she admires their work tremendously. Currently, she is wondering how to take the impact of the Boettcher Teachers Program on school culture and student achievement to a larger scale.

Susan R. McIntyre, PhD, is a professor and coordinator for the middle–secondary education program in the Department of Education Studies at the University of Wisconsin-Eau Claire. Her expertise emphasizes literacy development in adolescents and adults. McIntyre currently cofacilitates a cohort-based preservice program that integrates collaborative leadership dispositions, knowledge, and skills into a set of thematic experiences for future 6–12 teachers. In addition to teaching undergraduate and graduate courses in literacy development, McIntyre is an active researcher and materials developer in health literacy. She has published multiple articles examining the barriers to health care that exist as a result of gaps between the literacy skills of patients and the literacy level of materials and discourse used by medical professionals.

Helen Meyer, PhD, is an associate professor and the program coordinator for curriculum and instruction in the School of Education at the University of Cincinnati. She earned her degree in curriculum and instruction from the University of Wisconsin-Madison. During her doctoral work, she researched the development of teacher education curriculum and its implementation in newly independent Namibia. The majority of her current work is focused on science education reform and development. She has published in *Science Education*, *School Science and Mathematics*, and *Science Education Review*.

Abdou Ndoye is assessment director for the Watson School of Education. He works across the faculty and programs to develop assessment plans linked to national and state standards and program learning outcomes. His research focuses on the impact of teacher education, with a focus on success with diverse learners and closing achievement gaps. Recent scholarship includes investigating student achievement in charter schools, analyzing key variables in teacher working conditions, and the implementation of e-portfolios in candidate assessment.

María del Carmen Salazar, PhD, is an assistant professor at the University of Denver Morgridge College of Education. Her research and scholarship center on teacher residency programs that combine rigorous research and promising practices in teacher recruitment, preparation, and induction for urban schools. Her research and teaching fields include teacher education, linguistically diverse education, culturally responsive teaching, and college readiness for English language learners. She has authored numerous academic journal articles and book chapters, and given more than fifty scholarly presentations focused on her research areas. In addition, she is the lead author of a widely circulated policy document titled "The State of Latinos 2008: Defining an Agenda for the Future." This document was presented to members of the U.S. Congress in Washington, DC, and distributed to all members of the U.S. Congress. She also serves on the Colorado Quality Teachers Commission and the Interstate New Teacher Assessment and Support Consortium (INTASC).

Robert Smith, EdD, is a professor of secondary education and serves as the coordinator of the undergraduate secondary education program in the Watson School. He teaches foundations and graduate courses in the master of education and master of arts in teaching programs. His research focuses on high school reform, equity, and social justice. He is an advocate for small learning communities with a focus on teacher quality and engaging curriculum. Other current research is related to racial biases of beginning teachers and studying the early college and freshman academy initiatives.

J. Todd Stephens, PhD, is a professor in the Department of Special Education at the University of Wisconsin-Eau Claire. Stephens's expertise lies in cognitive disabilities, characteristics of learning and educational needs, and applied behavior analysis. As coordinator of the cognitive disabilities licensure program, Stephens teaches undergraduate and graduate courses in behavior analysis, challenging behaviors, and cognitive disabilities. Stephens consults with schools and families and is an active researcher with multiple publications, examining the way children with cognitive disabilities learn and use action concepts as well as investigating the validity of identification procedures in the field of ADHD.

Karen S. Troup is a field service assistant professor at the University of Cincinnati. She earned her master's degree in early childhood special education at the University of Cincinnati in 2000. After fourteen years of successful work as an intervention specialist, Troup has served as the field coordinator for the Special Education Program since 2006. Her role is to coordinate field placements with the University of Cincinnati's secondary and middle school program coordinators in order to establish coteaching placements at urban and suburban schools. As a result of her involvement in the coteaching placements, she has presented her work with fellow faculty members at the International Reading Association Conference, Council for Exceptional Children, Teacher Education Division, and American Reading Forum conferences for the past three years.

Jonatha W. Vare, PhD, currently chairs the Department of Curriculum and Instruction in the Richard W. Riley College of Education at Winthrop University. For the past nine years, she directed the college's Center for Pedagogy, a department whose unique mission focused on achieving goals related to the moral dimensions of education in a democracy. She holds a doctorate in educational psychology from the University of North Carolina at Chapel Hill. Her research interests include measuring dispositions of equity in teacher candidates, evaluating curriculum and policies that influence educational equity for diverse learners in public schools, assessing the impact of professional development school partnerships, and analyzing ways in which school–university collaboration transforms partnership culture.

Index

definition of dispositions, 179
diversity assessment in foundations
course, 87
future plans, 90
gap between valued dispositions and actual
performance, 76
identifying essence of how to teach content
to diverse learners, 88
illustration of a how "caring" can be evaluated, 79–82
illustration of commitment inhibited by
personal history, 76–79
illustration of how competence can inhibit
interaction, 82–84
inclusion of an underlying moral aspect in
the definition of dispositions, 180
lessons requiring redesign and earlier introduction, 85
organization of identified dispositions,
75–76
problem of candidates' preconceptions,
186–88
problem of enactment, 189
process of enumerating dispositions, 183
psychological barrier when candidates'
backgrounds differ from their students,
85–86
response to new NCATE accreditation
requirements, 74–75
revision of courses for special education
licensure, 87–88
shortfalls in the teacher preparation
program, 74
understanding supervisors' and cooperating
teachers' roles, 82
university supervisor and cooperating
teacher roles, 89
University of Denver. *See* Boettcher Teachers
Program
University of Illinois at Chicago (UIC)
about, 163–64
cooperating teachers and, 165–66
DECA-UT assessment use (*see* Development
of Ethical and Caring Actions in Urban
Teaching)
definition of dispositions, 179
elements in the development of desired
dispositions, 175
expectations for teacher candidates, 164
importance of conversations between
candidates and mentors, 175

justifications for the dispositions enumerated, 184
learnings applied to urban teaching, 176
problem of complexity met with collaboration, 192
reflections on missing elements of assessments, 166–67
settings for opportunities for dispositional
work, 166
University of North Carolina Wilmington
(UNCW)
about, 141
challenge of developing a statement of
dispositional expectations, 146
committee outreach during change process,
155
definition of dispositions, 179
desire to revisit fundamental basis of their
work, 147–48
dispositional assessment plan, 159–60
dispositions in content standards, 148, 149t
dispositions seen as malleable and able to
be cultivated, 180–81
earlier approaches to dispositions, 144–45
five pillars of new framework (*see* pillars of
new dispositions framework at UNCW)
impact on secondary program, 158–59
impetus for changing existing program,
142–43, 144, 147
involving colleagues in change process,
156, 157t
involving state level administrators in
change process, 157–58
justifications for the dispositions enumerated, 184
lack of understanding or focus on broad
dispositions, 146
professional literature regarding leadership,
caring, and diversity, 148–50
redesigns' focus on leadership and caring
about diversity, 148
team members, 143
Watson School of Education, 141
University of Southern Maine (USM)
about, 95
admissions-level assessments of moral
dispositions, 98–99
assessing candidates' moral dispositions,
98–101
assessment of disposition for collegiality,
109–12